STRONGHOLDS
of the SAMURAI

JAPANESE CASTLES 250–1877

OSPREY
PUBLISHING

STRONGHOLDS
of the SAMURAI

JAPANESE CASTLES 250–1877

STEPHEN TURNBULL

First published in Great Britain in 2009 by Osprey Publishing,
Midland House, West Way, Botley, Oxford OX2 0PH, United Kingdom.
443 Park Avenue South, New York, NY 10016, USA.
Email: info@ospreypublishing.com

Previously published as Fortress 5: *Japanese Castles 1540–1640*, Fortress 34: *Japanese Fortified Temples and Monasteries AD 710–1062*, Fortress 67: *Japanese Castles in Korea 1592–98* and Fortress 74: *Japanese Castles AD 250–1540*, all by Stephen Turnbull. Now revised and expanded.

For Yuko Sawata and everyone else at Akita International University

A CIP catalogue record for this book is available from the British Library.

Stephen Turnbull has asserted his right under the Copyright, Designs and Patents Act, 1988, to be identified as the author of this book.

ISBN 978 1 84603 413 8

Page layout by Ken Vail Graphic Design, Cambridge, UK
Index by Alison Worthington
Typeset in Bembo, Optima, Papyrus
Originated by United Graphic Pte Ltd., Singapore
Printed in China through Worldprint

09 10 11 12 13   10 9 8 7 6 5 4 3 2 1

For a catalogue of all books published by Osprey please contact:

NORTH AMERICA
Osprey Direct, c/o Random House Distribution Center
400 Hahn Road, Westminster, MD 21157, USA
E-mail: uscustomerservice@ospreypublishing.com

ALL OTHER REGIONS
Osprey Direct, The Book Service Ltd, Distribution Centre, Colchester Road,
Frating Green, Colchester, Essex, CO7 7DW, UK
E-mail: customerservice@ospreypublishing.com

www.ospreypublishing.com

Cover image: Shizugatake Castle, as it appears on the Shizugatake Screen in the Osaka Castle.

Contents

CONTENTS

INTRODUCTION

Although best known for the individual skills of horsemanship, archery and sword-fighting they displayed on the field of battle, the samurai, the warriors of old Japan, conducted many battles either from or against fortified positions. These strongholds ranged from simple wooden stockades to the magnificent castles that are such an attractive feature of Japan today.

The first Japanese fortifications of any sort appear to have been the fences and towers built along the perimeters of villages in about AD 250, but it is not until the 7th century that we see the creation of buildings that have an unmistakeably defensive purpose. These were castles with long, low stone walls in the Korean style, built because of fears of an invasion from continental Asia. None were ever tested in battle; instead the forts that saw military action were located at the opposite end of Japan, where the aboriginal *emishi* (the original inhabitants of northern Japan) raided the settlements of the Japanese state as it sought to push its boundaries further north. Two centuries later the descendants of the *emishi* chieftains, now officials of the Japanese government, and the great-grandsons of the warriors who had once been sent to control them, fought each other from elaborate wooden stockades in the first samurai wars.

Apart from providing the raw material for several myths and traditions about samurai behaviour, these wars set a pattern for fighting around strongpoints built mainly of wood that was to last until the mid–16th century. In 1185 one samurai clan, the Minamoto, triumphed over its rivals and created the post of *shōgun*, Japan's military dictator. In 1274 and 1281 Japan faced an invasion by the Yuan (Mongol) dynasty of China, which it fought off from behind simple stone walls built along the seashore, while during the 14th century an unsuccessful attempt to restore imperial rule was carried out from the protection of *yamashiro* (mountain-top castles).

In 1467 a civil war began within the streets of the capital that the *shōgun* was unable to control. As the fighting spread to the provinces local lords, who had once ruled as the *shōgun*'s deputies, took the opportunity to create petty kingdoms of their own, calling themselves *daimyō* (great names). Thus began the century and a half known by analogy to Chinese history as the Sengoku

Jidai or Age of Warring States. The *yamashiro* was a key component in Sengoku warfare, and the design of mountain-top castles grew more elaborate as the fighting became more extensive.

Along with the *daimyō*'s samurai armies, communities of farmers and small landowners banded together in leagues called *ikki*. They too erected fortifications, the most elaborate ones being built by the communities united by the religious beliefs they held in common. As early exponents of firearms, the religious armies made a considerable contribution to Japanese warfare and to the development of the Japanese castle, and the Ishiyama Honganji, the headquarters of the Ikkō-ikki (the armies of the Shinsū sect of Buddhism), withstood a siege of ten years' duration.

As samurai domains grew, so did the castles that protected them. These fortresses acquired new roles as commercial and administrative centres, but also as a symbol of the owner's power. Stone, once used only for foundations, was now employed to create massive stone bases that enclosed an earth core, often laboriously carved out of a hillside. These stone bases, the hallmark of

The restored entrance and gatehouse towers to Sumpu, the castle of Tokugawa Ieyasu, which now lies within the city of Shizuoka. Of the buildings which make up a castle's superstructure, the ones that a visitor first encounters are the gatehouses that would create quite a complex micro-system of defence.

Opposite: This larger gateway at the Esashi Fujiwara Heritage Park represents a more elaborate form of entrance to a stockaded fortress of the Heian Period. We may imagine Kanazawa, the main battlefield of the Later Three Years' War, looking very much like this.

The restored gateway and bridge of Sakasai Castle, the finest of the reconstructed Hōjō fortresses.

the developed castle form, supported gatehouses, towers and keeps, and many long and bitter sieges were conducted against them.

The reunification of Japan out of the chaos of the Sengoku Jidai came about as the result of the military prowess of three powerful *daimyō*, each of whom made use of prominent castles. Oda Nobunaga built Azuchi Castle in 1576 with a tower keep that impressed even European visitors. His successor Toyotomi Hideyoshi, who completed the unification of Japan, took over the site of the fortified cathedral of the Ikkō-ikki and built Osaka Castle there in 1586. Hideyoshi then made the fatal mistake of invading Korea, an ultimately doomed operation for which the line of coastal fortresses or *wajō* provided Japan's last toehold on the continent until the war ended in 1597.

The triumph of Tokugawa Ieyasu at the battle of Sekigahara in 1600 led to the re-establishment of the shogunate and a major change to the administrative map of Japan. The *daimyō* were moved to different provinces in a bewildering programme of relocation. Many new castles were built, but many more were destroyed so that control could be exerted locally from one castle in any one province. These castles with their vibrant castle towns eventually became the great cities of modern Japan, and during the peaceful Edo Period they were the nucleus of a thriving civic life.

Towards the end of this time of peace we see the building of new castles against the threat posed by Western nations who sought to end Japan's self-imposed isolation. The Meiji Restoration of 1868, although popularly portrayed as a bloodless coup, in fact saw a brief but violent civil war during which many fine castles were destroyed. When peace was restored, most of the castles that had survived were demolished as symbols of an outdated approach to warfare and politics. More were burned down during the air raids of 1945, and only 12 Japanese castles now survive in their original form. Others have been reconstructed, some during the 1960s in concrete, others more recently in natural materials. The sites of several early castles have also been subjected to archaeological investigation, so that we may now enjoy and understand better than at any time the strongholds of the samurai.

Next page: The choice of Kasagi as the first refuge for Emperor Go-Daigo may have had more to do with its religious significance than with the actual or potential strength of its defences. This pictorial map at the entrance to Kasagidera, the temple that is now built in the site, shows how it was a typical Japanese yamashiro. Note the massive rocks at Kasagi that have images of the Buddha carved into them. These rocks are described in Taiheiki, but did not hinder a night attack against Go-Daigo.

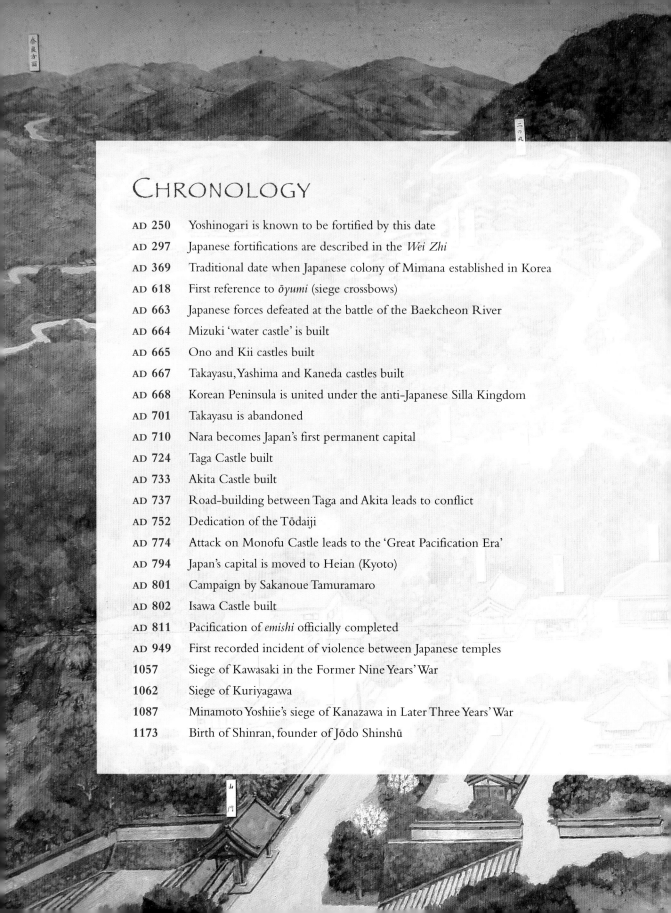

CHRONOLOGY

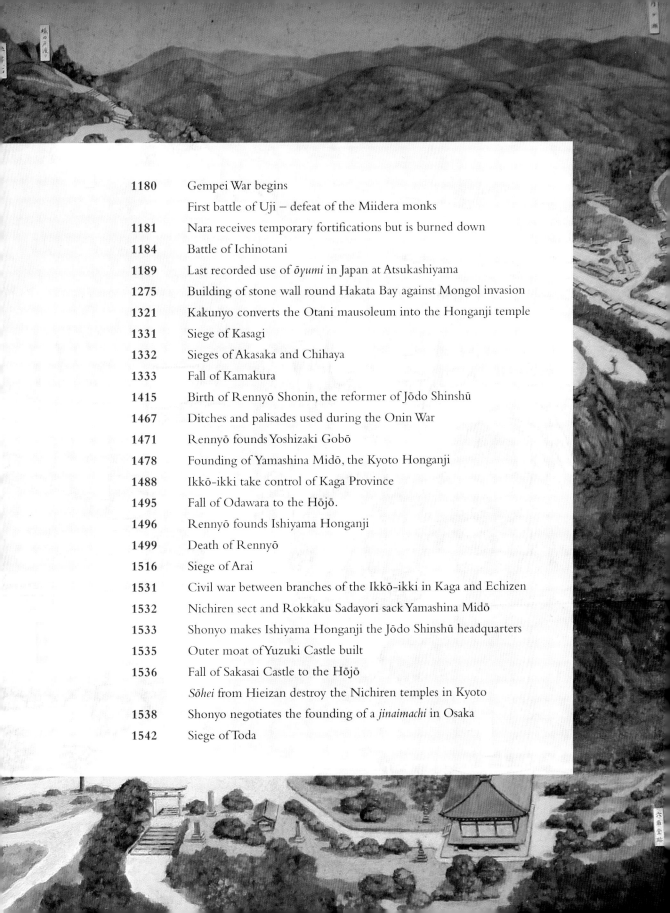

1180	Gempei War begins
	First battle of Uji – defeat of the Miidera monks
1181	Nara receives temporary fortifications but is burned down
1184	Battle of Ichinotani
1189	Last recorded use of *ōyumi* in Japan at Atsukashiyama
1275	Building of stone wall round Hakata Bay against Mongol invasion
1321	Kakunyo converts the Otani mausoleum into the Honganji temple
1331	Siege of Kasagi
1332	Sieges of Akasaka and Chihaya
1333	Fall of Kamakura
1415	Birth of Rennyō Shonin, the reformer of Jōdo Shinshū
1467	Ditches and palisades used during the Onin War
1471	Rennyō founds Yoshizaki Gobō
1478	Founding of Yamashina Midō, the Kyoto Honganji
1488	Ikkō-ikki take control of Kaga Province
1495	Fall of Odawara to the Hōjō.
1496	Rennyō founds Ishiyama Honganji
1499	Death of Rennyō
1516	Siege of Arai
1531	Civil war between branches of the Ikkō-ikki in Kaga and Echizen
1532	Nichiren sect and Rokkaku Sadayori sack Yamashina Midō
1533	Shonyo makes Ishiyama Honganji the Jōdo Shinshū headquarters
1535	Outer moat of Yuzuki Castle built
1536	Fall of Sakasai Castle to the Hōjō
	Sōhei from Hieizan destroy the Nichiren temples in Kyoto
1538	Shonyo negotiates the founding of a *jinaimachi* in Osaka
1542	Siege of Toda

1543	Arrival of Europeans in Japan
1545	Night battle of Kawagoe
1546	Founding of Oyama Gobo in present-day Kanazawa
1549	Arquebuses used at Kajiki siege
1553	First battle of Kawanakajima
1554	Siege of Muraki – volleys of arquebuses used
	Kennyo Kosa becomes the 11th *zasu* of Ishiyama Honganji
1557	First siege of Moji
1562	Fire destroys much of the *jinaimachi* of Ishiyama Honganji
1564	Tokugawa Ieyasu defeats the Ikkō-ikki of Mikawa at the battle of Azukizaka
1570	Oda Nobunaga's first attack on Ishiyama Honganji
1571	Destruction of Mount Hiei by Nobunaga
1573	Death of Takeda Shingen
	Nobunaga's generals invade Echizen but are repulsed
1574	Siege of Nagashima
1575	Siege and battle of Nagashino
	Nobunaga's generals take main Ikkō-ikki sites in Echizen
1576	Shibata Katsuie captures Miyukizuka (modern-day Komatsu) in Kaga
	Building of Azuchi Castle
	Siege of river complex of Ishiyama Honganji
	Building of Maruoka Castle
1578	Death of Uesugi Kenshin
	Nobunaga breaks Mori's supply lines at the battle of Kizugawaguchi
1579	Siege of Miki
1580	Surrender of Ishiyama Honganji
1581	Katsuie retakes Torigoe and Futoge

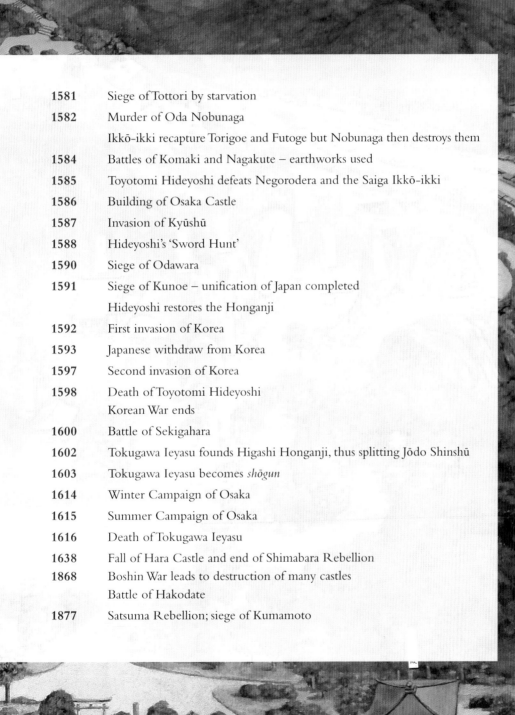

1581	Siege of Tottori by starvation
1582	Murder of Oda Nobunaga
	Ikkō-ikki recapture Torigoe and Futoge but Nobunaga then destroys them
1584	Battles of Komaki and Nagakute – earthworks used
1585	Toyotomi Hideyoshi defeats Negorodera and the Saiga Ikkō-ikki
1586	Building of Osaka Castle
1587	Invasion of Kyūshū
1588	Hideyoshi's 'Sword Hunt'
1590	Siege of Odawara
1591	Siege of Kunoe – unification of Japan completed
	Hideyoshi restores the Honganji
1592	First invasion of Korea
1593	Japanese withdraw from Korea
1597	Second invasion of Korea
1598	Death of Toyotomi Hideyoshi
	Korean War ends
1600	Battle of Sekigahara
1602	Tokugawa Ieyasu founds Higashi Honganji, thus splitting Jōdo Shinshū
1603	Tokugawa Ieyasu becomes *shōgun*
1614	Winter Campaign of Osaka
1615	Summer Campaign of Osaka
1616	Death of Tokugawa Ieyasu
1638	Fall of Hara Castle and end of Shimabara Rebellion
1868	Boshin War leads to destruction of many castles
	Battle of Hakodate
1877	Satsuma Rebellion; siege of Kumamoto

JAPANESE CASTLES 250–1540

INTRODUCTION

THE FIRST JAPANESE FORTIFICATIONS

The earliest known use of fortified sites in Japan is believed to date from the Yayoi Period (c.300 BC–AD 300), which succeeded the Neolithic Jōmon Period (c.10,000–300 BC). Jōmon culture had been characterized by hunter/gatherer behaviour followed by primitive agriculture. Until quite recently, it was assumed that Jōmon communities consisted of no more than a dozen or so households, but excavation of the archaeological site of Sannai-Maruyama in Aomori Prefecture has revealed a large village containing what may have been a fortified structure. Six 1m-wide postholes were found, each of which formerly held a massive pillar of chestnut wood. This may indicate the presence of a lookout tower, which would imply defensive purposes, or it may even be a religious structure.

Unless further archaeological work is able to identify Sannai-Maruyama unequivocally as a fortified site, the introduction of fortifications to Japan must be dated to the succeeding Yayoi Period. The most important innovation associated with the Yayoi culture was the introduction of wet-rice cultivation by immigrants from the Asian continent. This resulted in the rapid development of food production and a consequent increase in population. The immigrants also introduced metals into the Japanese archipelago – first iron and then bronze – the reverse of the order found in other parts of the world. Iron was used primarily for tools, while bronze was cast into weapons and bells. Skeletal remains show that the people who brought the Yayoi culture were taller than the natives they displaced.

There is a wealth of archaeological evidence to suggest that warfare and fortifications played a part in the expansion of the Yayoi settlements. The discovery of broken tips of stone or bronze weapons lodged in the bones of Yayoi Period skeletons from the 2nd and 3rd centuries AD has been interpreted as indicating the onset of war and some of its likely victims. The frequency of weapon finds among bodies in the Yayoi Period is particularly striking when compared to burials in the Jōmon Period. Out of the 5,000 skeletons excavated

from Jōmon graves since 1947, only ten appear to have suffered violent deaths, yet among the 1,000 skeletons associated with Yayoi sites, 100 appear to have died as a result of wounds inflicted by weapons. One victim at Doigahama appears to have been killed when a stone arrowhead struck his skull. A female skeleton in Nejiko in Nagasaki Prefecture has a bronze arrowhead lodged in her skull, while several skeletons at Yoshinogari in Kyūshū are headless.

The development of warfare at this time has been explained as follows. As populations grew and more land was sought, neighbours may well have fought each other over scarce lands and reliable sources of water. We know that settlements were extended into the upper reaches of river valleys as well as the lower-lying areas, and it is at this time that we first come across evidence that some, but by no means all, communities sought to protect their interests by the creation of fortifications. The first phase of defensive considerations appears to have been simply the establishment of settlements located on high ground, because numerous Yayoi Period hamlets containing between three and five households have been identified some 200m or 300m above sea level. These 'highland settlements' (*kōchisei shūraku*) could of course merely have been bases from which the fertile lower ground could be cultivated without wasting any valuable space. This may well have been the original reason for their creation during the 1st century AD, but the discovery of weapons at some later sites, together with scorched earth and ashes (which may indicate the sites of beacons), has suggested an additional military role. Indeed, it is now accepted that most upland sites at least provided the function of a lookout post in case of an attack.

This reconstruction on the site of Heijō-kyō, the ancient capital known to us as Nara, shows the southern gateway and a section of the rammed earth walls.

17

This archaeological evidence for fortification and sporadic conflict is reflected in the earliest written accounts concerning Japan. These may be found in the Chinese dynastic histories, of which the first to refer to Japan is the *Wei Zhi*, the history of the Wei dynasty (AD 220–65), which was compiled about AD 297. The account of the country of Wa, as Japan was then known, appears in a section in which China's barbarian neighbours are described, and, although the description is brief, it includes the mention of a fortified place:

> The country formerly had a man as ruler. For some 70 or 80 years after that there were disturbances and warfare. Thereupon the people agreed upon a woman for their ruler. Her name was Himiko. She occupied herself with magic and sorcery, bewitching the people. … She resided in a palace surrounded by towers and stockades, with armed guards in a state of constant vigilance.

A very similar description occurs in the *Hou Hanshu*, the history of the Later Han dynasty, compiled in about AD 445. The suggestion by the author of the *Wei Zhi* that warfare developed in Japan in the 2nd and 3rd centuries AD tallies with the archaeological evidence noted above, which also shows that this was a time when arrowheads were being produced that were heavier and deadlier than those made for hunting. The spacing of the highland settlements allowed smoke signals to be sent from one base to another, and these hamlets frequently lay within a short distance of major Yayoi settlements.

These larger Yayoi sites have been well studied, and provide strong evidence of early Japanese fortifications. Important places such as Otsuka near Yokohama, Jizoden in Akita and Yoshinogari in Kyūshū were settlements protected by ditches (*kangō shūraku*). Ditches have also been found in certain highland sites, and half a century of excavation has revealed 79 such villages from Kyūshū to northern Honshū. Asahi in Aichi Prefecture provides a good example of a fortified Yayoi village. Three ditches provided defence. The outer one was between five and seven metres wide and 1.5m deep, while the inner two were between 1.5 and 2m deep. Inside the ditches stakes, planks of wood and twisted branches had been arranged to make access impossible except across the bridges the linked the various sections. Beyond the outer ditch was a thigh-high line of stakes and planking. All such sites are of the Yayoi Period, and none is later than AD 300.

THE KOREAN-STYLE FORTRESSES OF THE YAMATO STATE

The development of Yayoi culture culminated in the emergence of the unified Yamato state, the dominant clan lineage that was to become the Japanese imperial house. By the 3rd century AD the Yamato court had achieved supremacy within the area of modern Nara Prefecture and had begun to extend its influence much more widely. The eventual triumph of the Yamato over their domestic opponents is shown by the absence of fortified settlements in Japan beyond about AD 300. Their archaeological monuments are instead the huge *kofun*, keyhole-shaped burial mounds, which date from about AD 250. From the early *kofun* of Hashihaka, 286m long, to the enormous mid-5th-century Daisen *kofun* at 486m, the supremacy of the ruling lineage was asserted locally in no uncertain fashion. Yet other military challenges were to be made to the fledgling imperial hegemony as the centuries went by, and each received a response that involved the creation of different types of fortified positions.

The first challenge concerned Japan's overseas interests. For the first six centuries AD the Korean Peninsula was divided into three kingdoms: Goguryeo in the north bordering China, Baekje in the south-west and Silla in the south-east. The three kingdoms fought each other over the years; sometimes individually, sometimes in alliance with one another, and in the 7th century AD with the involvement in turn of the Sui and Tang dynasties of China. Japan became involved in these conflicts, fielding expeditionary armies to support its ally Baekje and to safeguard its colonial interests in Mimana, a small enclave in the south between Baekje and Silla established some time during the 4th century AD (the traditional date is AD 369). While the Japanese cannot be said to have ruled Mimana in any absolute sense, the limited control they exerted allowed them access to iron and the advanced continental culture. But the wars between the Korean kingdoms placed great pressure on Mimana, which was finally absorbed by Silla in AD 562. The Yamato court planned several expeditions to retake Mimana, some of which were actually put into operation. For example, a Japanese move against Silla in AD 602 is recorded in the *Nihon Shoki* (*Chronicles of Japan*), which was compiled in AD 720. A prince of the imperial house called Prince Kume, who commanded 25,000 men, led it. Yet by the middle of the 7th century AD

THE MOATED YAYOI SETTLEMENT OF YOSHINOGARI UNDER ATTACK: AD 250

The Yayoi Period site of Yoshinogari has been thoroughly excavated and has revealed several defensive features.
In this plate we see a hypothetical attack by a rival tribe on the Minami Naiku, the inner 'palace' to the south of the
complex. The outer ditch has been thoroughly breached, and there is fierce fighting across the inner moat and palisade.
The watchtower is playing an important role in the defence. The sources for the plate are the excavations and
reconstructions at Yoshinogari. (Peter Dennis © Osprey Publishing Ltd)

JAPAN, CHINA AND THE CASTLES BUILT AGAINST CONTINENTAL INVASION

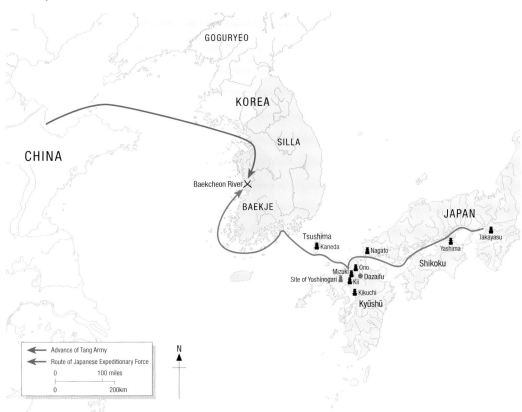

the Yamato court seemed to be content with a nominal recognition of sovereignty from whichever Korean kingdom controlled Mimana.

Japan's continental interests did not, however, decrease with the loss of Mimana. Indeed the Korean problem became more acute because of an increasing involvement by China in Korea's affairs. Towards the end of the 6th century AD the Sui dynasty had succeeded in unifying China after internal wars that had lasted for two and a half centuries. The Sui then turned their attentions towards Korea. A Goguryeo incursion into north-eastern China in AD 598 led to a prompt Sui retaliation into Korea and an apology by the Goguryeo king. Further Sui invasions of Goguryeo followed in AD 612, 613 and 614, but served only to weaken the Sui's influence at home, and the dynasty collapsed in favour of the Tang in AD 617. By the AD 640s the Tang felt secure enough to threaten Goguryeo for themselves. Their initial attempt ended in failure, and Goguryeo's success in defeating a Chinese army encouraged the northern Korean kingdom to become more belligerent against its neighbours.

Anxiety about developments on the continent and a lack of leadership at home led to a palace coup in Japan in AD 645. The new rulers soon turned their attentions to questions of national security and, although much of their attention was focused on the unsettled north-east of their own country, a matter described later, the Taika Reform Edict of AD 645 took in the need for vigilance against a possible foreign invasion from Korea against Japan's southern island of Kyūshū. Article One of the Edict specified that border guards (*sakimori*) should be provided, while Article Four stated that each recruit should supply a sword, armour, bow and arrows, a flag and a drum. In AD 646 another command was issued requiring the repair of arsenals throughout Japan. These arsenals, essentially stockpiles of weapons, did not necessarily imply fortifications, but this was a policy that was to change dramatically within the next two decades.

The reappearance of fortifications on Japanese soil came about because of a major military humiliation in Korea. The background to the disaster dates to AD 656, when Goguryeo armies in alliance with Baekje invaded Silla. Silla asked China for help, and the Tang responded positively with a very clever strategy. They concentrated first on Baekje, with the Tang advancing by sea and their Silla allies by land. Baekje fell in AD 660, but one of their generals survived to lead a resistance movement, and asked Japan for help. A Japanese expeditionary force to aid Baekje was mounted in AD 662 and was reinforced a year later, only to be utterly destroyed in a furious naval battle at the mouth of the Baekcheon River. It was Japan's worst military defeat until World War II. According to Chinese sources, as many as 400 Japanese vessels were sunk in the engagement of AD 663 and over 10,000 men were lost. The survivors limped home to Japan, where the news they conveyed and the sight of the Baekje refugees they brought with them created a state of panic in Japan. The fear of a Chinese and Korean invasion was much more acute than it had been in the AD 640s, and patriotic courtiers took to wearing weapons. More serious reactions appeared within a year of the disaster in AD 664, when the *Nihon Shoki* tells us that Emperor Tenchi gave orders so that: 'In this year guards and beacon fires were placed in the islands of Tsushima and Iki and in the Land of Tsukushi. Moreover a great embankment was constructed and water collected. This was called the *mizuki* [water fortress].'

Frontier guards and beacon fires had been a feature of Japan's earlier emergency preparations, but the construction of the *mizuki* was a dramatic departure from previous policy. As the above entry from *Nihon Shoki* tells us, the 'water castle' was a long, moated earthwork designed to provide protection for the Tsukushi region of Kyūshū, and in particular for the regional headquarters at Dazaifu. It was designed to stall a military advance after a seaborne landing, and was effectively Japan's first ever free-standing fortified structure. Amazingly, much of it can still be seen today. It was originally 40m wide and 15m high and lay between hills across the plain facing Hakata Bay. The reference to the fact that 'water collected' does not mean that it was

A view of Mizuki (the water fortress) as it is today. We are standing on the inner (Dazaifu) side of this remarkable earthwork, which dates from AD 664. The modern road passes through it, affording a cutaway view in the distance.

intended to store water. Instead its construction involved a higher inner moat in which water could accumulate and then be channelled through the rampart to top up the outer moat. The operation is described more fully in a later section. Two smaller versions were built nearby.

Fortifications more recognizable as castles began to appear very soon after the building of Mizuki (to which I have given a capital letter as it is now a recognized monument rather than a type of defensive structure), first in Kyūshū and then along a line along the Inland Sea leading to the centre of Yamato control near modern Nara. Ironically for defences built against possible Korean aggression, these stone structures, the first seen in Japan, were created in the Korean style. This was because Korean refugees from Baekje built them, and these refugees may well have been influential in the policy decision to use fortifications as part of the overall strategic plan against invasion. An entry in the *Nihon Shoki* for AD 665 tells us: 'Tappon Chunjo … was sent to the *kuni* [province or defined area] of Nagato to build a fortress. Ongnye Pongnyu … and Sabi Pokpu were sent to the *kuni* of Tsukushi to build the two fortresses of Ono and Kii.'

Ongnye Pongnyu, who was jointly responsible for the construction of the important Kyūshū fortresses of Ono and Kii, had fled from Baekje along with the survivors of the Japanese fleet in AD 663, and showed his gratitude by producing impressive castles modelled on the Korean *sanseong* (mountain fortresses) with which he would have been familiar at home. Embankments of earth or stone encircled prominent hilltops and ridges. Storehouses for rice were built within them to make a complex that was both a military base and a refuge for those living nearby. Ono and Kii were located on the tops of mountains to the north and south respectively of Dazaifu, and augmented the ground-level defence of Mizuki. The other castle referred to in the above quotation was built in Nagato Province at the western end of the Inland Sea.

Over the next few years the Tang Chinese went on to conquer Goguryeo, so that by AD 667 the Japanese rulers became more alarmed than ever and more fortresses were built. Kaneda (sometimes written Kanata) on

Kaneda Castle on the island of Tsushima was built in AD 667 to provide Japan's 'early warning system' for a possible invasion. In this picture we are looking up from the sea shore to the immense cliffs on which Kaneda was built.

Tsushima Island, located on a high mountain peak overlooking the sea halfway between Korea and the Japanese mainland, was clearly intended to provide Japan's 'early warning system'. Other castles formed a line of defence and communications between Kyūshū and Yamato along the Inland Sea, covering any likely advance in that direction, while Kikuchi in modern Kumamoto Prefecture provided logistical support for Kii and Ono. Yashima in Sanuki Province on Shikoku Island was built on high ground overlooking Takamatsu Harbour at the other end of the Inland Sea. Long after the castle had disappeared this was to become the location of the famous battle of Yashima in 1184. Finally, Takayasu was erected in the Yamato homelands. All appear to have been completed within a two-year period.

The castles continued to be maintained for over four decades, and there are records of construction and repairs of fortresses up to AD 701, but political changes on the Asian continent eventually made them redundant. After falling out with their Silla allies the Tang abandoned Korea altogether in AD 676, leaving the peninsula united under Silla. The Silla rulers were still very anti-Japanese, but without their powerful ally they were unable to pose a credible military threat. In AD 701 Takayasu Castle is noted as having been 'abolished', the immediate threat from China and Korea having subsided. There were to be further scares originating in China and Korea over the next two centuries, but none was sufficient to prompt a new phase of fortress construction. Threats to imperial stability now tended to come from the north of Japan, where some very different fortresses were built in response.

THE NORTHERN FORTRESSES

In addition to their involvement on the Korean Peninsula, the Yamato rulers faced a military threat in the north-east of Japan itself, where the strongest resistance to their assumption of control was to be found in Tōhoku, the distant territories that the Yamato called the provinces of Dewa and Mutsu. This was the land of the barbarians, whose savage ways precluded them from accepting the benevolent rule of the Yamato court. These truculent enemies are referred to as *emishi*, a term that does little to identify their racial origin, a matter that is still controversial to this day. They may have been identical to the Ainu, who still live on in Hokkaidō, but whatever their racial origins there is a clear implication that the *emishi* were 'beyond the pale' of Yamato civilization. The *emishi* were despised as blood-drinking, hole-dwelling savages by the Yamato rulers, whose written records show a great deal of contempt for them in every field except their military skills. In AD 724, for example, an *emishi* revolt took eight months to put down.

Yamato efforts to bring the *emishi* under their control began in the latter half of the 7th century AD, and accelerated following the creation of Nara as Japan's first permanent capital city in AD 710. From this time on the Yamato rulers may be referred to as the emperors of Japan. In an act of optimism over their future subjugation the designated provinces of Mutsu and Dewa were divided into administrative districts, and a long programme of conquest began. Its success was hindered by the policy of the imperial court of appointing submissive *emishi* chiefs as local rulers, a good idea that backfired when the process served to increase the chiefs' prestige and, as a direct consequence, their sense of independence and resistance.

Crucial to the pacification process was the establishment of fortifications. This time there were no Korean refugees to design fortresses for the Japanese, so instead of stone we find timber. The character '*saku*', which was often read as '-*ki*' and is usually translated as 'stockade' or 'fort', is the word that is used for them in contemporary literature. To refer to them in English by names such as 'Fort Akita' or 'Fort Monofu' conjures up appropriate images of frontier forts built from earth and wood, and the pictorial character itself resembles a wooden

The reconstructed one-storey barracks at Kikuchi Castle, which was probably built to provide logistic support for the other Korean-style castles of Kyūshū that were located on the 'front line'.

Left: Hotta no saku provides an excellent example of the northern model of a wooden stockade fortress surrounding an administrative complex. Hotta is built on a low hill, and was surrounded by a wooden palisade, of which this section, which includes a fine gateway, has been reconstructed.

Right: A drawing of an alternative means of construction for a northern fortress. Here the wall is made of rammed earth with a weatherproof roof. (From a drawing in the Tōhoku History Museum, by kind permission)

palisade. Later on the more familiar ideograph read as either 'shiro' or 'jō' was adopted, but was still read as '-ki'. This character may be derived from a combination of Chinese characters indicating 'tsuchi kara naru', or 'piling up soil', which was the action of creating an embankment from an excavated ditch.

Echigo Province, which bordered Dewa to the south, received two *saku* in AD 647 and 648. More were built in Mutsu and Dewa over the next two centuries, a slow pace of occupation that shows how cautiously the borders of Yamato civilization crept northwards. The larger forts were not simply military bases. Instead they were centres of imperial state administration that acted as the outposts of centralized rule in enemy territory. As both forts and offices, these defended locations did not merely administer a territory but actively facilitated its creation. Settler families, who were referred to as 'stockade households' (*kinohe*), were transplanted to Dewa and Mutsu to work the lands around the fortified places, which also provided them with security in case of *emishi* attack. A network of smaller stockades linked the major bases.

The most important large stockade base was Fort Taga, which dated from AD 724 and was located to the east of the modern city of Sendai at the southern end of Mutsu Province. It served for many years as the provincial government headquarters for Mutsu and eventually grew to be more of a fortified palace, becoming known as Tagajō or 'Taga Castle', the same name as the modern town that now surrounds the site, rather than a stockade (Taga no saku). It was originally the site of the 'pacification headquarters' (Chinjō, later called Chinjufu), a revealing term that indicates how tenuous was the hold on Mutsu exerted by the imperial court at that time.

The corresponding headquarters for Dewa Province was Fort Akita (in modern Akita City), which lay deep in the province and was established in AD 733. A major military operation began in AD 737 when the Yamato attempted to cut a road between the two bases. Over the next 50 years Fort Monofu in Mutsu and Fort Okachi in Dewa were added in a process involving a total labour force of 8,000 men. The completion of Fort Iji in

AD 767 was greatly resented by the local *emishi* and provoked an uprising. In AD 774, when these centres were all in place, a major initiative to crush the *emishi* began and lasted for 40 years. Five considerable expeditions followed in AD 776, 788, 794, 801 and 811, after which it was reckoned that the 'Grand Pacification Era', as it was dubbed, had come to a successful end.

CASTLES OF THE HEIAN PERIOD

In AD 710 Nara became Japan's first permanent capital city. Its design was copied from that of Chang'an, the capital of the Tang dynasty on the site of the modern city of Xi'an. Recent archaeological studies have indicated that the original palace complex at Nara, called Heijō-kyō, was defended by a large wall very similar in design and construction to the walls of Taga and Akita. A wall was begun around Heian-kyō (Kyoto), the capital city that succeeded Nara in AD 794, but was soon abandoned. Nor do we find any evidence of strong permanent watchtowers or heavily fortified gateways around Japanese capital cities. In the case of Kyoto this is perhaps surprising, because the Heian Period (AD 794–1192) belies its name as a time of 'peace and tranquillity'. A number of wars and revolts occurred, culminating in the Gempei War of 1180–85, but the only concession to defensive works within the capital itself would appear to be the erection of watchtowers on a temporary basis when imminent danger threatened, such as the revolt by the 'pirate king' Fujiwara Sumitomo in AD 940. On that occasion the climate of fear was such that the New Year ceremonies were conducted under armed guard. Otherwise the residences of the up-and-coming samurai class bore few defensive features.

There were nonetheless numerous incidents involving fortified places during the wars of the time, but these were fought around isolated stockade outposts that, like Kyoto's watchtowers, appear to have been erected initially as temporary strongholds while a campaign unfolded. The fortresses involved

Akita was the administrative centre for Dewa Province and has been extensively excavated. This is the reconstructed eastern gateway, looking out. The gateway is of wood with rammed-earth-plastered walls.

ANCIENT AND EARLY MODERN CASTLE SITES OF NORTHERN JAPAN

in these struggles were very different from the ordered headquarters complexes such as Taga and Akita. Compared to those regular long walls of beaten earth, they must have looked very rough and ready and resembled more the original *saku*, although some of the mountain strongholds could be very extensive, particularly if their use turned out to be prolonged.

One of the earliest examples of a stockade to see action, and one of the largest such complexes ever to be built, was Kuriyagawa (the site of which now lies within modern Morioka City), which was attacked during the

This useful reconstruction at the Esashi Fujiwara Heritage Park is an attempt to recreate the main gateway of Abe Sadatō's Kawasaki Castle, the site of much fighting in 1057 during the Former Nine Years' War. It is made completely from wood, with sloping parapets and a small guardhouse.

Zenkunen no eki, the 'Former Nine Years' War' (1051–62). The bitter siege of Kanezawa, which bore the brunt of most of the fighting during the Gosannen no eki, the 'Later Three Years' War' of 1083–87, also involved a stockade castle of considerable size. A century later the battle of Ichinotani in 1184, an epic struggle that became one of the most famous battles of the Gempei War, involved the defence of an elaborate stockade fortress between steep cliffs and the seashore near to modern Kobe.

The Former Nine Years' War and the Later Three Years' War were fought in the north of Japan, but unlike the earlier expeditions against the *emishi*, where Taga and Akita had played the role of the outposts of civilization in barbarian lands, the fighting in and around the military stockades was conducted by rival samurai. These men tended to be either the descendants of *emishi* who had submitted to the Yamato and become integrated into the Japanese aristocracy, or were descended from warriors who had pacified the *emishi* and acquired their lands as a reward.

For example, the Former Nine Years' War, the first such encounter in which fortified places played a prominent role, was conducted on and off over a period of 12 years against a man who was effectively the last of the *emishi* chieftains. Abe Yoritoki's family had ruled over the six districts of Mutsu for three generations. Yoritoki was a member of the Heian establishment, and now collected taxes and kept the peace in that remote part of Japan as its hereditary district magistrate. It was Yoritoki's refusal to hand over the taxes he had collected, rather than any 'barbarian uprising', that led the court to appoint Minamoto Yoriyoshi to the position of Governor of Mutsu and General of the Military Headquarters at Taga, with a commission to bring Yoritoki to heel.

Early on in the campaign Abe Yoritoki was killed, but his son Abe Sadatō continued to resist, and during the winter of 1057 entrenched himself within a stockade fortress known as Kawasaki. There Minamoto Yoriyoshi attacked him during a blizzard. Sadatō successfully drove away the besiegers, who carried out a fighting retreat under the command of Yoriyoshi's son Yoshiie, a man who was to become one of the greatest heroes of the Minamoto family. In 1062 the Minamoto, reinforced by a local samurai leader called Kiyohara Mitsuyori, mounted a further campaign against Sadatō from the protection of Taga. A series of sieges of stockade fortresses followed, the Minamoto taking Toriumi and Kurosawajiri with a final showdown at Kuriyagawa, where an epic siege took place.

The Later Three Years' War also involved samurai fighting in and around stockade fortresses. This conflict was not an official government commission to chastise a rebel but rather a private war between Minamoto Yoshiie, the son of the victorious Yoriyoshi from the Former Nine Years' War, and various members of the redoubtable Kiyohara family who had played a crucial role in ensuring the earlier Minamoto victory. The year 1086 was to find Minamoto Yoshiie besieging Kiyohara Iehira in the stockade fortress of Numa. While Yoshiie was regrouping Iehira was joined by his uncle Takehira, who advised a withdrawal to the stronger position of Kanezawa. It was a wise move, and Kanezawa held out until late in 1087. Many heads were taken during the fierce fighting, but as the government correctly regarded the operation as a private war no reward was forthcoming for Minamoto Yoshiie, so an angry Yoshiie threw the heads into a ditch rather than present them as trophies.

The family who benefited most from the wars in the north was the Fujiwara, whose 'northern branch', the Oshū Fujiwara, were very proud of their *emishi* descent. Their later descendants proclaimed their acceptance of civilization by creating a cultured mini-kingdom of their own in Hiraizumi that was regarded as a 'little Kyoto'. Tsunekiyo, the first of the northern Fujiwara lords, fought and died alongside Abe Yoritoki at the start of the Former Nine Years' War. Fujiwara Kiyohira, Tsunekiyo's son, was adopted into the Kiyohara family and gained his independence from them in 1083. This was the beginning of the 'golden age' of the Oshū Fujiwara. Kiyohira died in 1128, having established at Hiraizumi the great Buddhist temple of Chūsonji (with its wonderful surviving Konjikidō or Golden Hall). His son Motohira was responsible for the construction of the temple of Mōtsuji, while the third Fujiwara lord Hidehira developed the site of the family's riverside mansion of Yanagi no Gosho, which, although a palace complex, was defended by walls and ditches in the finest style of the times.

Fujiwara Hidehira died in 1187, and two years later his son Yasuhira was to experience the destruction of the family and much of its aristocratic culture. This was brought about by Minamoto Yoritomo, Japan's first hereditary *shōgun*, in what was to some extent the last campaign against the *emishi*, or at least against their direct descendants. Ironically, Yoritomo was the descendant of Minamoto Yoriyoshi who had fought the first Fujiwara lord over a century earlier.

The conflict between the two families came about as follows. Minamoto Yoritomo had become the victor over the Taira family in the Gempei War of

This simple model in Fukushima Prefectural Museum attempts to show the operation of the triple ditched earthwork erected at Atsukashiyama by Fujiwara Kunihira to frustrate the advance north by Minamoto Yoritomo in 1189.

1180–85, but his success had been brought about largely by his talented younger brother Yoshitsune. One of Minamoto Yoshitsune's most celebrated victories had been achieved against the fortified position of Ichinotani in 1184. The Taira had always been pre-eminent in sea fighting, due largely to their expertise in quelling pirates on the Inland Sea, and their base of Ichinotani was cleverly designed to give them ready access to ships from its stockade walls. These ships provided their means of escape when the Minamoto attacked along the beach and launched a surprise assault at the rear of the Ichinotani compound, where it was lightly defended. The only access to it was down a steep cliff path, so Yoshitsune led a daring assault using this dramatic entrance. The following year Yoshitsune's victory at Dannoura destroyed the Taira, but the jealous Minamoto Yoritomo then turned against Yoshitsune, who fled to the north of Japan and found sanctuary with the Fujiwara.

Faced by the advance north of Yoritomo's army in 1189, Fujiwara Kunihira, Yasuhira's eldest son, took charge of the task of stalling the advance. To do this he resorted to a bold defensive measure by excavating a triple embankment earthwork with a double ditch over a distance of about 3km between the mountain of Atsukashiyama and the Atsukashi River. It resembled ancient Mizuki in everything but the water; although it was reinforced with watchtowers and defended by siege crossbows for the last time in Japanese history, it succeeded in stalling the Minamoto advance for only a short time. Fujiwara Kunihira was killed in the fighting, and not long afterwards his family's illustrious refugee, Yoshitsune, was finally defeated by Yoritomo at the battle of Koromogawa.

CASTLES OF THE KAMAKURA PERIOD

Minamoto Yoritomo's triumph led to the establishment of Japan's first shogunate or military dictatorship under the nominal rule of the emperor.

Yoritomo moved the administrative capital from Kyoto to Kamakura, so that the time from 1192 to 1333 is known as the Kamakura Period. Kamakura fronted on to the sea and was surrounded on three sides by mountains, with the only access by land being a few easily defensible mountain passes or man-made tunnels carved out of the soft rock. A long earthwork that followed the line of the most prominent ridge augmented these natural fortifications. Two strategic stockade castles, at Sugimoto in the centre of the fortifications and Sumiyoshi at the eastern end of the beach, further strengthened the line. Kamakura thus became an unusual example of a Japanese fortified city, and its combination of natural and man-made defences served the place well when it was attacked in 1333. The investing army only broke in when a detachment under Nitta Yoshisada managed to make its way round the cape of Inamuragasaki at the western end of the beach at low tide. It was a move so unexpected by both sides that it was regarded as miraculous.

Hardly any use seems to have been made of stone at Kamakura, even though fortifications built of stone had recently made a brief reappearance on the Japanese scene as a result of the attempt by Kublai Khan, the Yuan (Mongol) emperor of China, to invade Japan in 1274. The experience of the first invasion prompted the Japanese to construct a number of long stone walls round Hakata Bay in 1275. Each had a sheer face on the outside but had a slope up from the rear, so that horses could be ridden on to the parapet. The walls provided an archery base when the Mongols returned in 1281. The walls' location was only a short distance from the site of Mizuki, designed, of course, to counter a similar possible landing six centuries earlier. It is believed that Mizuki played a role in stopping the Mongol advance in 1274, because their first invasion, a fairly brief reconnaissance in force, involved burning the Hakozaki shrine on the road from Hakata Bay to Dazaifu. They then turned back, probably in the vicinity of Mizuki. It may be that the presence of the earthwork encouraged the withdrawal, but no attempt appears to have been made to restore that structure in 1275.

During the Nanbokucho Wars (the Wars between the Courts) of the 14th century, several celebrated sieges were conducted against hill-top castles. Kasagi was the first such encounter, where the fantastically shaped natural rocks on Kasagiyama were augmented by man-made defences to provide a refuge for Emperor Go-Daigo, who had raised the standard of revolt against the *bakufu*, the shogunal government currently under the control of the Hōjō family. Go-Daigo then fled to the stronger position of Akasaka and then to Chihaya, where the mountain-top defences were in the capable hands of the great imperial loyalist Kusunoki Masashige. This was about the same time that the natural defences of Kamakura were being breached by the other imperial hero, Nitta Yoshisada, in 1333. The wooden stockade walls and lookout towers of Kasagi, Akasaka and Chihaya would not have differed greatly in appearance from the fortresses of the Gosannen War. Their particular identifying feature was the mountain-top location; hence the term *yamashiro* or 'mountain castle'.

MANSIONS AND MOUNTAINS

The heyday of the *yamashiro* was the latter quarter of the 15th century and the first half of the 16th, a time that was characterized by the gradual decline of the *shōgun*'s authority as a result of the Onin War of 1467–77, and its replacement by the new independent *daimyō*. Many *daimyō* had modest beginnings and very small territories of their own, and would set up bases for themselves in defensible locations such as high ground at a river's confluence or on top of a mountain. Various designs existed, their features being determined largely by the existing topography. Small mountain-top *yamashiro* provided lookout posts and 'last-stand' refuges in times of war, while larger castles became the nuclei of growing communities.

As many of the restored castle sites in Japan have been rebuilt only on the top of hills, the erroneous impression has sometimes been given that no other structure ever existed, but in addition to mountain-top stockade castles, the other characteristic defended structure to be found at this time was the fortified mansion or *yashiki*. They ranged from simple structures to elaborate complexes built along river valleys. These princely locations had fortified gatehouses and watchtowers, and towns evolved around the mansions where artisans worked and tradesmen were established under the protection of the nearby *yamashiro*. This evolution from the Kamakura warrior residences and mountain-top stockades to complex wooden castles continued as the locus of power moved from the centre towards the localized control exerted by the *daimyō*, so that by the mid-16th century these warrior bases had become important political and military centres. Ichijōdani, the seat of the Asakura family, and Tsutsujigasaki, the moated mansion of Takeda Shingen, are two excellent examples.

At the same time, almost inevitably, many mountain-top castles tended to become as important as the mansions they were designed to support, although, contrary to popular belief, they did not necessarily replace the mansions entirely. As late as the 1560s, for example, we find a dual system whereby the actual living quarters of most castle complexes were located around the base of a mountain and linked to the mountain-top site by a series of footpaths and levelled areas. Omi-Hachiman, for example, consisted of two very distinct sites: a *yamashiro* on top of the mountain and a growing castle town defended by moats and canals fed from Lake Biwa. Excellent examples are provided by the fortresses of the Hōjō family, whose castles in the Kantō plain, the area around modern Tokyo, show how cleverly the existing terrain could be utilized for defensive purposes. Hachigata made use of a prominent bluff overlooking a fast-flowing river, while Yamanaka dominated the narrow pass over the Hakone Mountains within sight of Mount Fuji. Takane Castle, a stronghold of the Takeda family, controlled a river valley in central Japan.

Design and Development

The following section covers the design and development of the different styles of Japanese fortified places introduced in the historical survey previously mentioned. It is illustrated by reference to certain key sites that are representative of their type either through preservation, written records, archaeological investigation or modern reconstruction. One important consideration to bear in mind about these early Japanese castles is that they rarely stood alone, but that each existed as one element within a complex defensive system.

THE FORTIFIED YAYOI SETTLEMENT

The best example of a fortified Yayoi site is the impressive Yoshinogari. Yoshinogari is not only a very important archaeological site, but is also one of Japan's newest and busiest tourist attractions. The small non-military Yayoi site of Toro, excavated just after World War II, had given the Japanese a sense of ancient identity that was sorely needed at the time. Yoshinogari, being a complex and wealthy settlement ruled by a king or chieftain, promised more richness of heritage, and has not disappointed. Speculation that Yoshinogari might actually be the capital of the kingdom ruled over by Princess Himiko has added enormously to the site's popularity.

Yoshinogari seems to have been settled throughout the Yayoi Period, but it is in the Middle and Late Yayoi that we find the key component of the Yoshinogari site, which is a large moated settlement with indisputably defensive features extending over an area of 25 hectares. The outer moat of Yoshinogari is V-shaped and fronted by a reverse-trapezoidal-shaped earth embankment constructed from soil brought up from the ditch. Wooden posts were set along this mound as a further defence. The maximum width of the moat was about 6.3m and about 3m deep. The embankment was between 2.5 and 3m wide and 2m high. An inner moat with a flat bottom encircles the inner settlement where more than 100 Middle to Late Yayoi pit buildings were found, while the

One of the finest reconstructed buildings in Japan is the drum tower at Kikuchi Castle. It is very much in the continental style, and resembles a contemporary Sui or Tang dynasty Chinese pagoda.

space between them was occupied by storehouses. The Yoshinogari storehouses are unusually large compared to other known examples.

There are also a considerable number of jar burials on the site. The broken points of stone swords were found in two of the jars, and were probably embedded in the corpses when they were interred. In one other jar were 12 arrowheads, while a further corpse was headless. All these finds have been accepted as evidence of warfare around the Yoshinogari site. The Minami Naiku (South Inner Palace) is believed to be the area where the *taijin* (rulers) of Yoshinogari lived and carried out their administrative duties. Houses, kitchens and an assembly hall have been identified.

Apart from the fence and ditches, the most striking defensive structures at Yoshinogari are the massive watchtowers. The identification comes from the strategic positions occupied by the posthole groups. The *Wei Zhi* account of

One of the four huge watchtowers in the South Inner Palace enclosure at Yoshinogari. It was the discovery of these towers that led to speculation that Yoshinogari might be the site of Princess Himiko's palace because similar structures are described in the Chinese dynastic histories.

Princess Himiko's domain says that she dwelt in a settlement surrounded by watchtowers, a description that is uncannily like Yoshinogari. There are two types of tower. The smaller type, built using four uprights, either acts as fortified gateways straddling the entrance across a moat, or is built immediately adjacent to an entrance. In the reconstruction they have been given no roofs, just a flat horizontal platform with a wooden parapet round the outside, and there are no actual gates in the gateway opening. The larger types are enormous roofed structures raised on six uprights. Here the horizontal platform is completely covered by a thatched canopy that extends just outside the parapet. In the process of reconstruction steps have been added for the safety of modern visitors, but are of a design that would probably not have been found during the Yayoi Period. There are four such watchtowers within the Minami Naiku. The northern watchtower is of different design from the others in that it has an offset central pillar that allows a larger deck on top. This unique design, and the fact that it overlooks the north burial mound and the north inner palace, has provoked suggestions that it had a special function.

THE KOREAN-STYLE FORTRESSES

Dazaifu, the regional seat of government for Kyūshū, was protected against a possible Chinese or Korean invasion by a complex defensive system. Aerial views of the area show how natural features were used and augmented to create a 'Maginot Line' – a planned battlefield where an invading enemy could be stalled and then driven back into the sea. Dazaifu, now a modern city of modest size, lies inland from the major modern metropolis of Fukuoka that sprawls around the shore of Hakata Bay. As Hakata Bay provides shallow water and a huge sheltered anchorage protected from the ocean by the island of Shiga, it was natural to assume that this would be the preferred landing point for a continental invasion. So it was to prove with the Mongol invasions of 1274 and 1281, but the defensive strategy adopted during the 7th century AD was very different. The whole accent was not on preventing a landing, but on containing an enemy's advance against Dazaifu.

Dazaifu itself was a palace-like complex surrounded by walls much like the arrangement found in Nara. Like Nara, it was built to a design copied from the Tang dynasty capital at Chang'an. It lay on flat land at the foot of a prominent mountain along the natural line of communication from Hakata Bay to the south. More mountains rose on its southern side, so the extraordinary Mizuki filled the gap between them. Two similar embankments, the Ko mizuki (little water fortress) and the Kasuga embankment, closed off the two valleys immediately to the west. Two further dry earthworks existed even further west.

As noted above, Mizuki was built in AD 664. It was originally 1.2km long, 80m wide and 10m high. The name 'water fortress' comes from the moat on the outer, Hakata side. This was originally 60m wide and 4m deep. The water level was kept topped up in two ways, first by the waters of the river that passed through a gap in the embankment on its way to the sea, and second by a clever drainage system that allowed water to flow down from the Dazaifu side under the structure. The huge pipes were made from massive wooden planks expertly dovetailed and held in place by iron clamps. The collecting channel ran at a right angle to the entrance to the pipe and was anchored by large tree trunks buried in the ground to give stability. The pipe (or pipes – it is unclear how many there were) would have been put in place before the embankment was finished, and archaeological study has shown how successive layers of earth were beaten down on top of one another. The finished Mizuki would have been crossed at least once along its length by a road protected by a gatehouse.

In addition to these earthworks, Dazaifu was defended by two castles built in the style of a Korean *sanseong* on the two adjacent mountains. Ono Castle lay on Shiōjiyama to the north and was built in AD 665. In typical Korean fashion, all the vegetation was cleared from the top of the mountain and a serpentine stone wall erected that followed the contours to give a complete defensive perimeter, 8km in total circumference. The walls would have been of two sorts: earthworks built from rammed layers of soil, as well as walls of dry stone construction at the most strategic points, such as gateway entrances along valleys. These stone walls had a smooth outer surface built with a gentle slope on the outside around a rammed rubble core. Very simple buildings were erected inside the enclosed area, although the gates would have been quite elaborate with pavilions on top. A simple wooden palisade existed outside the wall. Nowadays all that remains are small sections of the stone and earth walls, as well as the foundation stones of 70 buildings. Kii Castle to the south was very similar.

In the foreground of this view of Yoshinogari is the V-shaped moat and palisade that provided the main defence for the site.

Kii and Ono were the first castles to be built in a programme that was to see eight similar structures added over the next few years. The most dramatic location belonged to Kaneda Castle (Kanata no ki) on the island of Tsushima. It lies on the highest point of a promontory that projects in a northerly direction into the sea on the southern of the two islands that make up Tsushima. Dramatic slopes extend down on all sides, giving watch over the sea and the river valley to the south-east. The site is so inaccessible that it can have had little use other than as a defensible observation post. Nevertheless neat stone walls in the Korean style still survive, even though they are only accessible after a very steep 30-minute climb.

In marked contrast we find the fortress of Kikuchi in Kumamoto Prefecture, which is located on a low hill. This site has yielded a wealth of archaeological information, and now sports a number of reconstructed buildings, including storehouses and a spectacular octagonal wooden drum tower. Kikuchi Castle's function would appear to have been that of providing logistical support to Dazaifu in the form of food, weapons and soldiers from a location way behind the 'front line'. A posting to Kikuchi may well have been regarded as a 'cushy number' compared to windswept Tsushima! The complex appears to have been divided into a number of areas, modestly defended by wooden palisades and containing rice storehouses, weapon stores, barracks buildings and the like. A rammed earth wall enclosed the overall complex, strengthened at vulnerable points with stone walls and fortified gates just as in the case of Ono and Kii. The gates must have been very heavy, as shown by the holes of the pivots, which are carved into massive stones that have survived. The storehouses are built on raised piles and have thatched roofs. The barracks are one-storey buildings with shingle roofs. The drum tower is the most interesting feature of the site. It is of three-storey construction and resembles a Chinese pagoda.

THE NORTHERN CASTLES

The *saku* (palisaded forts) in Dewa and Mutsu were not the only buildings to be created by the Yamato on the borders of their civilization, because as the growing Yamato state expanded towards the north we begin to see the establishment of aristocratic dwellings in places far distant from the centre of power. Sometime around the middle of the 6th century AD Mitsudera was created in what is now modern Gumma Prefecture. Excavations have revealed it to be a moated settlement arranged on a very formal rectangular basis. But was Mitsudera a fortified place? This is by no means clear, and the safest term to use for places like Mitsudera is to describe them as 'elite residences', leaving the question of fortifications unanswered until further evidence becomes available.

By contrast, the identification of fortified places becomes less problematic at places where the Yamato civilization begins to encounter the *emishi*. Unlike the Dazaifu defensive complex in Kyūshū, which was designed to protect Japanese

territory against foreign aggression, the northern castles developed as a dynamic system designed to advance the borders of the Japanese state into hostile territory. Nevertheless, although different in intent, we see some striking similarities, particularly in the design of the administrative buildings located safely within the defensive walls. As the major forts of Akita and Taga grew to become regional centres, their outer walls began to shelter complexes of administrative buildings that resembled Dazaifu on a smaller scale. Most of the northern forts were built on flat land, although forts Taga and Hotta were built on hills.

The typical northern castle combined defensive works with an administrative centre, the usual arrangement being a long outer perimeter wall set some considerable distance from the civilian buildings within. At Fort Monofu the outer wall enclosed an area of 2.8km², while the inner wall measured 72m north to south and 116m east to west. Unlike the Korean-style fortifications of Kyūshū, these northern castles made no use of stone other than as foundations. Instead the main means of construction was rammed earth above a shallow foundation of undressed stone. It was a technique that was also to be found in the government buildings of Nara and Dazaifu. The soil, dug from a depth sufficient to guarantee that no seeds would be present, was carried to the site in a bag slung from a bamboo pole resting on the shoulders of two men. Here it would be mixed with water and carried up ladders to the latest layer. The overall shape of the wall, which was of trapezoidal cross section to give stability, was marked out by a series of scaffolding poles. When the mix was tipped, in wooden shuttering held it in place, just like modern concrete, but instead of simply waiting for it to set, each layer was rammed down by a team of men. The presence of sand and perhaps shells in the mix produced a very strong wall when it dried out. When one length of wall was complete the next along was begun, and the joins can still be discerned on excavated sections. The final stage was to give it a coating of plaster and add a tiled roof to weatherproof it. The tiles were laid across wooden trusses set at intervals along the wall. When done with precision the resulting construction was both neat and attractive, and its clean rectangular lines contrasted with the curved surface of the Korean-style stone walls in Kyūshū.

Left: An elevated rice storehouse reconstructed on the site of Kikuchi Castle.

Right: Hotta Castle was built on a low hill. The reconstructed gateway is just visible in the low foreground. The rectangular *seichō* is completely surrounded by an almost elliptical inner defence wall round the edge of the hill.

This model in the Tōhoku
Historical Museum is of the
seichō that formed a neat
rectangle in the Chinese
style within the immense
outer defences of Fort Taga.
The main building in the
middle was called the
seiden. The layout of
Dazaifu, the Regional
Headquarters in Kyūshū that
the Korean-style fortresses
were built to defend, was
very similar but on a much
larger scale. Every official
building complex dating
from the Nara Period can
trace its ultimate inspiration
to Chang'an, the capital of
the Tang dynasty of China.

Other buildings within the compound were made in a similar way, or could make more use of wood, whereby vertical posts resting on foundation stones gave the overall shape for the building, to which lath and plaster walls were added between the verticals, with a more extensive tiled roof. So, for example, the innermost part of Akita Castle – the *seichō* (government office) – consisted of five buildings within a precise rectangular courtyard arranged like a 'five' in dominoes. The building in the middle was called the *seiden*. The *seichō* lay in the middle of a wide area enclosing $550m^2$ and encircled by a defensive wall of beaten earth 2.1m high. Here no attempt was made to keep to a strict rectangular shape. There were two right-angled corners, but otherwise the wall was curved and followed the contours of the landscape as in the Korean models. The East Gate of Akita's outer wall has been reconstructed. It is of a simple but sturdy construction in the middle of a horizontal section of wall. The roof was given overhanging eaves that protect the actual entrance.

A very different style of outer wall is to be found at nearby Hotta. Here the modern reconstruction shows a wooden wall of stout vertical planking topped off by a horizontal beam. The fortified gate is a very impressive structure. It is built entirely of wood and is of two storeys. The lower part covers the entrance and is reminiscent of Akita except for its lack of colour. The upper storey has a projecting defensive walkway around it within a parapet. The inner *seiden*, however, is just like Akita's, being of rectangular shape although on a low hill. However, Hotta's *seiden* lies within not one but two outer walls, each the shape of an irregular ellipse. Archaeological investigation has revealed that some sections of this wall were of stone.

The most impressive *seiden* of all was to be found at Taga, which was founded in AD 724. Tagajō began life as a rough outpost and evolved into what was effectively a fortified town. As befitted the major fortress in northern Japan, the headquarters building of Taga was a splendid rectangular courtyard with gates at the four points of the compass and a fine two-storeyed building at its centre. Another office building lay just behind it. Several sections of Taga's very long perimeter wall have survived and show it to be of rammed earth construction, although use was also made of planking walls at places along its great length. Its fortified gatehouses were very similar to those at

Hotta, but Taga also sported fighting towers that straddled the walls. These simple openwork lookout towers consisted of a platform built over the length of the tiled wall, held in place by large vertical posts on either side of the wall. Access to the fighting platform was by means of a trapdoor and a ladder from the inside of the wall. Examples of similar towers have been reconstructed at the site of Shiwa Castle in Morioka. They are arranged at intervals of about 50m along the wall on either side of the main gate.

MANSIONS AND FORTRESSES OF THE HEIAN PERIOD

With the Heian Period two further types of defended buildings emerge. First, we see the development of quite sophisticated warrior residences. Some are the homes of low-ranking samurai and have only rudimentary defensive features, if they have any at all. A typical warrior's home would have been a fairly simple farmhouse of a size commensurate with his rank, and differed only from the homes of samurai in Kyoto in its more rural construction and its proximity to the owner's rice fields. These *yakata* (samurai mansions) would have been built on low ground or on an elevated plot near to the fields. Rough wooden fences marked their boundaries, which were often surrounded by water-filled ditches crossed by simple bridges. Gates had thatched roofs to protect them against the weather, as did the simple main buildings. Yet none of these features could be regarded as a military structure. This was a role exercised solely by the large stockades where the warriors gathered in times of war, and it was to be another century before the two types of building merged, as shown by the *yakata* that appears on a painted scroll called *Ippen hijiri e*, which dates from the 13th century. The scene is of the priest Ippen visiting a warrior's mansion, which is very well defended with strong wooden walls.

Two of the reconstructed towers of Shiwa Castle, one of the fortresses of Mutsu. The towers lie along the southern wall together with a gateway very similar to the one at Hotta. Shiwa now lies within the city of Morioka.

41

GUARD DUTY AT THE NORTHERN CASTLE OF TAGAJŌ: AD 700

Tagajō was the regional command centre for Mutsu Province in the north of Japan, built, like all the other northern stockades, to pacify and control the *emishi*. In this plate we see the outer wall of Tagajō, which is crossed by a large but simple lookout tower like those at Shiwa where an *ōyumi* (giant crossbow) has been installed. Built into the wall is a flushing toilet, which is currently in use. The sources for the plate are the excavations and reconstructions at Tagajō, Akita, Hotta and the Tōhoku History Museum. The crossbow is based on Chinese models that resemble the written descriptions of Japanese *ōyumi*. (Peter Dennis © Osprey Publishing Ltd)

This bas relief is to be found at the park near Gosannen that is built on the site of Minamoto Yoshiie's siege headquarters during the siege of Kanezawa in 1087. It is based on a section from the contemporary painted scroll of the Later Three Years' War. A defender is looking out from a watchtower that has sloping sides and is festooned with arrows that have been loosed against it. Important defensive features are the rocks secured by ropes that pass over a tree trunk. When the ropes are cut the rocks will fall on any attacker who may be climbing up.

The most important type of fortified building during the Heian Period was the temporary mountain stockade that emerged during the Former Nine Years' War and the Later Three Years' War. From the first of these conflicts we have a literary description of the fortresses, and from the second we have a pictorial record. The *Mutsuwaki* (*Tale of Mutsu*) is a near-contemporary literary work that was probably based on eyewitness reports from samurai who had served in the Former Nine Years' War. For pictorial sources we find fortifications featured three times on a contemporary picture scroll of the Later Three Years' War. The *Mutsuwaki* makes it clear that the defences associated with these fortresses could be quite extensive, when it notes that: 'The rebels had blocked the trails with felled trees and obstructed the roads with debris from the banks of the river, which persistent rain had swollen to flood stage'. There is also a good account of how the site of the fortresses made use of the local topography:

> Sadatō had built his stronghold, Kuriyagawa Stockade, on a site adjoined on the north and the west by a great swamp and on the other two sides by rivers with sheer impassable banks more than three *jō* [about 10m] high. Fierce warriors manned its towers, and it was separated from the rivers by dry trenches bristling with upturned knives. The surface of the ground was strewn with caltrops.

These literary descriptions are reflected in the pictorial sources. In one section of the *Gosannen kassen emaki* (*Picture Scroll of the Later Three Years' War*) we see a very clear depiction of a fighting tower. It projects over the wall like a smaller version of the ones at Taga. Its parapet walls are very solid and come up to the chest of the defender. They have a definite slope outwards to make it difficult for an attacker to climb, and in the course of the battle the outer surfaces have become festooned with arrows that have lodged in the planking. The tower appears to have no parapet on the inside, presumably to allow quick access by the defenders. The walls themselves are of rough plaster construction within a timber framework, probably made from 'wattle and daub' rather than beaten earth because they are quite narrow, and a temporary base such as this would not allow the time to construct elaborate walls such as those at Akita and Taga. The most interesting feature on the walls is a series of three square loopholes. These are apparently not for archers because they are placed low down on the wall's surface. Ropes pass through them, suspending heavy rocks. The ropes are passed over horizontal tree trunks and are tied to posts within the castle, so that they can be cut at the appropriate moment to let the rocks fall against attackers. In another section of the scroll a fight is going on around a tower. Here the details are not as clear, but the wall appears to be made from horizontal wooden planking rather than plaster. One rock is suspended by a rope through a very narrow hole. A further section of the scroll shows the fortress burning. Here we see plastered walls but with a loophole set at head height. Flames are billowing out of it and cracking the surface of the plaster.

For some remarkable reconstructions of these styles of fortress, one need look no further than the Esashi Fujiwara no Sato, the 'Fujiwara Heritage Park', built near the city of Esashi in Iwate Prefecture. This extensive site began life as a film set, and has been preserved to show visitors the architecture and lifestyles of the Oshū Fujiwara family. As it is not an archaeological site like Yoshinogari, the designers have had full rein to include numerous buildings that cover several styles of architecture over several centuries. The emphasis in the first section of the site is on Fujiwara Tsunekiyo, who died at the start

Left: This reconstruction at the Esashi Fujiwara Heritage Park is of the fortified east gate contemporary with Fujiwara Tsunekiyo, who fought during the Former Nine Years' War. It is very similar to the reconstruction of the gate of Kawasaki on the same site. We are looking from the outside in.

Right: This fine reconstruction of a Heian Period watchtower is at the Esashi Fujiwara Heritage Park. Such buildings would have been found at all Heian Period castles such as Ichinotani.

of the Former Nine Years' War, and his son Kiyohira, the first Fujiwara to set the family on the path to greatness. Their age, the late 11th century, is commemorated by a wooden fortress, of which visitors encounter first the purely defensive features.

Tsunekiyo's fortress is approached through its east gate. Like all the other gates in the display, this resembles the illustration in the picture scroll of the Later Three Years' War in that it has a parapet that slopes outwards. As it is a fortified gatehouse it is of strong construction, and has a guardroom above the gate. The parapet extends all the way round the tower, and a ladder through a trapdoor provides access. Other gates in the fortress are quite simple with supporting beams. All the walls of the fortress are of wood, either horizontal planking or rough vertical timbers. The separate gateways of the isolated fortresses are very similar in construction but wider and stronger.

This model of fortified tower gateway was to be used for the next three centuries, taking us into the Kamakura Period. Modifications that may be noted include the insertion of square loopholes into the sloping parapet, and the augmentation of the parapet wall by using the familiar large wooden shields set up on battlefields. These raised the height of the parapet by a small amount. Another defensive device was to increase the height of the outer walls by suspending rough bamboo or straw matting from wooden frameworks. Other pictorial sources show the hanging of heavy cloths bearing the defenders' *mon* (family crest) from frameworks above a gate. These curtains were called *maku*, and were used on a battlefield to mark off the general's field headquarters position. Just like the rough bamboo or straw matting, the *maku* would catch spent arrows and prevented an attacker from looking inside a fortress from any elevated position nearby. At the Fujiwara Heritage Park two almost identical isolated gateways are set away from the main fortress. They are supposed to represent the gateways of Kawasaki, where the Former Nine Years' War began, and Kuriyagawa, where it ended. All in all, it is a superb display of reconstructed Heian Period military architecture.

One addition to the overall fortification pattern that seems to have appeared later in the Heian Period was the free-standing multi-storeyed

These two linked buildings make up the *shinden* (chief dwelling) of the reconstructed residence of Fujiwara Kiyohira, who died in 1128, at the Esashi Fujiwara Heritage Park. They add a touch of comfort to what is otherwise a very austere frontier stockade similar to the fort owned by his father Tsunekiyo. The 'golden age' of the Oshū Fujiwara is regarded as having begun with Fujiwara Kiyohira.

watchtower. These structures would become very common during the Sengoku Period, when they were built to a considerable height. Those of the Heian Period resembled the watchtowers of Yoshinogari except that they did not have thatched roofs but planking, and had an outward-sloping parapet on the gatehouses. An example of a free-standing watchtower is included at the Fujiwara Heritage Park.

THE WARRIOR RESIDENCE AND THE *SHINDEN* STYLE

Within the defensive walls at the Fujiwara reconstruction we find a *shinden* (chief dwelling) in the classic domestic style of the early Heian Period. The *shinden* style, which is essentially an elaboration of the simpler samurai's *yakata*, was developed in the capital when the court nobility were given rectangular plots of land around and below the imperial enclosure. The size of the plot depended upon the recipient's rank. The resulting dwelling was based, like the imperial palace itself, on a Chinese model, with an initial symmetry from left to right but not from top to bottom. The mansion-estate centred round the actual 'chief dwelling', which faced south on to an open courtyard. Subsidiary buildings would be attached to the *shinden* by covered corridors, or could be free-standing within the courtyard. A garden might be included. Movable screens provided visual privacy within the *shinden*. The formal entrance to the courtyard was always the eastern gate, where the officers and guards were stationed. The courtyard inside the fortified gateway at Esashi is complete with living quarters, stables and gates, latrines and wells. The storehouses, which are raised on piles to keep the rice dry, stand in a separate compound outside the inner area. The lord's own living quarters consist of two one-storey buildings connected to each other.

Fujiwara Hidehira died in 1187, just two years before the glorious Fujiwara capital of Hiraizumi was attacked by Minamoto Yoritomo. It is to Hidehira that we owe the completion of the fortified palace of Yanagi no Gosho, which is represented at the Esashi Fujiwara Heritage Park by this stunning reconstruction of a mansion in the *shinden-zukuri* style.

Towards the end of the Heian Period, we see the building of large fortified palaces typified by the elegant Yanagi no Gosho of the Oshū Fujiwara. These are sophisticated residences placed securely within genuinely defensive walls and fortified gateways. As one purpose of the Esashi Fujiwara Heritage Park is to show that the northern branch of the Fujiwara was every bit as sophisticated and refined as their cousins in the capital, this elaborate style of mansion has also been reconstructed and represents the home of Fujiwara Hidehira, who died in 1187. Given the name of Kyara Gosho (Aloes Wood Palace) it is an attempt to realize the vanished glories of Yanagi no Gosho, the large fortified palace of the Fujiwara in their capital of Hiraizumi. It is built in the *shinden-zukuri* style, which represents an elaboration of the *shinden* style both in overall size but also in its introduction of native Japanese features to the original Chinese style. It was less of a clear-cut model than an ideal to be realized by incorporating features that expressed beauty and charm and demonstrated its integration into the natural or created environment. Yet even Yanagi no Gosho needed defending. A wooden palisade surrounded it with bridges over a moat. When danger threatened, security could be enhanced by the simple expedient of removing a section of planking from the bridge.

The best visual record of the *shinden-zukuri* style that has survived is the picture scroll *Nenjū-gyōji* of the 12th century. One section of it depicts a

The choice of Kasagi as the first refuge for Emperor Go-Daigo may have had more to do with its religious significance than with the actual or potential strength of its defences. This pictorial map at the entrance to Kasagidera, the temple that is now built in the site, shows how it was a typical Japanese *yamashiro*. Note the massive rocks at Kasagi that have images of the Buddha carved into them. These rocks are described in *Taiheiki*, but did not hinder a night attack against Go-Daigo.

cockfight inside the courtyard of such a mansion, but as the location is a nobleman's home in Kyoto no defensive features are to be found. They are also absent from the reconstruction at Esashi, making the point that the century that had passed since the Former Nine Years' War had seen the Fujiwara established as elegant aristocrats and patrons of the arts. Thus the reconstructed mansion of the Fujiwara has a pond garden across the courtyard from its main buildings, which are very elaborate compared to the earlier Fujiwara residence. Subsidiary living quarters are attached using short covered corridors that enclose small courtyard gardens.

THE 14TH-CENTURY *YAMASHIRO*

Some of the most vivid sections in *Taiheiki*, the epic about the 'Wars Between the Courts' of the 14th century, are concerned with the defence of mountain-top castles, the *yamashiro*. Go-Daigo's first refuge on top of the mountain at Kasagi may well have been chosen because of its spiritual power, symbolized by the huge carvings of Buddha on its cliff faces, rather than its military strength, because it fell quite easily to a night raid. This is described in the *Taiheiki*, which includes the following account of Kasagiyama. The 'rocks like folding screens' are still a feature of the site:

> ... The 50 men began to climb at the northern ramparts of the castle, a rock wall 450m high, where even a bird could not fly easily. By various ways they went up for 225m until with perplexed hearts they beheld rocks like folding screens, rising in layers above them in place of smooth green moss and ancient pines with drooping limbs.

The loyalist hero Kusunoki Masashige more successfully defended Akasaka and Chihaya. Several accounts deal with his clever stratagems, which will be discussed in the operational history section, although we find little actual description of the castles in *Taiheiki*. The following brief section, concerning Chihaya, emphasizes the steepness of the approaches to it:

> Now there were deep chasms eastward and westward of this castle, so that a man might not climb up, while northward and southward it stood over against Mount Kongō in a region of high and steep peaks. Yet the attackers looked upon it scornfully, for it was a small castle, barely 200m high and not a league around.

The construction of Akasaka and Chihaya was almost entirely of wood, and most probably they resembled the wooden stockades of the Heian Period, with use being made of wooden walls and fortified gateways in a series of interlocking baileys spread across several mountain peaks. Mountain paths would link the different sections. Chihaya was built upon a particularly high

This large-scale model of the Shimazu family's Tsurumaru (Kagoshima) Castle in the Reimeikan Museum in Kagoshima is an excellent illustration of how a major medieval *yamashiro* could be created by literally carving up the neighbouring peaks of a mountain and joining them together.

mountain ridge. As noted earlier, Kasagi, the first such fortress to be defended by loyalist troops, made use of the natural rock outcrops that exist on Kasagiyama, a feature absent from both Akasaka and Chihaya.

Each of the imperial loyalist fortresses stood alone, without any notion of a strategic defensive system. They were simply a refuge and strongpoint for the emperor or his followers. The accounts of Kusunoki Masashige's cunning ruses involved the use of suspended stones and ropes as noted earlier, with nothing in their overall design that indicates technological innovation. Indeed, these fortresses were largely a development of the earlier models found during the Former Nine Years' War.

THE EARLY SENGOKU *YAMASHIRO*

The castles of the Sengoku *daimyō* were called *yamashiro* if they were located on mountains or *hirajiro* if they were built on a flat plain. The *yamashiro* design was essentially a development from the rough-and-ready mountain-top castles of the Nambokuchō Wars, but ground preparation was crucial whatever surface the castle was built upon. For a *yamashiro*, the top of the mountain would be cleared of trees and levelled. On the resulting plateau there would be built quite intricate arrangements of wooden palisades, wooden towers, gateways and domestic buildings. The solid wooden walls of the palisades were pierced with arrow slits. Towers were enclosed at the top with wooden walls or portable wooden shields, and from these vantage points archers fired longbows or simply threw down stones, the only other missile weapons available before the introduction of firearms. Domestic buildings thatched with rice straw would also be built from wood and acted as quarters for the garrison as well as reception and command areas for the general, together with stables, food stores, weapon stores and the like.

By the mid-16th century, certain improvements had been introduced to the *yamashiro* model. Sometimes the forest cover was stripped away almost entirely over a large area of mountain and the gaps between adjacent ridges were deepened. In such a way, a roughly concentric series of mountain peaks could be converted into a number of natural inner and outer baileys, each overlooking the one below it. Ditches were strengthened by having vertical cross pieces through them, built at right angles to the inner walls. Very steep sections were made more dramatic by having long channels cut out of them, down which rocks could be rolled. Mountain streams were diverted into gullies to create moats and reservoirs, and entrances to gateways were offset to allow an enemy's approach to be covered completely.

Wooden walls were commonly of two types. The first were loose open palisades, designed to hinder an attacker's progress, slow him down and make him an easier target for missile fire. The second type was a stronger affair built from solid wooden planking, sometimes with loopholes cut into it. These wooden palisades would often be augmented by having strong supporting timbers on their inner side, along which planks could be laid to produce two levels from which the garrison could deliver missile fire. Trees were planted in castles to bind the soil and also to shield the castle from view, but too many trees in a castle's bailey could be inconvenient in a siege situation and would be cut down before an attack.

As time went by, castles grew larger to accommodate the increasing numbers of troops a samurai commander now employed. A wider area allowed more elaborate walls and buildings to be raised, and in place of the loose wooden palisades of the old days stronger walls could be built using a form of wattle and daub construction. Stout vertical wooden posts were driven into the earth at 2m intervals with bamboo poles placed between them and bundles of bamboo, lashed together with rope, as the core. The rope held the wooden skeleton together, and by a series of complex knots provided a firm key for the layers of plaster that would be applied. The resulting structures were plastered with a mixture of red clay and crushed rock, and were often whitewashed, giving a Japanese castle its characteristic appearance. Alternatively the wall would be finished with a 'skin' of black-painted wood. Arrow ports were cut at regular intervals. To keep weather damage to a minimum the walls were topped with sloping thatch, wooden shingles, or even tiles.

The expansion of a site caused its own problems on a restricted and uneven mountain top. To bind the soil on exposed sections rough bamboo grass was allowed to grow, but the torrential rain experienced in Japan took a heavy toll of foundations and structures alike. Even if there were no typhoons, earthquakes or sieges to create additional havoc, normal wear and tear demanded that the plastered walls be routinely repaired at least every five years.

It is in the increasing use of stone, however, that we see the greatest development in castle design. Initially stone was used as a strengthening material for the slopes or as foundations for buildings, but as time went by

THE *YASHIKI* (MANSION) AND CASTLE TOWN OF THE ASAKURA AT ICHIJŌDANI: 1520

The settlement of Ichijōdani that grew up around the *yashiki* (mansion) of the Asakura family within a narrow river valley provides an excellent example of an early castle town. There is busy commercial life in the streets of the town where the residences of the Asakura samurai are located. Just like their lord's mansion, these buildings are lightly fortified, and depend upon the strength of the mountain-top *yamashiro* nearby. The sources for this plate are the excavations and reconstructions at Ichijōdani. (Peter Dennis © Osprey Publishing Ltd)

stone became the most prominent feature of a Japanese castle, a trend that will be discussed in detail later.

THE EARLY DEVELOPMENT OF THE CASTLE TOWN

The *yamashiro* on a mountain peak was a successful model, so we see this put into operation for the purposes both of defence and expansion. But as the *daimyō*'s confidence grew, we also see the development of low-lying areas for commercial expansion that had little defensive capacity in themselves and were dependent upon the nearby *yamashiro*. These settlements grow increasingly more complex until the two types of *daimyō* headquarters merge

to give the familiar 'Japanese castle' that we know so well. Takeda Shingen
ruled from Kofu, then called Fuchu, which is now the prefectural capital of
Yamanashi Prefecture, but in spite of his military prowess, his headquarters
in Kofu was not a castle. Instead Shingen ruled from a *yashiki* called
Tsutsujigasaki. It was of rectangular ground plan and was defended only by
a wet moat. The distinguished Confucian scholar Ogyu Sorai (1666–1728)
visited the site of Tsutsujigasaki and was amazed at how small it was. The site
of Tsutsujigasaki is now the Takeda shrine in Kofu City, and the apparent
weakness of its defences came to symbolize Shingen's confidence in his armies
and his subjects to defend him, rather than placing his trust in stone walls.

The excavated site of Ichijōdani, near the city of Fukui in the former
province of Echizen, is a good example of a collection of residences and
workshops built beside a *daimyō's* mansion along a river valley from the late
15th century onwards. It is a fortified town that utilizes the topography of the
narrow valley in which it is built. The town stretches along the banks of
the Ichijōdanigawa down to the point where it joins the Asuwagawa. At each
end of the town the valley is particularly narrow, and here were two gates,
the upper and the lower castle gates. In between them is the town, which is
associated with the Asakura family. Asakura Toshikage fought during the Onin
War, and on being made governor of Echizen by the *shōgun* he established
himself at Ichijōdani, where he died in 1475. His son Norikage (1474–1552)
fought constantly against the Ikkō-ikki in Echizen. The next generation,
Asakura Yoshikage (1533–73), defeated the Ikkō-ikki and forced them to be
content with neighbouring Kaga Province. His end came at the hand of Oda
Nobunaga, who defeated him at the battle of the Anegawa in 1570 and then
besieged him inside Ichijōdani in 1573. Here Asakura Yoshikage killed himself.

The stone walls, moat and other artefacts of Ichijōdani were discovered by archaeologists along a 200m stretch, and represent a new phase in the development of the samurai class. The largest-scale residences are those of samurai. As retainers of the Asakura family, they live adjacent to their lord's mansion. The most important difference between their residences and those of the *yakata* of the Heian and Kamakura Period is that the farming element in their role is much diminished. These men are almost professional soldiers, whose duties anticipate the great changes that would come about when Hideyoshi ordered the separation of samurai and farmers, a new legal status to be rigidly enforced by the Tokugawa.

These social changes are reflected in the site itself, because Ichijōdani is a prototype castle town, and the samurai residences bear a great resemblance to the settlements that were to be such a characteristic of the Edo Period. Each residence is like a smaller and poorer version of their lord's own mansion. The walls are of beaten earth, with simple roofed gateways opening on to the street and tiles for weatherproofing. Their defensive features are very modest, and there are not even right-angled turns through the gateways. Instead the model is that of a community designed for peacetime use, which could be temporarily abandoned for the *yamashiro* on the mountain nearby when danger threatened.

The same considerations applied to the *daimyō*'s own mansion. It has a more elaborate gateway and a moated embankment, but Yoshikage's last stand was made from the mountain-top *yamashiro* rather than this poorly fortified mansion that looks more suited to the streets of Kyoto than to a river valley out in the country. The *yamashiro* site has also been excavated, and is revealed to be a long set of four linked baileys of about 600m from end to end. It is only reached by a stiff climb up narrow mountain paths, making it the perfect observation station and 'last stand' outpost, but totally unsuited for daily living. Defensive features include several *unejō tatebori*, a series of parallel trenches running up the sides of the excavated mountain. These provided man-made gullies down which stones could be rolled, but more importantly forced an

Left: A small section of the reconstructed street of the castle town of Ichijōdani. The wall are plastered and built over stone foundations. Drainage ditches run along the walls.

Right: A cross section through the wall surrounding a samurai residence at Yuzuki Castle in Matsuyama. The different layers that have been added and rammed down can be clearly seen, as can the outer layer of rough plaster.

attacking army to advance in column up their inner slopes, thus exposing them to concentrated fire from the defenders.

Yuzuki Castle, in the Dogo Onsen (Dogo Hot Spring) area of Matsuyama in former Iyo Province on the island of Shikoku, is a small site that provides another excellent example of a *yamashiro*, yet is of a design that is very different from the Ichijōdani complex. Yuzuki is associated with the Kōno family. Its outer moat was built by Kōno Michinao, the father-in-law of Kurushima (Murakami) Michiyasu, from the famous pirate family of Iyo Province. Yuzuki resembles the small castles of the pirate families of the Inland Sea that were usually built on islands, and like them succumbed to the invasion of Shikoku by Toyotomi Hideyoshi in 1585.

Yuzuki was the cultural and military heart of the Kōno domains for 250 years. It probably began life during the early 14th century as a modestly sized *yamashiro* on the hill that is at the centre of the site. The defences were expanded over the next two centuries, but this was done within the constraints imposed by the topography. The castle hill was isolated from other high ground, so expansion was made by building on the flat lands around and enclosing the castle within a double wet moat and a double earthwork, producing a *hirayamashiro* (castle on plain and hill). The samurai retainers of the Kōno family lived in the space between the two moats. The dwellings of the highest-ranking retainers have been identified on the east of this area, while the lower-ranking samurai lived to the west. Their houses were simple wooden constructions with thatched roofs and were surrounded by beaten earth walls on stone foundations, plastered and topped with tiles that were similar to those at Ichijōdani. A very dramatic contrast to Yuzuki is provided by the mighty Matsuyama Castle, which was built a few miles away after Yuzuki had been abandoned. For this castle, one of the classic early modern stone-based castles of Japan, the low-lying site of Yuzuki was spurned in favour of a high mountain ridge.

One of the low-ranking samurai houses at Yuzuki that lay between the inner castle and the moat.

THE HŌJŌ FAMILY'S *YAMASHIRO* OF YAMANAKA: 1540

The Hōjō family used a system of castles to defend their territory and to consolidate new gains. The *yamashiro* of Yamanaka is a prime example of the process, because it guarded the western approaches to the strategic Hakone mountains beneath Mount Fuji. As a classic *yamashiro* Yamanaka illustrates many features of the style, and is particularly noted for its *shogi* ditches, divided into small sections like a checkerboard (see top inset). The sources for this plate are the site of Yamanaka itself, to which typical castle buildings of the period have been added. (Peter Dennis © Osprey Publishing Ltd)

THE SENGOKU *YAMASHIRO* AND THE SATELLITE CASTLE SYSTEM

As time went by, the small *yamashiro* of minor *daimyō* were usually abandoned when their owners became the prey of more successful rulers. As an alternative, however, the sites could be incorporated by the victors into their own strategic network of defence. Thus it was that the Hōjō family, the archetypal castle builders of the Sengoku Period, thought in terms of a strategic defensive system, not merely individual castles. This was expressed by having one provincial *honjō* (main castle) supported by several *shijō* (satellite castles) that were manned by family members or highly trusted retainers. Most of the Hōjō warriors were known by the company to which they were attached, each of which bore the name of the satellite castle. Many of the *shijō* were modest affairs and were not designed to withstand a siege. Instead they were communications points or muster stations with guardrooms and armouries.

At the zenith of their power the provinces of the Kantō were dotted with Hōjō fortresses large and small. The *shijō* might consist of little more than a signalling station, but what mattered was how the various fortresses related to each other. To aid communications between their castles, the Hōjō introduced a post station system in 1524 linking Odawara in Sagami Province with their fortresses in Musashi Province.

Odawara may well have been one of the most impressive castles of the 16th century in all Japan, ranking with Osaka and Azuchi. Although it did not reach the sophistication of the castle towns of the Edo Period, it was built on an extensive site near to the sea, dominating the narrow neck of land between the Hakone Mountains and the Pacific Ocean. Primarily a fortress, Odawara withstood two sieges, by Uesugi Kenshin in 1561 and Takeda Shingen in 1569, and only capitulated to Toyotomi Hideyoshi in 1590 after a 100-day blockade. The first fortress on the site was built by the Omori family in 1416, and succumbed to Hōjō Sōun, the first of the five Hōjō *daimyō*, in 1495. Sōun kept his capital at Nirayama, which was abandoned in favour of Odawara by his son Hōjō Ujitsuna on Sōun's death.

We are fortunate that several of the Hōjō castles' sites have been excavated and preserved. In some cases there have been reconstructions of parts of the sites. At Hachigata, for example, a wooden fortified gatehouse has been constructed inside the museum. It is very similar to the classic Kamakura Period models described above. A small gateway and walls have been restored outside. One of the most interesting defensive features of all has been carefully preserved at Yamanaka Castle. This is the curious 'checkerboard moat', so-called from its resemblance to the playing board for the Japanese game of *shogi*. The moats are criss-crossed by raised sections to hinder an attacker's progress. If they were flooded the upper surfaces would be invisible, and an enemy soldier would have to haul himself up to proceed, thus exposing himself as a target. Overall, Yamanaka Castle is an extensive *yamashiro* covering the mountain road from the Hakone barrier down to the sea on the western side of the Izu Peninsula. From the top of its Nishi-no-maru (western bailey) there is a magnificent view of Mount Fuji.

Sakasai, located to the north of Tokyo, is the finest of all the reconstructed Hōjō castles. Sakasai is built on a low hill, and thus has the predominant characteristics of a *hirajiro* (castle on a plain). It was defended by a wet moat, much of which survives, and the local council have restored the section of wall immediately above this moat, together with an openwork tower, a bridge and a couple of buildings, so that when a visitor arrives it looks as though the entire castle is still there. The walls, which run along the grassy bank above the moat, are made from wattle and daub and wooden planks. They are weatherproofed using shingles and have rectangular loopholes. A fine three-

storey tower building stands next to the roofed gateway. The ground floor is fully enclosed with narrow windows and sloping roofs. The top storey has a walkway around it beneath a similar sloping roof. There are two lookout towers on the site. Each is built from long wooden beams and has a roof to protect against the rain. There is an interesting gatetower on the other side of the site that controls a bridge over the moat.

The Takeda family used a similar satellite system to the Hōjō, although the Takeda *honjō* was not a castle, just the mansion of Tsutsugjiasaki. Indeed, Shingen's heir Katsuyori's decision to build a 'proper' castle was regarded as a very bad omen by the surviving Takeda retainers. 'Proper' castles, of course, were needed on the fringes of the Takeda domains where they came into contact with the territories of the Hōjō and the Uesugi. Just as in the Hōjō model, there was a network of satellite castles and signalling stations, the latter consisting of smoke-signal posts. One Takeda satellite castle to have been excavated is Takane, built overlooking a river valley near the modern town of Misakubo on one of the strategic approaches to the Takeda lands from the Pacific coast. Takane is located on Sankakuyama, a 420m-high mountain with a 150m vertical drop on one side. It was first settled by the Okuyama family early in the 15th century, and fell to the Takeda as they expanded outwards from Kai. It appears to have been in use until about 1576. Takane has the usual structure of three baileys carved out of the hillside, although, in accordance with the period of development, it does not appear to have been reinforced with stone. Nor does stone play any part in the design of the buildings on site, which are instead all of wood and are defended by wooden palisades and modest plastered wattle and daub walls. The central building on the site, and one which has now been reconstructed, is a fine lookout tower (*seirō yagura*). Unlike the openwork towers rebuilt at Sakasai, this one is covered on all sides with wooden planking.

Left: A corner of the Sakasai Castle site, showing a watchtower and an elegant domestic building within the courtyard.

Right: Unlike the openwork towers of Sakasai, the main tower of Takane Castle is completely enclosed.

THE LIVING SITES

CASTLES AND CONSCRIPTS

The men who garrisoned the castles of Kyūshū in anticipation of a Korean invasion were all conscripts, an idea copied from China. A *heishi* (soldier) was assigned to a particular *gundan* (regiment) and served for part of the year, the rest of the time being spent on agricultural duties. Every soldier carried a bow and quiver and had a pair of swords. Much use was made of heavy wooden shields as battlefield protection.

In AD 684 Emperor Temmu issued a decree ordering all civil and military officials in his court to become skilled in the martial arts, because 'in government, military matters are the essential thing'. These men would be the core of his army and could control any recalcitrant regional official who was not acting loyally. To further ensure this overwhelming central control, Temmu began the confiscation of weapons from anyone not employed in his government. These were issued to the conscript infantrymen who were drafted to the area around the imperial capital of Nara or to the fortresses of Kyūshū. Temmu's successors continued his work, culminating in AD 702 with the Taiho system, which finally succeeded in creating a large and reliable Japanese army conscripted on the Chinese model.

These decisions by a series of emperors resulted in hundreds of men being uprooted from their homes and moved to distant fortresses where very little happened. Such service was therefore a lonely and boring occupation. Mononobe Akimochi, a border guard sent from eastern Honshū to Kyūshū in AD 755, composed the following poem about his unenviable situation:

> The dread imperial command
> I have received; from tomorrow
> I will sleep with the grass
> No wife being with me.

The system of conscripting peasants was finally ended in AD 792. The official reason given was that the decision had been made to reduce the burden on

farming communities of impressed labour. There was much truth in this, for it had long been recognized that if a household breadwinner was drafted, the whole family would suffer. There was even a saying that if a man was conscripted for *heishi* duties then he was unlikely to return until his hair had turned white! But with the pacification of the *emishi* and improved relations with Korea, Japan's borders were more secure than they had been for centuries. In AD 835 even the guards mounted on the strategic islands of Iki and Tsushima were withdrawn, and the sad poems written home by soldiers became a thing of the past.

Compared to the Kyūshū fortresses, life in the northern stockades was much livelier because *emishi* raids kept the garrisons on their toes. Otherwise the soldiers would grow their own food, and archaeological finds within the northern stockades have confirmed their dual role as military bases and defensive locations for people who were both soldiers and farmers. At Fort Akita, digs in pit dwellings have revealed not only iron knives and arrowheads but also axes and reapers, which would be expected from a frontier 'colony'. Other information about daily life in the castles comes from the numerous finds of *mokkan*, the wooden writing slips that were used much more frequently than paper at that time. Inscriptions on them, which are often dated, refer to troop numbers and movements and all the minutiae of the

Details of the outer wall of the inner bailey of Takane Castle, a classic satellite *yamashiro* owned by the Takeda family.

bureaucracy associated with being a frontier provincial capital. Some paper that was lacquered to make it weather resistant has also survived.

EARLY ARMS AND ARMOUR

We know quite a lot about the armour worn by the garrisons of the early castles of Kyūshū and the north because of examples excavated from Japanese burial mounds. The earliest type was called *tanko*, and was made of heavy iron, the plates being fastened together with leather thongs. Almost all the surviving examples fitted closely to the body and had a pronounced waist so that they sat firmly on the hips. They were provided with an opening down the front that was fastened by ties of cloth. The deep cut-outs for the arms left an extension at the front reaching to the upper chest, and a similar, rather higher section at the back, to which were fastened a pair of cloth shoulder straps which transferred some of the not inconsiderable weight from the hips to the shoulders.

Protecting the lower body and tying over the flanged lower edge of the body armour was a flared skirt, called the *kusazuri* (grass rubber), because it reached to just above the knee. Like the neck guard, it was made of ten or more horizontal pieces, laced to internal leather thongs and split down either side to allow some movement when walking. No protection was provided for the lower legs at this date, but long baggy trousers were worn, tied with a drawstring just below the knee.

The shoulders and upper arms were covered by an arrangement of curved plates, running from front to back and extending as far as the elbow. Completing the outfit were long, tubular, tapering cuffs of plate fitted with a small panel of leather-laced scales which formed a defensive cover for the back of the hand. As was normal on all later styles of armour, the metal surface was given a coating of natural lacquer as a protection against the humidity of the Japanese climate. Some slight decoration was afforded by leather thongs sewn through holes along the sharp edges of all the major elements, and by a bunch of pheasant-tail feathers tied to iron prongs provided for that purpose on top of the helmet, which had a pronounced beaked front. A typical armament for a *tanko*-wearing soldier was a large wooden shield, a spear and a straight-bladed sword. Other soldiers were trained as archers or crossbowmen.

Although the *tanko* continued to be made, a new style of armour was developed called *keiko*. These armours were made by combining numerous small scales of metal or leather rather than large plates. The result was a flexible defence whose efficiency lay in its ability to absorb the energy of a blow in the lacing sandwiched between the rows of scales before penetration could begin. The body of a *keiko* resembled a sleeveless coat opening down the front and provided with a flared skirt extending to mid-thigh. With the *keiko* came a new style of helmet with a very prominent pierced horizontal peak riveted to the front lower edge. The neck guard fitted to these helmets was made of metal strips arranged exactly like the earlier ones.

CROSSBOWS AND CATAPULTS

Until the end of the 12th century, both the Korean-style castles of Kyūshū and the northern stockades were defended by a mysterious weapon called the *ōyumi*. The name was written using the same ideograph (*nu*) used in China for 'crossbow'. Although there is some controversy about whether *ōyumi* means hand-held crossbows, because the Japanese expression literally means 'great bow', it is generally accepted that they were large-scale siege crossbows operated by a team of men. Unfortunately none has ever been excavated, but written records lamenting the lack of skilled operators strongly suggest that these were large and complex machines, not just simple infantry weapons.

The first mention of an *ōyumi* occurs in an entry in the *Nihon Shoki* for AD 618 referring to the defeat of a Sui invasion by Goguryeo forces. The ruler of Goguryeo sent two Chinese captives to Japan along with a small number of crossbows and a camel. By the time of the next mention in the *Nihon Shoki* in AD 672 their use appears to be well established. On this occasion they were 'discharged confusedly, and the arrows fell like rain'. For the next two centuries we read of *ōyumi* being deployed, usually as the result of the latest scare about an invasion by the Silla Kingdom of Korea from the AD 860s onwards, although the threat never seemed to be sufficiently strong to restart the fortress-building programme that had been wound down from about AD 700. Instead *ōyumi* were set up at possible landing sites such as the island of Tsushima and the province of Hōki, where a crossbow expert was funded in AD 871. Crossbows were used at sea in a battle with Silla ships in AD 894, but it is not clear whether these were handheld weapons or *ōyumi*.

The larger variety was certainly present in the northern stockades, as shown by the records of an attack in AD 880, probably by bandits rather than *emishi*, which was directed against Akita Castle. The insurgents burned the fortress and destroyed the crossbows that they found inside. The chronicler of the event usefully makes a clear distinction between the 100 handheld crossbows and the 29 *ōyumi* that were seized. It is also in the north of Japan that we note the final recorded use of an *ōyumi* in Japanese warfare. This happened at the Atsukashi earthwork during Yoritomo's advance against the Oshū Fujiwara in 1189. The chronicle *Azuma Kagami* tells us that during an attack on one of the strongpoints along the line Yoritomo's men took 18 heads in spite of deadly arrows from an *ōyumi*. Yet from this moment on *ōyumi* vanish from the Japanese scene, and their swansong at Atsukashi, a unique occurrence not found in any other campaign of the Gempei War, may indicate that in their northern fastness the Oshū Fujiwara had simply failed to move with the times.

As no example of an *ōyumi* has survived, we can only speculate as to their actual design. Did they use one bow, or were they like the powerful siege crossbows of ancient China that combined two or even three bows pulling together? Did they fire one massive arrow or a volley? Did they have wheels or were they always permanently mounted? An entry from AD 835 mentions a new type that was supposed to be able to be rotated in all directions. They were certainly complicated and specialized machines, because several records from the 9th century AD complain that the *ōyumi* in their arsenals were going to waste because no one knew how to use them.

As well as discharging arrows, the *ōyumi* were used for projecting stones. There are records of such use for the Former Nine Years' War and the Later Three Years' War. When used for this purpose the *ōyumi* are sometimes referred to as *ishiyumi* (stone bows). One warrior fighting in the Later Three Years' War was hit on the helmet by a stone from an *ishiyumi* and knocked to the ground. In 1156 a certain Kiheiji Taifu is praised for his ability to throw stones over a distance of three *chō* (about 300m).

HEALTH AND HYGIENE

The supply of fresh water was very important in any fortified site. A Nara Period well that extends 5m underground has been found at Fort Akita, while a Heian Period well on the same site still has water flowing into it today. The food that people ate in the Nara and Heian Periods and the ingredients that they used are described in detail in literature. All that is missing are recipes, so we cannot be quite sure how meals were put together for castle garrisons. Nobles had the luxury of consuming dairy products as well as such speciality items as abalone (sea snails), while the diet of commoners was much simpler. Historical records seem to indicate that people consumed two meals a day, but

This beautiful reconstruction in the Fujiwara Heritage Park at Esashi shows Fujiwara Hidehira (centre) entertaining his son Yasuhira (to the viewer's left) and their fugitive guest Minamoto Yoshitsune to dinner inside the main hall of the *shinden-zukuri* within the fortified palace of Yanagi no Gosho in about 1186.

this was not considered sufficient for those engaged in heavy manual work or fighting. We know this from surviving wooden *mokkan* slips on which requests were written for more meals and in-between meal snacks. Earthen vessels for storing such snacks have been found at Akita Castle.

Important beliefs in ritual purity related to the religious ideals of Shintō, as much as notions of hygiene, probably lay behind the strong emphasis on sanitation that we find associated with early Japanese castles. Dung beetles have been found in the moats of Yayoi Period sites, suggesting that the ditches were not just military structures but also latrines, and may also have been designed to allow heavy rainfall to wash away excrement. Fresh water was obtained from wells within the site.

A HIGH-RANKING SAMURAI'S FORTIFIED *YAKATA*: 1200

This plate recreates the domestic life of a high-ranking retainer of one of the powerful clans of the Heian and Kamakura Periods. Although the walls are quite modest in defensive terms, they have an outer moat and a very strong fortified gateway that is typical of the times. The mounted samurai loosing arrows at it will receive a suitable welcome from the archers in the tower. Inside the compound the owner enjoys a comfortable living area in the *shinden* style that includes a Japanese garden. The sources for the plate are the painted scroll *Ippen hijiri e* and the reconstructions at the Fujiwara Heritage Park at Esashi. (Peter Dennis © Osprey Publishing Ltd)

Apart from this separation between fresh water and polluted water, there is no evidence of the provision of toilets as such, but all this changes with the establishment of the fortresses of the 7th century AD. Sophisticated archaeological work on early military sites has yielded fascinating information about sanitation, and has even allowed conclusions to be drawn about the diet of the people who lived in the northern stockades and the provincial headquarters. For example, cesspit toilets have been found at the site of Yanagi no Gosho, the fortified palace of the Oshū Fujiwara in Hiraizumi. Cesspit toilets allowed human waste to be recycled as fertilizer for the fields. Literary evidence is available for this practice from the Kamakura Period onwards, and the Portuguese Jesuit Luis Frois described it happening during the 16th century. Analysis of specimens found in the toilets showed the prevalence of a large number of eggs of a fish tapeworm, an infection caused by eating raw or incompletely cooked salmon from the nearby river. Other finds of eggs of tapeworms associated with pigs and cattle contradict the popular notion that meat eating ceased with the introduction of Buddhism.

At some early sites, wooden structures to convey water have been found, and for many years it was assumed that these were for ritual purposes. However, analysis of parasitical remains around them has shown most convincingly that these are in fact flushing toilets, and that the ritual objects such as beads found there were probably lost when the owner was otherwise engaged! One version (at the Makimuku site, a non-military site of the Kofun Period) involved a reservoir to store water, including a filter for leaves and other debris. The collection tank into which the water flowed via a wooden conduit would have had manual flushing devices such as ladles and pails. Here also are stones upon which users could squat. Water overflow passed over a lip and joined the water washed manually downstream. A large number of lung-fluke eggs were found at this site, suggesting the eating of river crabs. Exactly this type of flushing toilet has been excavated at Akita Castle, showing that sanitary facilities existed even on the fringes of Yamato civilization. There is no ambiguity over the identification of the site as a toilet because of the presence of several *chugi*, the small wooden slips that were used instead of toilet paper.

Flushing toilets have also been identified at the sites of the city of Fujiwara, which preceded Nara as Japan's first permanent capital, and at Nara itself, where long narrow buildings were provided as public conveniences. The job of keeping the sewage gutters clean fell to prisoners, as directed by the contemporary Penal Code:

> The person sentenced to penal servitude shall be directed to carry out construction work on roads and bridges and other miscellaneous work. Furthermore, the government office shall direct prisoners to sweep out the outside of the Palace every six days, and clear up sewage in the Palace, and the gutters of toilets on the day after a rainy day.

A glimpse of daily life within a high-ranking samurai's home in the castle town of Ichijōdani. One servant is filleting a fish for *sashimi* (raw fish), while another prepares the trays of food that will be taken in for the samurai.

Similar concern about hygiene in castles was still to be found in the Sengoku Period. The Hōjō specified that for their castles: 'Human waste and horse manure must be taken out of the castle every day and deposited at least one arrow's flight from the castle.'

This implies cesspit toilets rather than a flushing system, but sanitary concerns were made very clear, because health and safety considerations necessitated a twice-daily inspection regime by the castle commander, as recorded in Hōjō Sōun's 'Twenty-One Articles':

> Before washing your hands in the morning, inspect the latrine, stable, garden and outside the gate. …
>
> When you return in to your residence in the evening, time permitting, inspect the back of the residence and stable, repair the four walls and fences of the compound, and make sure that even holes only a dog can get through are closed up and repaired. …

That health depended on more than ritual purity is shown by the presence in Akita Castle of buried *enatsubo*, earthenware vessels whose name literally means 'placenta jars'. As an offering for the health and success of a newborn baby, parents would put money, writing brushes, knives and other assorted objects into an *enatsubo* jar and bury it. One placenta jar excavated at Akita Castle contained five coins, a few articles of clothing and other metal objects. A similar religious belief lay behind the discovery in a well of two *bokusho*, papers on which prayers were written. One was a petition for plentiful water, the other a prayer for the banishment of evil spirits.

OPERATIONAL HISTORY

SIEGES OF EARLY CASTLES

As there are no written records from the Yayoi Period, any operational activity around the Yayoi stockades has to be inferred from the archaeological finds. The anti-invasion castles of Kyūshū, of course, never saw any action, and although the northern stockades were subjected to raiding by the *emishi* there is again a lack of any detailed written account of such operations. One account simply tells us: 'They swarm like bees and gather like ants. ... But when we attack, they flee into the mountains and forests. When we let them go, they assault our fortifications. ... Each of their leaders is as good as 1,000 men.'

It is not until the Heian Period that we come across reliable contemporary accounts of operations involving fortifications, and here the source material is very rich. For good accounts of fighting around Heian Period stockades we need look no further than *Mutsuwaki* (*Tale of Mutsu*), the near-contemporary account of the Former Nine Years' War. The first battle involving a stockade occurs at Komatsu:

> Since the date was inauspicious and twilight had already fallen, Yoriyoshi had not intended to attack at once, but while Takesada and Yorisada were conducting a preliminary reconnaissance, their footsoldiers set fire to some buildings and reeds outside the stockade. The men inside responded with vengeful yells and barrages of rocks. Accepting the challenge, Yoriyoshi's men competed enthusiastically to be the first to scale the ramparts.

At first both groups of attackers were held back by the deep blue waters that flowed beside the stockade on the east and the south, and by the mossy cliffs towering sheer above it on the north and the west. Presently, however, a band of 20 gallant men, led by two warriors named Fukae Korenori and Otomo Kazusue, began to chisel into the banks with their swords. They hauled themselves over the rocks with their spears, tunnelled underneath the stockade, and burst into the fortress with their weapons bared, to the utter confusion of the defenders.

The fight ended with the victorious army setting fire to the stockade. In the next siege section, which deals with the attack on Kuriyagawa, we first encounter the *ōyumi*, but the account is more notable for its stark savagery. The action is a far cry from the popular idea of a samurai battle, where elite fighters maintained the gentlemanly notion of giving challenges to honourable opponents. Instead the killing is completely anonymous, and when the attack is frustrated the besiegers resort to the indiscriminate weapon of fire: 'When the enemy were far away, the defenders shot them to death with their *ōyumi*; when they were close, they struck them down with rocks. If by any chance someone reached the base of the fortress they cut him down with swords after scalding him with boiling water.'

The men in the towers beckoned to Yoriyoshi's men, calling 'Are you warriors', and several dozen servant girls climbed up to the towers to sing songs. Yoriyoshi was much displeased.
The battle began at the hour of the hare on the 16th day. All day and night the *ōyumi* twanged and arrows and rocks flew like rain. Yoriyoshi's army sacrificed hundreds of men in a futile attempt to bring down the stoutly defended stockade. Finally, during the hour of the sheep on the 17th day, the general directed his warriors to fill the trenches by demolishing houses in the village, and to pile cut reeds along the riverbanks.

The bridge and walls of Hachiōji Castle, one of the most important satellite castles of the Hōjō family. It was totally destroyed in 1590 during Hideyoshi's Odawara campaign, and has recently been thoroughly excavated.

A section from the painted scroll of the Later Three Years' War. This is a copy of the original in the museum at the site of Kanezawa Castle in the village of Gosannen. A wounded samurai falls from the parapet of the wooden defences, which are covered with arrows. In the epic *Mutsuwaki* such a cloak of arrows provided kindling for a successful attempt at burning the castle down. Note the suspended rock.

The section continues to tell us how Yoriyoshi then prays to his family patron, Hachiman the god of war, to send a strong wind that will fan the flames he is about to ignite. He himself grasps the first torch, assuring his men that it is the will of the gods, and then tosses it on to the pyre. At the same instant a dove flew up from the neighbouring woods. As the dove was believed to be the messenger of Hachiman, this is regarded as a very good omen. The god is placing his seal of approval on to the means whereby the battle will be ended. The little point of detail in the quotation that follows about the arrows stuck into the outside of the stockade acting as kindling gives the episode an air of great authenticity:

> A strong wind suddenly sprang up and sent smoke and flames spreading towards the feathers of the arrows previously released by Yoriyoshi's men, which blanketed the outer sides of the stockade and its towers like straws in a raincoat. As the towers and buildings caught fire, a great lament rose from the thousands of men and women inside. Some of its frantic rebels flung themselves into the watery depths; others lost their heads to naked blades.

Yoriyoshi's warriors crossed the river and attacked. In desperation several hundred rebels put on armour, brandished their swords, and tried to break through the cordon. Since they were resigned to death, they made no effort to protect themselves, and they had exacted a frightful toll from Yoriyoshi's warriors before Takenori finally commanded, 'Let them through'. Once the encirclement was opened, they fled without a struggle. The besiegers then attacked their flanks and killed them all.

> Inside the stockade dozens of beautiful women coughed in the smoke and sobbed miserably, all dressed in damask, gauze and green stuff shot with gold. Every last one of them was dragged out and given to the warriors, who raped them.

That was how sieges were conducted against the stockades of the Heian Period, with fire, cruelty and utter ruthlessness.

THE SIEGES OF THE 14TH CENTURY

The accounts in *Taiheiki* of the sieges of Akasaka and Chihaya during the Wars between the Courts are very different in content from the harsh realism of the *Mutsuwaki*. The accent is very much on the skills and heroics of Kusunoki Masashige as he defends his fortresses using a mixture of bravery and cunning. At Akasaka an extra outer wall fools the attackers:

> From within the castle not an arrow was released, nor was any man seen. …
> At last the attackers laid hold of the wall on the four sides to climb over it, filled with excitement. But thereupon men within the castle cut the ropes supporting the wall, all at the same time. For it was [a] double wall, built to let the outside fall down. More than a thousand of the attackers became as though crushed by a weight, so that only their eyes moved as the defenders threw down logs and boulders on to them.

Akasaka eventually had to be abandoned when the besiegers cut off its water supply, so Kusunoki moved to the stronger and more remote castle of Chihaya. Its formidable appearance made the enemy cautious:

> At first for two or three days they forbore to build positions against it, nor prepared their attack, but with upheld shields climbed together as far as the gate, each striving to be first. Undismayed, the warriors within the castle threw down mighty rocks from the tower tops to smash the enemy's shields to pieces; and while the attackers were afflicted thereby, the defenders shot them terribly with arrows.

A stratagem appears shortly:

> But although their hearts were valiant, they could not climb up that high and steep side. They stood vainly glaring at the castle, helpless to do aught but swallow their anger. Just at that time the warriors within the castle let

In this section of the Later Three Years' War scroll we see the conclusion of a siege by the burning down of the wooden buildings. Flames are pouring out of the loopholes in the plastered walls, which are resistant to fire. Samurai lie dead on the approaches to the castle.

fall ten great trees laid down flat against the ditch in readiness, by which four or five hundred attackers were smitten, who fell over dead like chessmen. And while the remainder clambered discomfited, seeking to escape the falling trees, the castle warriors shot at them according to their will, from towers on all sides.

We also read of Kusunoki Masashige creating a dummy army of straw, and then releasing rocks by cutting ropes as the enemy drew near, and countering an equally ingenious ploy by the besiegers to create a bridge that could be dropped across one of the chasms. This was done by dropping combustible material on to the bridge and setting it on fire.

OPERATIONS AGAINST EARLY SENGOKU *YAMASHIRO*

Siege operations involving Japan's three rivals for the Kantō plain between the 1490s and 1540s, the Takeda, Hōjō and Uesugi families, provide excellent examples of attacks on Sengoku *yamashiro* where wood is still a more important building material than stone. It was during the siege of Un no kuchi in 1536 that Takeda Shingen, then aged 15, had his first combat experience, taking the garrison by surprise after marching through thick snow. The following year the Hōjō besieged the Uesugi castle of Musashi-Matsuyama, when the garrison tried to summon help from outside by sending a message through the siege lines attached to the collar of a dog. Psychological pressures on a garrison may be noted at the siege of Shika in 1547, where Takeda Shingen had the freshly severed heads of the victims of the battle of Odaihara displayed in front of the castle walls.

The progress made by the Hōjō family from being obscure provincial *daimyō* to controlling the Kantō was carried out almost exclusively by conducting successful sieges against rival castles. The system of control by satellite castles followed on from these successes, with the Hōjō's new possessions being defended against all comers until the siege of Odawara in 1590.

Hōjō Sōun, the first of the five generations of Hōjō *daimyō*, captured Odawara in 1495. At this battle he made use of an unusual stratagem in the form of 'fire oxen', an idea he probably picked up from his reading of the

THE CASTLE OF AKASAKA UNDER ATTACK: 1333

In this plate we see Kusunoki Masashige, the great imperial loyalist, putting into action one of his celebrated stratagems in defence of Emperor Go-Daigo. His men erected a dummy outer wall round Akasaka above one of its steepest slopes. As soon as the enemy were climbing up it, the wall was allowed to collapse. The sources for this plate are the description of the action in the *Taiheiki* and research undertaken into contemporary castle design. (Peter Dennis © Osprey Publishing Ltd)

Chinese military classics. Pine torches were tied to the horns of a herd of oxen, which were launched in a stampede against the outer defences of Odawara.

One of the most interesting accounts of a Hōjō acquisition of an enemy castle concerns the long war that Hōjō Sōun waged against the Miura family, which was carried out by a process of isolation and progressive control, and ended with a furious attack. The defeat of the Miura was essential if the Hōjō were to control the whole of Sagami Province and expand to the east, because the Miura controlled Okazaki Castle that overlooked the Tōkaidō road not far from Odawara Castle. They also had a number of outposts on the peninsula that bore their family name, which juts out into the sea further to the east and includes the former capital of Kamakura on its western shoreline.

The Miura were allied to the Ogigayatsu Uesugi, but their *daimyō* Miura Yoshiatsu's failure to capture any Hōjō possessions and internal strife between the Ogigayatsu and Yamanouchi branches of the Uesugi allowed Hōjō Sōun to take the fight to the Miura, and in 1512 he captured Okazaki. Two months later he attacked Sumiyoshi Castle, which had once been part of the defences of Kamakura. This gave the Hōjō control of the old capital and drove the Miura back to their castle of Arai. The building of Tamanawa Castle to the north of the Miura Peninsula meant that the Miura were now surrounded.

Arai was located almost at the very end of the Miura Peninsula, with rocky cliffs on nearly all sides of the castle site, which the Miura had made into an island by cutting a channel through the narrow isthmus than had joined it to the mainland. The only access to this artificial *umijiro* (sea castle) was a large wooden drawbridge that led to an open bailey, beyond which lay the main castle. Hōjō Sōun believed that the Miura, now isolated in Arai, would 'wither on the vine' as the *Hōjō Godaiki* puts it, but the Miura were initially supremely confident because they could be supplied from the sea by their own navy and had on the island what they described as a great cave known as the 'thousand horsemen tower', where large quantities of supplies could be stored. Four years later Sōun's isolation of Arai appeared to have had no effect, so he decided to mount a decisive attack upon them in 1516.

Two thousand soldiers defended Arai, against whom Hōjō Sōun, who was now 84 years old, brought between 4,000 and 5,000 men. Once Sōun had cut Arai off from fresh supplies it did not take long for the 2,000 defenders to consume the rice intended for only 1,000 men. The final Hōjō assault involved a landing on one side of the island and a fight up a path, while the main attack went against the channel under the drawbridge. Tons of rock and rubble were poured into the gap until it could be crossed, and then the Hōjō samurai fought their way up beneath the raised drawbridge.

Realizing that all was lost, Miura Yoshiatsu and his son Yoshioki prepared to sell their lives dearly. It was a dark night because clouds obscured the moon. Father and son drank a final cup of *sake* together and led a furious charge out of the castle gate that smashed through the Hōjō lines to a depth of 200m. Young Yoshioki wielded an enormous iron-studded wooden club, until, entirely surrounded by enemies and unable to defend himself further, he performed the most dramatic act of suicide in Japanese history. If the story is to be believed, it was done by cutting off his own head. This greatly impressed the victorious Hōjō, who took the head back to Odawara and interred it under a pine tree.

In 1545 Hōjō Sōun's grandson Hōjō Ujiyasu took part in a celebrated night battle when he went to the aid of the castle of Kawagoe. Communication was established with the garrison inside, who made a sortie to coincide with the attack by Ujiyasu on the Uesugi siege lines. Ujiyasu took every precaution against the obvious hazards of a night attack. First, he made sure that his men could recognize each other by issuing them with insignia in the form of white paper 'jackets' shaped like *jinbaori* (surcoats) that they wore on top of their armour. He also ordered them not to gather in one place but to roam around, and most importantly of all, no one was to take heads. Any heads cut off from the Uesugi samurai were to be 'cut and tossed'. As head collection was a great samurai tradition, it is testimony to the control the Hōjō had over their loyal samurai that these instructions were followed to the letter.

JAPANESE FORTIFIED TEMPLES AND MONASTERIES 710–1602

PART 2

THE DEVELOPMENT OF
THE FORTIFIED TEMPLE

SŌHEI AND MONTO

Parallel to the development of Japanese castle design that was led by the samurai, another trend was taking place because of the pressure that the samurai brought to bear on other sections of Japanese society. From the 8th century AD onwards, the challenge posed by the growing influence of powerful samurai families provoked sporadic military responses from farmers (many of whom were 'part-time samurai'), priests and monks. Although this response was frequently manifested through brief riots or raids, organized communities often resorted to fortifications. The most important of these were created by communities that shared identical religious beliefs, resulting in the development of fortified temples and monasteries. These walled and moated religious establishments were castles in all but name, and their pre-eminent example, Ishiyama Honganji, withstood the longest siege in Japanese history.

The expression 'warrior monk', which is often used of the inhabitants of the fortified temples and monasteries, is the popular translation of the word *sōhei*, which literally means 'priest soldier', and refers specifically to the armies maintained by the monasteries of Hieizan and Nara from about AD 970 until the 16th century. It can also be applied to the temple called Negorodera in Kii Province. A helpful comparison is with the military religious orders of Europe that emerged during the Crusades. Indeed, this provided a useful analogy for the only European visitor ever to make their acquaintance, the Jesuit missionary Father Caspar Vilela, who visited Negorodera early in the 1560s and described its adherents as being like the Knights of St John.

The *monto* (followers, believers or disciples) of the populist Jōdo Shinshū (True Pure Land Sect) communities, however, were very different, and to describe the *monto* as 'warrior monks' is highly misleading. Their communities attracted samurai, farmers and townsmen in associations of shared religious

Previous page: A painting of the Edo Period depicting the jinaimachi of Tondabayashi beside the Ishikawa River. We see a bridge across the river, and the natural defences provided by trees and water.

beliefs led by ordained priests. The Ikkō-ikki, as the armies of Jōdo Shinshū were known, were certainly warriors but never warrior monks. In fact the teachings of Shinran (1173–1262), with whom the sect originated, had revolutionized Japanese Buddhism by doing away with the duality of monasticism and laity and replacing it with a new emphasis on spiritual egalitarianism. So, rather than comparing the Ikkō-ikki to the Knights of St John, a better European analogy would be the Hussites of Bohemia, or the extreme Puritan communities that arose a century later during the Reformation. Linked by zeal for their beliefs, and under the leadership of charismatic preachers, they formed self-governing communities defended by armies. So it was with Jōdo Shinshū and its fortified temples.

THE RISE OF THE WARRIOR MONKS

The original Buddhist priest soldiers were formed as a result of the rivalries that existed between the temples of Nara, the old capital of Japan, and of Hieizan, the mountain that lay near to Kyoto, the

Soldier monks of the Negorodera prepare to defend their temple. They have portable wooden shields and are carrying firearms along with more traditional weapons such as bows, swords and *naginata* (spears with curved blades).

city that replaced Nara as capital in AD 894. The great temples of Nara such as Tōdaiji and Kōfukuji resented the move to Kyoto, and were particularly jealous of Enryakuji, the temple that was located on the summit of Hieizan. There were also major arguments over the right of the Hieizan clergy to ordain new monks, instead of this being performed exclusively in Nara.

The first major incident of violence involving priests happened in AD 949. It began as a protest demonstration by a delegation from Tōdaiji to Kyoto, and ended with a brawl during which some of the participants lost their lives. Other incidents followed, so, in about AD 970 Ryogen, the *zasu* (chief priest) of Enryakuji made the decision to create a permanent fighting force to defend Hieizan and its growing wealth. These men soon became involved in inter-temple disputes, some of which were fought between Enryakuji and its daughter temple Onjōji, or Miidera, which lay at the foot of Hieizan. Over the next 100 years there are references to fighting between Enryakuji, Miidera and the temples of Nara. By 1006 the Kōfukuji of Nara could field an army numbering some 3,000 *sōhei*. There were also several instances when *sōhei* marched down to Kyoto to place their demands in front of members of the imperial court, whom the *sōhei* intimidated as much with their curses as they did with their weapons.

There were no permanent fortifications associated with these *sōhei* sites. Enryakuji was defended solely by its position on a high wooded mountain. The temples of Nara were more open to assault, and were forced to erect temporary fortifications when they were faced with attack in 1181. This was at the start of the Gempei War, the struggle for supremacy between the samurai families of Taira and Minamoto. The *sōhei* involvement was brief, tragic and almost totally destructive of them as an entity. The monks of Miidera supported the imperial claimant put forward by the Minamoto family, but were heavily defeated at the first battle of Uji in 1180 as they were heading south from Kyoto to join up with their fellow *sōhei* from Nara. The victorious Taira took terrible retribution, and after a desultory defence Miidera was burned to the ground. In 1181 the Taira burned down most of the buildings in Nara, including Tōdaiji and its huge statue of Buddha. The destruction of Nara was such a shock to the priests of Hieizan, who had been standing aloof from the conflict, that there was almost no more *sōhei* activity for the rest of the Gempei Wars.

Minamoto Yoritomo, the victor in the Gempei Wars, became the first *shōgun* of Japan and established the principle of samurai rule. His religious sensibilities, however, encouraged him to rebuild the Nara temples, and it was not long before the monks rediscovered their military skills. In 1221 we read of warrior monks from Nara being involved in the brief Shōkyū War. Monks from Hieizan fought in the Nanbokucho Wars of the 14th century, and were active until their final destruction in 1571.

JŌDO SHINSHŪ AND THE FIRST FORTIFIED TEMPLE

Around about the time of the Shōkyū War, an important new development was taking place in Japanese Buddhism through the teachings of Shinran, the founder of Jōdo Shinshū. The new sect's beliefs contrasted sharply with the monastic approach of the older institutions of Nara and Kyoto and proved highly attractive to the lower orders of society. Its features included local membership centred around village meeting places, a charismatic leadership under the headship of Shinran's lineal descendants, who were free to marry, and a fundamental independence from traditional regimes, whether aristocratic or military. In 1272 Shinran's daughter Kakushin-ni (1221–81) built the Otani mausoleum in Kyoto to house the ashes of her father, and in 1321 Shinran's great-grandson Kakunyo (1270–1351) developed it further, naming it the Honganji, the 'temple of the original vow'. From then on the expression 'Honganji' came to refer not only to the building that was its headquarters, but to the dominant faction in Jōdo Shinshū. At Otani Honganji, Kakunyo began to develop the ideas of Shinran into a coherent religious system.

In spite of it being the location of the grave of Shinran, recognition and power came very slowly to Otani Honganji during the first century and a half of its existence. Much of Shinran's original missionary work had been in the Kantō provinces, the area around modern-day Tokyo, so the Kantō temples such as Sensuji in Takada in Shimotsuke Province were unwilling to defer to the wishes of the Honganji. All was to change with the tenure of Rennyō (1415–99), the eighth head of the Honganji and Jōdo Shinshū's great revivalist.

The second half of the 15th century, when Rennyō led the Honganji, was a period of great instability in Japan. This was the time that saw the Onin War and the rise of the independent local *daimyō*, and one consequence of the breakdown of law and order was that the lower orders of society were no longer content to be ruled by an impotent *shōgun* or an ambitious *daimyō*. Instead, groups of peasants and low-ranking samurai took the opportunity to assert their own autonomy. Popular uprisings and riots became a common feature of the times. They ranged from local disturbances to province-wide revolts, incidents that were generally referred to as *ikki* (riots), the original use of the word that was later used to designate those who took part in them. Into this turmoil walked Rennyō and his Jōdo Shinshū followers, who were to contribute to the political history of Japan in a way that none of them could have envisaged.

Rennyō's personal charisma and his effectiveness as a preacher and proselytizer go a long way to explain why the Honganji branch of Jōdo Shinshū grew at the expense of other factions. But there was another factor involved, and the stimulus came, ironically, from the warrior monks of Enryakuji. They were enraged by the influence that Otani Honganji was having on their traditional control of the religious life of the capital, so in 1465 an army of *sōhei* descended upon Otani Honganji and burned it to the ground. Rennyō escaped from their clutches and took refuge with a few followers in nearby Wakasa Province. Not long afterwards the Hieizan monks pursued him there, but were attacked and driven off by the local Honganji members. This was the first manifestation of the military capabilities of the Jōdo Shinshū *monto* that would make them so feared in the years to come.

In 1471, to put even greater distance between himself and the warrior monks of Hieizan, Rennyō moved to Yoshizaki in Echizen Province on the coast of the Sea of Japan. The area had already been thoroughly evangelized by Rennyō's uncle, so Rennyō was enthusiastically welcomed by the local *monto*. They helped him to build a new headquarters called Yoshizaki Gobō, which was completed in just three months. Here Rennyō produced some of his most important writings. He encouraged the local believers to set up *ko* (fraternities) that would not only be prayer organizations but would lay the foundations of future self-governing communities. But Yoshizaki Gobō was not just a Jōdo Shinshū temple. It was built on a defensible plateau overlooking the sea, and Rennyō personally attended to the details of its fortification. He also urged the *monto* to be prepared for unhesitating sacrifice in defence of their faith. The first permanently fortified temple in Japan had been created.

A drawing of 1847 showing Yoshizaki. Yoshizaki Gobō, which lay on the plateau, has by this time been replaced by the temple buildings at its foot. These still exist.

Although Rennyō made it clear to his followers that resort to arms was justified only in the most extreme cases where the survival of Jōdo Shinshū was at stake, to fortify a temple was a radical departure from the original teachings of Shinran, who had simply advocated moving to another place in the event of persecution. But this was the Sengoku Jidai, a time of great conflict. Unfortunately, although Rennyō's attitude was realistic, it left his organization open to possible abuse by militant *monto*, who saw the ideological and military strength of the Honganji as a way of advancing their interests. Rennyō soon became alarmed by the belligerence shown by some *monto* who, incited by militant priests, began to attack other sects and challenge the civil authorities. Membership of Jōdo Shinshū also proved attractive for low-ranking members of the samurai class, who were able to combine their own small forces under a common banner to produce an effective army. They became the fighting core of Jōdo Shinshū's Ikkō-ikki armies. The pacifist Rennyō, however, viewed all samurai with distaste, and wrote on one occasion that they were the 'enemies of Buddhism', but increasing numbers of samurai became *monto*. Their fighting skills were to prove useful in the years to come, with very dramatic results.

THE IKKŌ-IKKI TAKE CONTROL OF KAGA PROVINCE

The great breakthrough for the *monto* of Yoshizaki came from the direction of the neighbouring province of Kaga, where the Kaga Ikkō-ikki came into being, not to defend the Jōdo Shinshū faith per se but to assist a second-rate *daimyō* regain his position. In a long campaign the Ikkō-ikki ousted the Togashi family and took over the province themselves. They ruled Kaga for the next 100 years in a unique demonstration of 'people power'.

In spite of this success, Rennyō feared that the Ikkō-ikki of Yoshizaki would now be known for their military activities rather than for their religious lives. He was informed that the *sōhei* of Hieizan had quietened down, so he decided to return to Kyoto, where in 1478 he founded Yamashina Midō. It was completed after five years of work and became his new headquarters. Sources tell of Yamashina Midō being of 'unsurpassed magnificence', and it was likened to the Jōdo (Pure Land) itself. Like Yoshizaki Gobō, Yamashina Midō had to be fortified, but it would be many years before it had to face any attack.

THE FOUNDING OF ISHIYAMA HONGANJI

Kyoto's Yamashina Midō was completed in 1483. In spite of some residual rivalry, particularly from the Takada Sensuji in the Kantō, Rennyō had effectively realized the unfulfilled aspirations of his ancestor Kakunyo in making the Honganji the undisputed centre of Jōdo Shinshū and the authority for the authentic teaching of Shinran.

Rennyō was now nearing the end of his life, but did not lack descendants to carry on his work, for he left 15 daughters and 13 sons, the last born when he was 84 years of age. So, with his succession secure, Rennyō retired in 1489 and handed over the headship of the Honganji to his son Jitsunyo. Rennyō spent the first few years of his retirement within the compound of Yamashina Midō, but in 1496 he began to yearn for solitude, so he built a hermitage on a sweeping bend in the Yodo River downstream from Kyoto. It lay on a long, sloping, wooded plateau, and the 'long slope' gave the place its name: Osaka. A contemporary account noted how Rennyō had established his chapel 'on Ikutama manor, at a place called Osaka', the first documented use of the name of what is now Japan's second city.

Left: Warriors of the Ikkō-ikki leave their fortified temple, which has gun ports in its walls.

Right: A rare illustration of a fortified temple in *Ehon Toyotomi Gunki,* an illustrated biography of Toyotomi Hideyoshi. It depicts a temple fortress called Saginomori, which was besieged by Niwa Nagahide in 1582.

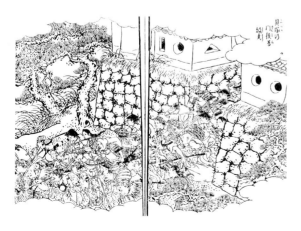

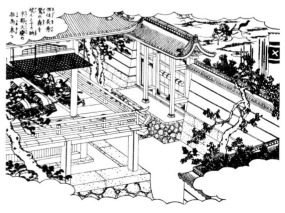

Osaka provided tranquillity for only a short time, however, because even in retirement Rennyō commanded a huge and loyal following. Thousands flocked to pay homage to him, so his simple hermitage was soon replaced by great prayer halls, residences for visiting Jōdo Shinshū priests and extensive gardens. The growing complex was surrounded by formidable moats and walls. Tradesmen moved in, and by the time of Rennyō's death in 1499 the new foundation, now called Ishiyama Honganji, was beginning to take on its final shape. By the 1520s at least six residential neighbourhoods had grown up around the religious complex. Jōdo Shinshū continued to grow and prosper under Shonyo, the tenth leader of the Honganji, who took over following his father Jitsunyo's death in 1525. Shonyo had friends in very high places, and in 1528 he was adopted into the family of an imperial regent. Such connections were to prove highly valuable in the turbulent years that lay ahead.

In spite of the growth of Osaka, Kyoto's Yamashina Midō was still regarded as the sect headquarters until a dramatic incident occurred. By the early 16th century Kyoto had become the city of a rising urban class who were rebuilding their capital from the ashes of the Onin War. Most of these merchant families were adherents of the Nichiren sect of Buddhism, otherwise known as the Hokkeshu or Lotus Sect. Jōdo Shinshū and Nichirenshu had much in common in terms of their defensive mentality, but they were complete opposites when it came to recruitment. Jōdo Shinshū was largely drawn from peasants and country samurai, while Nichirenshu appealed to the townspeople. There were 21 Nichiren temples in Kyoto, and their members organized themselves by neighbourhoods for self-protection and mutual regulation.

During the 15th century, spontaneous peasant mobs had frequently attacked the city, but by the 1530s similar attacks were being carried out by the Ikkō-ikki, who had turned to militancy in much the same way as their comrades in Kaga had done. In 1532 Shonyo showed his personal belligerence by leading an attack against Kenponji, one of the main Nichiren centres in the port of Sakai. Following on from this success the Ikkō-ikki even burned Kōfukuji in Nara, one of the traditional centres of the *sōhei*, and ransacked the Kasuga shrine. News of the destruction caused considerable apprehension within Kyoto when it was rumoured that the capital was the next target, but the Nichirenshu members rallied round the flag of the Holy Lotus and, after some initial setbacks, fought off an Ikkō-ikki assault. Much aggrieved, the Nichiren believers decided to retaliate against the Ikkō-ikki. They were not lacking in sympathetic samurai allies, and towards the end of 1532 they joined forces with Hosokawa Harumoto and Rokkaku Sadayori in an attack on Yamashina Midō, which they thoroughly sacked and burned. Shonyo was forced to take refuge in Ishiyama Honganji.

The abandonment of Yamashina Midō and the flight of Shonyo resulted in Ishiyama Honganji becoming the sect's headquarters for the next 50 years. Its strength was soon tested, because Hosokawa Harumoto and the Nichirenshu attacked it in 1533. To the great relief of the Ikkō-ikki, their massive temple complex, set within a natural moat of rivers and sea, withstood the assault and indeed appeared to be impregnable. This welcome demonstration of its strength and safety encouraged further commercial settlement, and the surrounding merchant community experienced considerable growth over the next few years. Ishiyama Honganji's wealth increased, and in 1536 the priests of the Honganji even paid all the expenses for the enthronement of Emperor Go-Nara. It proved to be money well spent, because in 1538, the leaders of Ishiyama Honganji negotiated a deal with the imperial court and the local military governor to make the surrounding merchant community into a *jinaimachi* (temple town), with immunity from debt moratoriums and from entry by outside military forces.

THE FORTIFIED TEMPLES OF THE IKKŌ~IKKI AND NOBUNAGA'S CAMPAIGNS AGAINST THEM 1569–80

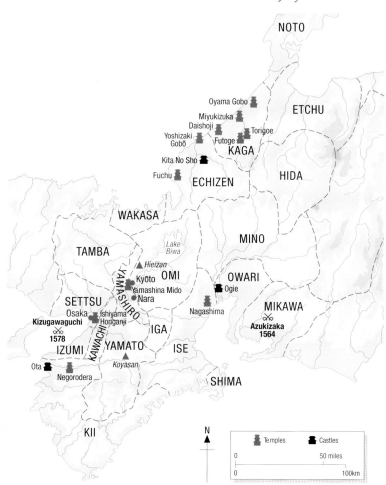

A *jinaimachi* had been developed in Yoshizaki, but Osaka was to eclipse it both in size and concept. The Osaka *jinaimachi* area was officially recognized as being within the Ishiyama Honganji compound, so the Honganji levied its own land tax from the inhabitants and provided all their police and judicial functions as well as their spiritual and military needs. The self-contained community was such a success that by the middle of the 16th century a dozen or so smaller but similar *jinaimachi* had arisen in the provinces of Settsu, Kawachi and Izumi that now make up the modern metropolitan district of Osaka. All of them were commercial and military strongpoints defended by walls and ditches, and each had obtained from the outside authorities a package of self-governing privileges 'just like Osaka's'. The days of the Ikkō-ikki as a simple rural peasant army had passed into history.

While these developments were taking place in Osaka, the triumphant Ikkō-ikki of Kaga had been suffering a series of factional disputes that eventually resulted in a civil war in 1531. The leadership of the Honganji faction proved victorious, and grew richer through confiscation of land, much of which was returned to the defeated factional members as fiefs when they pledged loyalty to the Honganji. The result was that by 1546 the sect's responsibilities in Kaga had become so great that it had to create a permanent local headquarters within the province. The site they chose became known as Oyama Gobo and was the beginning of the city of Kanazawa. Its population numbered between 3,000 and 5,000 people. From this headquarters the leaders of the Kaga Ikkō-ikki ruled their province in a manner that any *daimyō* would have recognized, and many would have envied. On one occasion they fought the powerful Uesugi Kenshin to a standstill and blocked his access to the capital. Not bad for a *hyakusho no motaru kuni* ('a province ruled by peasants'), to use a popular phrase.

The Oyama Gobo, like the other branches of Jōdo Shinshū, still recognized Ishiyama Honganji as its head and Shonyo as the leader. When Shonyo died in 1554 he was succeeded by his 11-year-old son Kennyo, who proved to be the most militant of all the Honganji leaders. Cometh the hour, cometh the man, because Kennyo was soon to face the fiercest onslaught in all of the Honganji's history.

CHALLENGE TO THE HONGANJI

The 1560s and 1570s in Japan were dominated by the ambitions of Oda Nobunaga, who entered the capital in 1568 to set up his nominee Ashikaga Yoshiaki as *shōgun*. But his relations with Yoshiaki deteriorated so quickly that Nobunaga dismissed him, thus abolishing the post of *shōgun*, so the dispossessed ruler sought allies elsewhere. They included the Ikkō-ikki. Up to this point Nobunaga's victims had been rival *daimyō*, but in 1570 he experienced his first clash with the Ikkō-ikki after Kennyo issued a call to arms. Nobunaga was fighting Miyoshi Yoshitsugu near Osaka when forces from Ishiyama Honganji, including 3,000 armed with arquebuses, reinforced the Miyoshi and forced Nobunaga to withdraw. Soon afterwards they struck a more personal blow. The previous year, Oda Nobunaga had placed his brother Nobuoki in charge of Ogie Castle in Owari Province. In the 11th lunar month of 1570, the Ikkō-ikki of the Nagashima delta took advantage of Nobunaga's departure for northern Omi and attacked Ogie, forcing Nobuoki to commit suicide. That same winter of 1570–71, when Nobunaga was driving back the Asai and Asakura armies, his flank was attacked by *sōhei* from Enryakuji.

The threat to Nobunaga from Ishiyama Honganji and its allies was not just one of actual fighting. It was also strategic and economic, because the power base of the Ikkō-ikki coincided precisely with Nobunaga's own primary sphere of interest. The sect was particularly well entrenched within its fortified temples of Owari, Mino and Ise, the places where Nobunaga's own regime had been born. It lay across every approach to the capital save the west, from where the sympathetic *daimyō* Mōri Motonari happily supported and supplied them from his coastal base. But the creation of *jinaimachi* had also lifted Jōdo Shinshū from its peasant roots into a position of economic power, so that the Ishiyama Honganji could confront Nobunaga on commercial terms as well. It is therefore no exaggeration to say that the greatest challenge Nobunaga faced lay with the Ikkō-ikki and their allies.

It must have seemed to Oda Nobunaga in 1571 that he was totally surrounded by religious fanatics, and when the time came to hit back he began with an easy target. In an operation so one-sided that it does not deserve the appellation of a battle, his troops moved against the *sōhei* of Hieizan. In an orgy of fire and slaughter the samurai moved steadily up the mountain, killing everyone and everything in their way. No religious sensibilities stood in the way of the total destruction of the Hieizan temples. The threat to Nobunaga's flank was neutralized, and the long history of the Hieizan *sōhei* came to a bloody end.

As for the Ikkō-ikki, a long and bitter war had now started that was to last until Nobunaga's death 12 years later. He also brought some subtle politics into the equation that were to have an indirect effect on the development of the fortified temple. First, he pursued a policy of disarming the rural population from which the Ikkō-ikki had traditionally drawn their strength. This went a long way towards separating the farming class from the samurai class, a development that is usually regarded as having begun with Toyotomi Hideyoshi's 'Sword Hunt' of 1588. So, for example, in 1575, when the Ikkō-ikki of Echizen had been subdued, we read of regulations forbidding peasants to seek new masters or to leave their villages, and ordering them to confine themselves to tilling the soil. In 1576 Nobunaga's general Shibata Katsuie conducted a Sword Hunt of his own in Echizen, just to make sure.

Secondly, Nobunaga made clever use of religious rivalry. It was not too difficult to persuade the Nichiren temples of Echizen to oppose the Ikkō-ikki, but Nobunaga also made use of the jealousy that still existed between the

Honganji and the smaller rival branches of Jōdo Shinshū. Any Honganji *monto* who survived his attacks were given the opportunity to change their allegiance. For example, a surviving letter from Nobunaga to the Senpukuji in Mino Province in 1572 gives the temple two days to renounce its affiliation to Osaka. Similarly, the three Takada faction temples of Echizen were promised protection if they would publicly acknowledge their difference from Osaka and provide 'loyal service'. It proved to be a successful policy, because some from the Takada faction in Echizen went so far as to capture and kill Shimotsuma Hokkyo, one of the Ishiyama Honganji's principal deputies in that province.

THE LAST STAND OF THE IKKŌ-IKKI

Oda Nobunaga's first campaign against Ishiyama Honganji was launched in August 1570. His last campaign against it finished in August 1580, after exactly ten years of intermittent but bitter fighting that involved many features beyond siege-work and assault. Both sides made considerable political efforts and a prolonged naval campaign was designed to cut the supply lines until, isolated from any support, Ishiyama Honganji eventually surrendered. On the night that it capitulated, the entire complex burst into flames and was utterly destroyed, probably on the initiative of the Ikkō-ikki leaders themselves, who did not wish their glorious headquarters to become a prize for the man they had defied for so long.

Nobunaga's war against the Ikkō-ikki is commonly regarded as having finished with the surrender of Ishiyama Honganji in 1580. However, there were a few more years of bitter fighting left, and the first action was to be directed against Kaga Province. As early as 1573, forces commanded by Akechi Mitsuhide and Toyotomi Hideyoshi had driven through Echizen and on into the southern part of Kaga. In 1574 a fierce counter-attack by the Ikkō-ikki blunted this advance, so Nobunaga took personal command of the response. In 1575 he left his base at Tsuruga and swept through Echizen, recapturing the province from Ikkō-ikki forces. Mitsuhide and Hideyoshi then continued their advance into Kaga, taking in rapid succession the three fortified temples of Daishoji, Hinoya and Sakumi. By the end of 1575, the year that also saw Nobunaga's celebrated victory at Nagashino, the southern half of Kaga was firmly under Nobunaga's control and the Ikkō-ikki federation was beginning to fall apart. In November 1575 Nobunaga boasted to the *daimyō* Date Terumune that he had 'wiped out several tens of thousands of the villainous rabble in Echizen and Kaga'.

Nobunaga assigned the newly pacified Echizen Province to Shibata Katsuie, one of his most trusted and experienced generals. In 1576 Katsuie's nephew Sakuma Morimasa advanced deeper into Kaga and captured Miyukizuka (modern-day Komatsu). Four years later, as the spearhead of his uncle's forces, Sakuma Morimasa devastated the Ikkō-ikki of Kaga by destroying their headquarters of Oyama Gobo in Kanazawa.

THE FORTIFIED TEMPLE IN THE AGE PRIOR TO GUNPOWDER: YOSHIZAKI GOBŌ 1474

Yoshizaki Gobō, founded by Rennyō when he fled from the *sōhei* of Hieizan in 1471, was Japan's first permanently fortified temple. It was built to resist attacks by bows and arrows, fire and edged weapons, and is shown as it would have appeared when it came under attack by Togashi Kochiro in 1474. This reconstruction is based on a model on display in the Rennyō Kinenkan in Yoshizaki, which was constructed using a contemporary scroll painting in the possession of Yoshizakiji and archaeological investigation. (Peter Dennis © Osprey Publishing Ltd)

In that same year of 1580 the Osaka Ishiyama Honganji surrendered. The war in Kaga should have been over, but diehard elements among the Ikkō-ikki abandoned the flat plains of Kaga and entrenched themselves in fortified temples in the mountainous areas nearby. The most important locations were two sites in the foothills of the mighty Hakuzan Mountains. They were called Torigoe and Futoge and were located on top of forested hills on either side of the river valley of the Dainichigawa, a branch of the Tedorigawa. The sites were to change hands three times within the following two years until these final outposts of the Kaga Ikkō-ikki were wiped out.

Oda Nobunaga died in 1582, and three years later his successor, Toyotomi Hideyoshi, finally quelled militant Buddhism. The last Jōdo Shinshū enclave was located in Kii Province to the south of Osaka, around the area where the castle and city of Wakayama now stand. They were called the Saiga Ikkō-ikki from their location, where the strongest point was a castle called Ota. Owned by a *daimyō* who belonged to Jōdo Shinshū, the castle had resisted an attack by Nobunaga in 1577. Not far away was the other remaining religious army in Japan: the *sōhei* of Negorodera, who had very unwisely supported Tokugawa Ieyasu against Hideyoshi during the Komaki campaign of 1584. This folly brought about terrible retribution on them the following year. The result was the almost total destruction of the Negorodera complex in as thorough a job of destruction as Nobunaga had performed on Hieizan. Hideyoshi then turned his attentions towards the Saiga Ikkō-ikki. Just as in Kaga a number of villages, 26 in all, had banded together for mutual defence and economic power, but when their main base at Ota was destroyed they surrendered, and thus the last armed enclave of Jōdo Shinshū disappeared from Japan.

FROM WARRIORS TO WORSHIPPERS

To underline his triumph in Kii Province in 1585, Hideyoshi sent the following warning to the Shingon temples on Koyasan that same year:

> Item: The monks, priests in the world and others have not been prudent in their religious studies. The manufacture and retention of senseless weapons, muskets and the like is treacherous and wicked. Item: In as much as you saw with your own eyes that Hieizan and Negorodera were finally destroyed for acting with enmity against the realm, you should be discerning in this matter.

The authorities on Mount Koya were not slow to grasp the point. In 1588, when Toyotomi Hideyoshi enacted his famous 'Sword Hunt' to disarm the peasantry, small landowners or anyone who might possibly oppose him in future, the monks of Koyasan were the first to respond by handing over their cache of arms.

After the destruction of Ishiyama Honganji, Kennyo Kosa sought every opportunity to restore the cathedral of the sect, but only as the religious headquarters of Jōdo Shinshū, not as a fortress. Permission was granted after Kennyo sent some of the few remaining Ikkō-ikki warriors to harass Shibata Katsuie's rear during the Shizugatake campaign in 1583. In gratitude to the *monto*, Hideyoshi eventually made a parcel of land available in Kyoto in 1589, and the Honganji headquarters were rebuilt there in 1591. This was the same year that Hideyoshi finally achieved the reunification of Japan.

The absence of *sōhei* or *monto* from Hideyoshi's last campaigns would seem to indicate that the problem of sectarian violence had been solved forever. But his successor, Tokugawa Ieyasu, who became *shōgun* as a result of his victory at Sekigahara in 1600, was not a man to take any chances. Not only did he take steps to emasculate any potential rivals from among the ranks of defeated *daimyō*, he took very seriously any possibility of an Ikkō-ikki revival. Ieyasu

gave high priority to the issue, which he solved in 1602, the year before he was officially proclaimed *shōgun*.

The results may be seen by any visitor to Kyoto today. On leaving the station one is struck by the fact that there are two Jōdo Shinshū temples, Nishi (Western) Honganji and Higashi (Eastern) Honganji, both of which appear to be the headquarters of the same organization, and which are situated almost next to each other. The explanation is that Tokugawa Ieyasu, who had suffered personally at the hands of the Mikawa *monto*, deliberately weakened Jōdo Shinshū by splitting it in two. A dispute between Junnyo, who headed the Honganji, and his older brother Gyonyo provided Ieyasu with the pretext he needed to divide the sect. Ieyasu backed Gyonyo and founded Higashi Honganji to enable him to rival the existing temple, built by Hideyoshi in 1591 and henceforth called Nishi Honganji. This weakened the political power of the sect, leaving it as a strong religious organization, but never again capable of becoming the monk army of the Ikkō-ikki.

Jōdo Shinshū is today the largest Buddhist organization in Japan, a worthy acknowledgement of the genuine populist roots that Shinran and Rennyō laid down so many centuries ago. However, Toyotomi Hideyoshi had already paid the greatest compliment ever to the Ikkō-ikki. He had admired the *monto* for their fine strategic eye, particularly in choosing the sites for their formidable fortified temples. To hold out for ten years against Oda Nobunaga proved that the site of Ishiyama Honganji was a superb strategic and defensive location. Recalling how it had frustrated his master for so long, he chose it as the site for his new headquarters in 1586. Japan's largest castle was established on the site, and in 1615 it required the country's biggest-ever siege using European artillery to crush it. Nowadays it lies at the centre of Japan's second city – the great modern metropolis of Osaka.

Left: The view today from the keep of Osaka Castle, the site of Ishiyama Honganji.

Right: The armoured monks of Negorodera attempt to save their temple when Hideyoshi burns it in 1585. (From *Ehon Taikōki*)

THE SACRED SPACE

SACRED AND SECULAR FUNCTIONS

Unlike ordinary Buddhist temples, every fortified temple had both a sacred and a secular function to perform, and in the turbulent times of medieval Japan this effectively meant the performance of a role associated with peace and a role connected to war. The structure and design of the buildings and their layout reflect the interplay between the two roles.

We will look first at the peaceful role that a fortified temple performed. The sacred role of the buildings of any Buddhist institution, either in medieval Japan or today, first consists of providing an area where the ritual demands of Buddhism may be exercised. Second, there is a need for space wherein the material needs of its clergy, such as food and living accommodation, may be met. In a monastic situation the space needed for the latter function might be quite large, but it would never detract from the primacy of the former, to which the finest architectural and decorative design would be directed. The populist nature of Jōdo Shinshū added a third sacred role: that of providing adequate room for worship for a large congregation of lay people. As homes and workplaces were often provided for them within the defensive perimeter, this final function led ultimately to the creation of the *jinaimachi* or temple town.

Surviving plans and illustrations, and the results of archaeological investigation of fortified temple sites, show that by and large there was a total separation in architectural terms between the buildings associated with the sacred function and the other parts of the temple complex concerned with providing its defence. There were exceptions and variations to this depending on the size of the site available and its topographical layout, as we will see, but effectively we can study the layout of a Japanese fortified temple as if it were two separate units. These were the temple, laid out according to a fairly standard model depending largely on the Buddhist sect to which it owed its allegiance, and the defensive perimeter that resembled in most particulars the contemporary castles of the secular samurai warlords.

THE DESIGN FEATURES OF A TYPICAL JAPANESE BUDDHIST TEMPLE

Buddhism came to Japan by way of China in the middle of the 6th century AD, so it is not surprising to find that the model adopted for the general layout of the temples where the new faith was practised was based on Chinese antecedents. The architecture of Chinese Buddhist temples derived in turn from that of the Chinese palace and, by and large, the overall pattern of a Buddhist temple compound that it gave rise to persists to this day. There are numerous variations, many of which we will note specifically in relation to the examples discussed here, but certain features have stubbornly persisted over the centuries.

The usual pattern of a Buddhist temple is based on the model of a courtyard, which is entered through a formal gateway. Because this gate symbolically marks the entrance to the precincts it may not even have closing doors or walls on either side. It may also contain a pair of huge statues called *Nio*. These half-naked giants, who stand guard over the temple entrance, are derived from Hindu deities incorporated into Buddhist cosmology. One *Nio* has its mouth open, while the other's mouth is closed.

The buildings arranged within the courtyard are solidly framed wooden structures standing on masonry terraces and crowned with graceful tiled roofs. They are built round a framework of massive vertical timbers, with large cross pieces and very intricate bracketing to support upper storeys and roofs. Each vertical support usually rests on one very large stone.

The main hall within the courtyard is called the *hondō* (or sometimes the *kondō*). The *hondō* is the focus of the layout, although this may not always be immediately apparent from the overall temple layout. The *hondō* invariably has overhanging eaves protecting an outside walkway that will stretch right around the building. This walkway is reached via a flight of stairs. The interior of the *hondō* is entered at the front by some form of door. This may be a sliding or hinged wooden door, or a set of doors, with additional sliding *shoji* just inside. *Shoji* are the instantly recognizable light-framed doors with translucent paper covering them. Alternatively, the doors may be hinged at the top, so that they can be lifted up and propped open.

The main image in the temple occupies a central place within the *hondō*, while around it is the space for the priests or monks to perform services, together with some provision for lay worshippers to gather. In Jōdo Shinshū temples this latter area is made deliberately large. The floor will probably be of wooden planking, augmented by *tatami* (straw mats). There will be some form of barrier to divide the sanctuary of the image from the outer area.

Outside in the courtyard there may be some or all of the following features. Lanterns are always popular. A pagoda is often to be found in the temples of the older sects, but is unusual in Jōdo Shinshū temples. Pagodas came to Japan with Buddhism itself. They were originally towers for housing the remains of the Buddha as relics, but were developed for other purposes, such as markers for holy places. A very common feature in nearly all temples that had obvious defensive uses was the bell tower. Unlike European bell towers, a typical Japanese example is a free-standing open wooden structure from which the huge bronze bell is suspended. It is rung using an external wooden clapper. A drum tower may also be included, although these are often enclosed two-storey structures. Temples that are also monasteries are most likely to include a lecture hall, together with other similar buildings concerned with the education and ordination of monks. We may find a Sutra repository (place for Buddhist scriptures), various dormitories, living quarters and a refectory. These buildings usually stand alone, but may be connected to each other using roofed wooden corridors. Further features may include a garden and a cemetery, because Buddhist funeral rites have always been very important in Japan. A final feature could be a nearby Shintō shrine

Opposite: The bell tower of Sokusoji, a Tendai mountain temple in Mie Prefecture. This is a typical Japanese bell tower based round the design of a simple wooden frame beneath a protective roof. As in all Japanese examples, the bell hangs inside the bell tower, and is rung by using a heavy wooden external clapper, which is swung by a rope.

associated with the temple's foundation. Shintō is the indigenous religion of Japan, and for most of Japanese history Shintō shrines and Buddhist temples have happily co-existed, with their adherents sharing their religious lives between the two.

THE EARLY ARISTOCRATIC TEMPLES OF NARA

The first Buddhist temples in Japan were founded in the area around Nara, the place that became Japan's first permanent capital in AD 710. The city of Nara was laid out on a grid plan in imitation of the capital of the Tang dynasty of China, from which Japan's rulers drew their inspiration.

The statesman Fujiwara Fuhito (AD 659–720) encouraged the move to Nara by founding the Buddhist Kōfukuji temple and the Shintō Kasuga shrine as the spiritual guardians of the new capital. Fuhito also protected his family's position by methodically marrying off his daughters to Japanese emperors, and it was his grandson Emperor Shomu who was to provide Nara with its largest and most glorious monument: Tōdaiji, built to house a colossal image of Buddha. In the buildings of Tōdaiji and Kōfukuji we see the sacred function being exercised on a grand scale that befitted the capital of Japan. In AD 752 Tōdaiji, which rivalled the greatest Chinese monuments, was inaugurated in the most splendid ceremony ever witnessed in Japan.

THE DEVELOPMENT OF ESOTERIC MOUNTAIN TEMPLES

In AD 794 Japan's capital was moved from Nara to Kyoto via the short-lived Nagaoka. Kyoto was originally known as Heian-kyo, which gave its name to the Heian Period in Japanese history. The motive behind the move was the desire of the imperial court to free itself from the stranglehold of the great Nara monasteries. As if in answer to their prayers, not only was a new site for a capital found, but no fewer than two Buddhist sects also arose and rapidly became associated with the new city.

Saicho (AD 762–822), known to posterity as Dengyō Daishi, founded the Tendai sect on top of Hieizan, to the north-east of Kyoto, where he had established a monastic community in his younger days. Chinese *feng shui* taught that the north-east was the direction from which evil spirits proceeded, so Hieizan was regarded as the spiritual guardian of the new capital. It was richly endowed at Nara's expense, although Saicho was to die before he could realize his dream of having Hieizan regarded as an independent institution that ordained its own monks. After his death his temple was raised to official status and given the name of Enryakuji.

Saicho's colleague Kukai (Kobo Daishi, AD 774–835) founded the Shingon sect of Buddhism. In AD 823 Emperor Saga presented him with Toji, one of only two Buddhist temples allowed within the city precincts. In terms of physical influence, therefore, the new Heian government seemed to have succeeded in controlling Buddhism – but there was a catch. The new Buddhist sects were esoteric in their approach. Their *mikkyō* tradition stressed the active quest for enlightenment through strenuous austerities and secret rituals. Their monks would undertake arduous mountain pilgrimages and perform long mysterious rituals in their temples. As no institution was more dependent upon ritual than the imperial court, the influence of Buddhism continued, even if it was exercised in more subtle ways.

In architectural terms, independence from Nara led to the diminution of Chinese styles in the design of the Heian temples, and the emergence of a national style. There were also two other factors that led to the Hieizan temples looking very different from their predecessors in Nara. The first was the association with mountains. For an esoteric sect, sacred and mysterious mountains were the obvious places to build monasteries where aspiring monks could practise rituals and undergo austerities. The result was that the courtyard model of Buddhist temple seen at Nara had to be modified because of the mountainous terrain. Halls were built on different levels and joined

The Daibutsuden (Great Buddha Hall) of Tōdaiji, the world's largest wooden building under one roof.

by mountain paths through secret valleys. Enryakuji, for example, was spread out over a vast area of the summit of Hieizan, on its peaks and in its wooded valleys.

Another difference was found in their interior layout. The *mikkyō* sects stressed gradual initiation into secret rites, so the *hondō* of *mikkyō* temples acquired a central barrier that divided the interior into an outer part for the uninitiated and an inner sanctum.

The Tendai and Shingon temples also took very seriously their role of serving the populace, as distinct from emphasizing the needs of the aristocracy. This requirement of being available to the laity in order to instruct and enlighten them caused further problems of space that the old Nara models could not accommodate. Pictorial evidence suggests that, like vassals in an imperial audience, any congregation in a Nara temple, even a high-ranking one, had to make do with the open air of the courtyard, with perhaps some form of temporary shelter if the weather was inclement. To cope with the conflicting demands of secrecy and education, three improvements to the plan of the *hondō* were evaluated during the Heian Period. The first was to add an aisle across the front, covered by an extension of the main roof. This is the model found in the most important Tendai building of all: the Konponchūdō (Central Main Hall) of Enryakuji, founded in AD 788. The second was the provision of a building just in front of the *hondō*, either free-standing or joined to it by a gallery. This was already common in Shintō shrines, where it was known as a *raido* or *haiden*. The third improvement, which was to become very important in Jōdo Shinshū, was to construct a *raido* as the fore-hall in contact with the main building of the *hondō*, or more simply as an integral part of it under one roof. This model gave the Heian monks the best of both worlds. The laity could be accommodated with ease, while sliding partitions enabled the monks to exclude them just as easily from anything deemed improper for their eyes.

THE 'PEOPLES' TEMPLES' OF JŌDO SHINSHŪ

The populist nature of sects like Jōdo Shinshū inevitably led to changes in the architecture of its buildings. The first change was the shift in orientation from a south-facing *hondō* to one that looked towards the east, because Amida Buddha, the focus of devotion in Jōdo Shinshū, faces east from his western paradise. Other major changes arose from the fact that Jōdo Shinshū temples were not monasteries but popular temples served by comparatively few priests. There were no cloistered corridors, lecture halls or pagodas. Nor do we see formal dormitory and refectory blocks. The quarters for the married priests were more like private houses, walled off from the public area in their gardens.

But the most striking difference concerned the *hondō*. First, it was likely to be dedicated not to any conventional figure in the Buddhist pantheon but to Shinran Shonin as a *goeidō* (founder's hall). Second, a very common feature in the larger Jōdo Shinshū establishments was the existence of two main halls instead of just one. The second hall was dedicated to Amida and was smaller, although it often had two storeys rather than one and appeared richer in detail. The *goeidō* would have had a more imposing gateway, but the gate of the *amidadō*, although smaller, may have had the special elaboration of an ornate roof with curved gables. The size of both halls was intended to make their *raido* spacious enough for a crowd of worshippers. The rear was closed off by a partition while the congregation assembled, but the partition was then drawn back. So, although the *raido* style was derived from esoteric Tendai worship, it served a religion in which the ceremonies were performed in public.

THE TEMPLE AS A DEFENSIVE SYSTEM

THE TEMPORARY FORTIFICATIONS OF THE *SŌHEI*

The earlier monastic institutions of Nara and Hieizan had nothing in the way of permanent fortifications. We will therefore study their buildings in relation to the natural defensive features of the sites chosen for them and the temporary fortifications, such as walls and ditches, that were erected in times of war.

The two centres of *sōhei* activity in early medieval Japan could not have been more different in terms of their layout and defensive capability. The temples of Nara lay in their own grounds within a fine city on a flat plain. The temples of Hieizan were hidden within mountain valleys or stood proudly upon mountain peaks. Temporary fortifications for Nara are mentioned in the *Heike Monogatari* account of Taira Shigehira's attack on Nara in 1181. We read how the monks dug ditches across the roads and erected breastworks and palisades. The breastworks would probably have been earthworks made from ditches, with the soil piled up behind to make a parapet. Fences of stakes could have been added, and they would also have made use of rows of wooden shields. These solid wooden shields, made familiar in many picture scrolls of the period, were often erected on battlefields. They had a hinged strut at the rear for support, and were often decorated at the front with the samurai leader's *mon* (family crest). Monastic armies, however, would often paint *bonji* (sacred Sanskrit ideographs) on the front of their shields.

When Miidera, which lay at the foot of Hieizan, was threatened, similar precautions were taken, and the ready supply of wood from the forests on its slope provided extra means of defence. Trees would be cut down and laid with their branches facing towards the enemy. Logs could be cut and piled, ready to roll down a path against an advancing column. However, the haughty Enryakuji on Hieizan's summit seems never to have made use of any artificial defence in

all its history. Its self-confidence as the protector of Kyoto and the alma mater of the founders of almost every Buddhist sect in Japan gave it an arrogance and self-importance that saw no need for walls. This happy state of affairs was to be rudely shattered in September 1571 when Nobunaga's armies swept up the holy mountain, allowing no time for even a shield wall to be erected.

THE DEFENCE OF THE IKKŌ-IKKI TEMPLES

It is in the design of the defences of their fortified temples that we find the best evidence that the Ikkō-ikki were not just a rabble composed of ignorant peasants. Part of the secret behind their remarkable success lay in sophisticated military technology and its uses that matched any of the contemporary *daimyō*. This military prowess was illustrated by their early enthusiasm for firearms and their skills in castle-building. In this and the following section we will see how the two achievements came together.

The Ikkō-ikki sites first made skilful use of their natural positions, be they a mountain (as at Torigoe), a plateau and sea cliffs (Yoshizaki), a swampy estuary (Nagashima), or a combination of all three (the mighty Ishiyama Honganji). Upon these sites were raised walls, towers and gates that resembled a *daimyō*'s castle in every particular bar one: at the heart of the complex, instead of a keep and a mansion, lay the buildings of the Buddhist temple to which its followers owed a fanatical adherence.

The original *kondō* of Negoroji, now at Daigoji near Kyoto. It was first built early in the Kamakura Period (1185–1392) in the developing national style. It is an excellent example of an early temple hall, and contains a main image of Yakushi Nyorai which is probably contemporary with the building. The survival of the *kondō* and images is quite remarkable after Hideyoshi's fire attack on Negoroiji in 1585.

This remarkable life-sized diorama in the Heike Monogatari Museum in Takamatsu shows the fallen head of the Great Buddha of Nara after Taira Shigehira's attack on Todaiji in 1181.

Throughout their history, the design of the fortified temples of the Ikkō-ikki paralleled or even led the advances in defensive technology introduced by samurai. The earliest Ikkō-ikki fortified temples, therefore, would have been identical to the predominantly wooden samurai castles described earlier. Just as in the case of the samurai castles, Ikkō–ikki fortresses grew even larger to accommodate the increasing numbers of *monto* drawn to their flags. Eventually we see the introduction of great stone bases, the fundamental design element of the developed Japanese castle. Gatehouses, towers and bridges appear, but not the tower keeps found in some samurai castles. In their place stood the sacred temple buildings.

The Ikkō–ikki and the Negorodera monks were among the first to appreciate the use of gunpowder weapons, and one of the earliest examples of volley firing in the defence of a castle occurred when Oda Nobunaga was driven away from the Ishiyama Honganji during his first attack on it in 1570. All subsequent operations involving the Ikkō–ikki saw a considerable use of firearms on both sides, and the reconstruction of Ishiyama Honganji, discussed in detail in the next section, strongly suggests that the Ikkō–ikki designed their later fortified temples in a way that allowed clear fields of defensive fire with a minimum of blind spots. The result, when resources and topography allowed it, was a series of stone walls topped by low plaster walls that interlocked and covered each other like a Japanese folding screen. From loopholes in the plastered sections hundreds, even thousands, of arquebuses could be brought to bear.

The final innovation that can be credited to the Ikkō-ikki lies in their creation of the temple town or *jinaimachi*. From the outset the *jinaimachi* was seen as an integral part of the fortified temple's community, and therefore played a role in its defence. The outer defensive perimeter would be located around the *jinaimachi*, which itself was located in a defensible space. Thus rivers and other natural features were used. Natural slopes, rivers and streams, forests and bamboo groves provided cover and defence, while the design of the streets of the *jinaimachi* was always a deliberately complex one intended to mislead the attackers.

REPRESENTATIVE FORTIFIED TEMPLES OF JAPAN

In this section I shall describe key sites of the *sōhei* and *monto* as they were in their heyday. Some no longer exist, whilst others were destroyed and rebuilt several times over and are reconstructed on the basis of literary, pictorial and archaeological evidence.

THE SŌHEI TEMPLES OF NARA

Kōfukuji, the centre of the Hosso sect of Buddhism, was begun in AD 710 and completed by about AD 730. It was assigned a four-block square in Nara's gridiron pattern, within which the main buildings stood inside a rectangle one block wide by two blocks deep. At the time of the warrior monks, the *hondō* arose from the centre of this area and gave the impression of great size. It was nine bays across by six bays deep, 41m by 26m. There were also two lesser halls known as *kondō* (golden halls). Kōfukuji boasted just one pagoda, the magnificent five-storey structure that stands to this day.

The area allotted to the Tōdaiji, eight city blocks on each side, was four times the area of Kōfukuji and equalled that of the imperial palace precincts. All of its elements were built on the same impressive scale. The Nandaimon (Great Southern Gate) was a masterpiece of its kind, with huge *Nio* in the niches. The compound had two pagodas, each seven storeys tall and some 108m to the tip of each spire. The Daibutsuden (Great Buddha Hall) was a colossal wooden structure of 11 bays by seven, half as large again as its present replacement, which is the largest wooden building in the world. The temples of Nara had no military involvement in the whole of the Sengoku Jidai, so any further changes to the designs arose from calamities such as fires and earthquakes.

A hanging scroll showing Yoshizaki Gobō displayed in the Yoshizakiji Museum in Yoshizaki. The Amida hall is the simpler structure with an open roofed area. The *goeidō* is fronted by a gateway. In the case of Yoshizaki Gobō these buildings have been joined by a third, smaller structure on the rear (western) side, presumably to provide private accommodation for Rennyō himself.

YOSHIZAKI GOBŌ – THE FIRST PERMANENTLY FORTIFIED TEMPLE

Yoshizaki Gobō, which lies on the historical border between Echizen Province and Kaga Province, was founded by Rennyō in 1471 after he had fled from Kyoto. The land on which Yoshizaki Gobō was to be built was owned by the samurai Oei Yoshihisa, the local village head. A convert to Jōdo Shinshū, he donated a parcel of land to Rennyō that included Chitoseyama (Mount Chitose). While the temple was being constructed Rennyō lived in his benefactor's house, the site of which is now occupied by Yoshizakiji. In 1474 the patron performed a further valuable service to Jōdo Shinshū when he rescued Rennyō from a fire, carrying the older man to safety on his back.

In a letter of 1473 Rennyō wrote that he had selected the site of Yoshizaki Gobō on account of its scenic beauty, but that was only part of the story. Chitoseyama, the focal point of the site, had obvious defensive possibilities, being the highest point on a peninsula that projected into Lake Kitagana. The lake was connected to the sea by a narrow waterway, protected at its exit from the lake by a small forested island called Shikajima.

Our sources for the reconstruction of Yoshizaki Gobō are a contemporary scroll painting displayed in the Yoshizakiji Museum, a woodblock drawing of 1847 and archaeological investigations. The plateau of Chitoseyama covered 33,000m², and was surrounded on all sides by cliffs. There was a path on the eastern side leading down to an area of flat land on the northern side, the only

Some of the best pictorial evidence for the day to day life during the siege of a castle comes from the painted screen depicting the Shimabara Rebellion of 1637–38. A strong wooden palisade is shown here in a section from the Shimabara Screen, together with a gate that the attackers have knocked to one side. Note also here the stumps of trees.

such path on the whole site, where boats could be launched into the lake. The southern side was also defended by cliffs, leaving only a narrow neck of vulnerable land at the extreme eastern side. The buildings of Yoshizaki Gobō on the plateau have long since disappeared and have never been replaced. Land has been reclaimed from the lakeside, and this is where the modern village is located.

The plateau of Chitoseyama was the location of the temple buildings. Taking the scroll painting as a guide, we recognize the common feature of a *goeidō* and *amidadō* connected by a covered walkway. The Amida hall is the simpler structure with an open-roofed area. The *goeidō* is fronted by a gateway. In the case of Yoshizaki Gobō, these buildings have been joined by a third, smaller structure on the rear (western) side, presumably to provide private accommodation for Rennyō himself. The only other structure within the courtyard is a smaller building that was probably a bell tower. A low temple wall divides the courtyard area from other buildings outside on the southern side.

From this cluster of buildings a winding hairpin path led down to the lake on the western side of the plateau, while a gentler path led around the slope to descend on the eastern side amongst more buildings. A steeper descent could be made by means of two flights of stone stairs on the vulnerable, but steep, eastern side. The side was defended by sloping stone walls identical in design to those commonly found in Japanese castles. The walls overlooked the flat lakeside area. Beyond the landing stages and beach were more houses, rice fields and narrow paths that made up Yoshizaki's *jinaimachi*. They were surrounded on the lake fringes by dense woods. We know from Rennyō's own statement that during the two years after his arrival, well over 200 separate residences were built to accommodate the flow of pilgrims attracted to the site by its famous newcomer.

NAGASHIMA – DEFENCE OF RIVER AND SEA

The Ikkō-ikki base at Nagashima is the easiest to envisage in outline and the most difficult to reconstruct in detail. The overall picture presented by descriptions of Nagashima is of a community located on a vast, remote and lonely river delta where three great wide rivers, the Kiso, Nagara and Ina, enter the sea. There was no high ground for miles, and its inhabitants were clustered on to a series of islands amid sea, river and marsh, with numerous creeks and inlets. Sandbanks shifted as the years went by. Islands disappeared or were saved as *waju* (dyked communities), while the whole area was regularly battered by typhoons and high tides. Little was visible from sea level because of the maze of reed beds, whose dense fronds waved in the wind, now and then blowing to one side to reveal simple wooden palisades concealing basic wooden buildings. Here and there the roof of a higher building, perhaps a temple, protruded above the monotonous landscape, while tall wooden watchtowers gave the only indication from a distance that this was a military establishment.

This was the environment from which the Ikkō-ikki of Nagashima defied Oda Nobunaga for several desperate years until his combination of naval control and the deadly weapon of fire stripped Nagashima of its defences. The wooden walls of Nagashima were augmented by other unique defensive devices when danger threatened. The shores of the reed beds were booby-trapped by the simple addition of old pots and vases buried up to the necks in the sand to provide a trap for ankles. Ropes tied on to stakes just below the water level were the contemporary equivalent of tripwires. The heart of the religious community was a fortified temple called Ganshōji, which has since been rebuilt.

Left: The well and gatehouse of Torigoe.

Right: Torigoe, where a fortified temple is almost indistinguishable from a samurai's castle.

HONSHŌJI – FORTIFIED TEMPLE AS *HIRAJIRO*

Near the modern city of Anjō in Aichi Prefecture lies the Honshōji temple, a Jōdo Shinshū establishment that was once one of the most important Jōdo

The fortified drum tower of the Honshōji near Anjō. This is one of the finest restored fortified Jōdo Shinshū temples.

Shinshū sites in Mikawa Province. Together with the Joguji and Shomanji, it provided a focus of opposition to Tokugawa Ieyasu during his early rise to power. The overall layout of the site has been preserved, and resembles the Ganshōji of Nagashima in its rectangular layout that is here contained within a narrow moat. Even in its subsequent rebuilding it still has the air of a fortified temple. One striking feature of the Honshōji is the corner drum tower which is identical to a castle tower with narrow windows suitable for defence.

TORIGOE – TEMPLE AS *YAMASHIRO*

Reference was made earlier to the strong resemblance between the defensive elements of a fortified temple and the contemporary samurai castle. This is no coincidence, because many of the prime movers within the Jōdo Shinshū sect and its Ikkō-ikki armies were samurai. Like their secular counterparts, the

Ikkō-ikki commanders faced the same challenges posed by contemporary fortress technology and the strict rigours of the Japanese landscape.

Nowhere is the solution to these problems better seen in the fortified temple context than at Torigoe, the archetypal temple/castle. It is the only temple/castle site to have been comprehensively excavated. The published results, the findings displayed in the nearby Ikkō-ikki Museum (the only one of its kind) and some sensitive on-site restorations provide much valuable information about the last important Ikkō-ikki *yamashiro*.

Torigoe is located in the southern part of modern Ishikawa Prefecture, the old province of Kaga, about 19km from the city of Komatsu. It lies on the top of a 312m-high mountain overlooking the Tedorigawa (Tedori River) at a strategic point where it is joined by the Dainichigawa. Together with its sister fortress of Futoge across the valley at the slightly lower elevation of 286m, the site of Torigoe dominates the area, and in 1582 it was to provide a suitably dramatic location for the last stand of the Kaga Ikkō-ikki.

Excavation of Torigoe was carried out between 1977 and 1995 and has yielded very valuable results that allow us to appreciate the nature of an Ikkō-ikki *yamashiro*. The Jōdo Shinshū temple, the heart of the community, would have been located within the wooden walls of the highest and innermost of three irregularly shaped baileys: the *san no maru* (third bailey), the *ni no maru* (second bailey) and the *hon maru* (innermost bailey). Each was built on slightly higher ground than the preceding level, in keeping with the Japanese practice of levelling a mountain top to give good defensive space. The complete defensive area covered about 2,000m², almost one-sixteenth the size of the Yoshizaki Gobō.

The reconstruction of small sections of various military structures allows us to envisage the castle as a whole, although unfortunately no reconstruction has been carried out for the religious buildings. The appearance of these may however be inferred from the archaeological findings (mainly post holes)

The gateway and *koguchi* (barbican) that defend the perimeter of the *hon maru* at Torigoe.

and by comparison with other similar buildings elsewhere. When the dig commenced numerous post holes were discovered. These would have held the large single-stone foundations on which each upright wooden pillar of the temple buildings was individually supported. The *hon maru* was a near perfect rectangle that narrowed slightly towards the rear because of the presence at the front of the enclosure of a watchtower. It measured approximately 50m by 21m. A layer of black ash was found from the time of the castle's final fall and subsequent destruction.

The archaeologists concluded that at the time of the sieges of 1581–82 there were three buildings within the *hon maru* courtyard. The largest building, probably a *goeidō*, covered an area seven postholes by six, thus giving the building an approximate floor size of 15m by 10m deep. The postholes make a perfect rectangle, indicating that the *goeidō* was a simple building without any projecting porch. It would therefore seem reasonable to assume that the *goeidō* was very similar in appearance to the contemporary Shorenji in Takayama.

The other two buildings within the *hon maru* were probably the living quarters for the garrison, or had other military purposes. One is directly in front of the entrance, suggesting a role as a guardhouse when the location of the *goeidō* was planned. Also within the *hon maru* is the castle well, now surrounded by a low wooden fence. Preparations for a siege may be seen in the large earthenware storage jars sunk into the ground of the *hon maru*. Two of the jars are on show in the Ikkō-ikki Museum.

The *hon maru* was enclosed by an inner wooden palisade, reconstructed on site as an open fence of sharpened stakes. There is also an earthen wall. The key to the defences of the *hon maru* was the corner tower and the gateway. The gatehouse is offset from the centre of the wall and is a simple two-storey affair of square plan using four large-diameter timbers as the vertical supports. The solid wooden gates swing back on hinges underneath the guard tower that is open at the rear, but which has narrow window slits at the front. There is a low balustrade running round it, and the whole has a sloping wooden

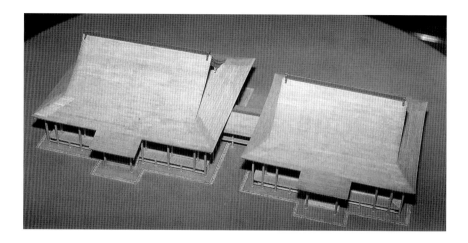

A model of the *goeidō* and the *amidadō* of Ishiyama Honganji in the Osaka Castle Museum.

roof. A wooden palisade stretches out on either side of the gate to join the earthwork in a staggered fashion. The outline of the base of the corner tower is indicated on the ground, and would probably have been the simple three- or four-storey version found in many contemporary castles, enclosed at the top in a fashion similar to the gateway.

The ground drops away sharply from the *hon maru*, where there is an extra line of defence in the form of a quite sophisticated dressed-stone *koguchi* (barbican). At Futoge Castle across the valley there is a square *koguchi*. Seen from above, the Torigoe *koguchi* has the appearance of a small conventional castle wall with sloping outer surfaces. The *koguchi* has a gateway, again offset, requiring attackers to turn to the right before entering the *hon maru*. This gate is of a different design from the *hon maru* gate. It is one storey high and has no guardroom above it, but the gates swing open under the shelter of two small roofs.

Beyond the *koguchi* we are in the *ni no maru*, the defensive perimeter of which consists of a planking fence with firing places above a ditch that continues down to the natural slope of the mountain. It also extends around the edge of the *ni no maru* to face back on itself against the *hon maru* area. Thus cover could be provided against any attackers ascending the slope between the *hon maru* and the *ni no maru*.

The reconstructed *ni no maru* fence is pierced by two very simple gateways consisting of two uprights but no gate. However, at the point where the *ni no maru* is left to begin the long journey down a steep mountain top, we find what are effectively the outer defences of the 'citadel'. A low earth mound around the site provided cover, while the path is individually guarded by a very solid gate. It is very similar to the *hon maru* gate but is stronger, with an enclosed gatehouse

The interior of the Amida Hall of Nishi Honganji in Kyoto, which is of colossal size to house large congregations.

and a small postern gate to its side. There is no balustrade around the outside, but once again the solid fence is integrated with the earth mound.

ISHIYAMA HONGANJI – THE FORTIFIED CATHEDRAL

Ishiyama Honganji was the headquarters of the Ikkō-ikki for most of the time the organization was involved in war. It was the largest establishment within Jōdo Shinshū, lasted a full century, and presented an amalgam of defensive features that enabled it to withstand Oda Nobunaga for an entire decade.

Not a single trace of Ishiyama Honganji's walls or buildings remains today. The one general fact known about it is that it occupied the site now filled by Osaka Castle. The precincts of Osaka Castle today are a welcome expanse of grass and water within the modern city with its gleaming skyscrapers, but because of this it is very difficult to appreciate that Rennyō's hermitage for his retirement was built upon a 'long slope'. Yet this is what lies under 21st-century Osaka: a long slope leading up to the Uemachi plateau.

By the time Rennyō moved to Osaka, the place already had a long history of settlement. Known first as Naniwa, it had been the site of one of Japan's transient capital cities before Nara was made the permanent capital in AD 710. Naniwa was built along the Uemachi plateau and offered a convenient port in the inner recesses of a bay fed by a major river, the Yodogawa. Recent archaeological discoveries have established that Rennyō founded Ishiyama Honganji on the site of the old imperial palace of Naniwa. The overall area was probably about 4km from the beginning of the slope at the south to the edge of the plateau where it overlooked the estuary to the north. The natural edge to the plateau provided good defence on the northern side, and would have been progressively strengthened as it levelled out. It also had its own defended

A view from the courtyard of Shorenji in Takayama, showing the *hondō* that dates from 1504.

harbour where the north-western quarter of the plateau sloped down to the estuary. But the Uemachi plateau was only part of Ishiyama Honganji's outer defence system, because this high ground, the only elevation for miles around, lay at the heart of a landscape similar to that of Nagashima, although it was much more developed. There were plenty of reed-covered islands, creeks, rivers, forests and rice fields to confuse any enemy who chose unwisely to leave the well-trodden road north to Kyoto or east to Nara, or to abandon the well-navigated Yodogawa and the busy navigation at the entrance of the Inland Sea.

Except perhaps for the steeper northern side, the original 15th-century Ishiyama Honganji would have been defended by an additional earthen embankment behind an excavated ditch. A wooden palisade of some sort would have topped the embankment, and the defences on the flat southern side would have been made the strongest. The Jōdo Shinshū temple would have been located at the centre of the plateau with earthwork walls and gates of its own. No extra water defences were provided beyond those already supplied by nature. The *jinaimachi* grew within the outer walls.

The drum tower of the Takayama Shorenji.

Several attempts have been made in recent years to reconstruct the appearance of Ishiyama Honganji's innermost citadel. As a great deal of speculation is involved there is some variation in the conclusions drawn, but on three points there is broad agreement:

1. Ishiyama Honganji began as a simple stockade fortress but evolved in size and design over the century of its existence in a way that reflected the development of Japanese castles in general.

2. By the time it was attacked by Oda Nobunaga's army, the Jōdo Shinshū temple at Ishiyama Honganji's heart lay within concentric baileys as strong as any contemporary castle. It had sloping stone walls, plastered parapet walls, gatehouses and corner towers that would have presented the exact appearance from the outside of a strong *daimyō*'s castle.

3. The main buildings of the Jōdo Shinsh temple consisted of a *goeidō* and an *amidadō* that were linked by a covered corridor.

The most important source for information on the appearance of the final Ishiyama Honganji in the 1570s is a contemporary map showing the disposition of the rival forces at the time of the final siege. In 1987 this map was used to build a model of the fortress area that is now on show in Namba Betsuin, a Jōdo Shinshū temple in Osaka. This model has provided the basis for the accompanying plate that shows Ishiyama Honganji at the time of Oda Nobunaga (see p.116). The builder of the model in the Namba Betsuin subdivided the central island on the map into a number of smaller islands that were created using moats. This is a perfectly reasonable conclusion to draw in view of the ease with which this could be done, and the pattern of moats used later when Hideyoshi built Osaka Castle on the site. The original 15th century layout of Ishiyama Honganji, whereby it simply filled the space available on the Uemachi plateau with minor additions, had by this time disappeared, and a fortress that heralded the future Osaka Castle had emerged in its place. Now that moats and walls had been constructed, the sloping plateau was much less discernible.

The structures of Ishiyama Honganji look increasingly formidable the nearer one moves to its religious centre. The outer moats that divide the inner fortress complex from the rest of the *jinaimachi* and the rice fields beyond have a natural curve, and the stone walls on either side of them are comparatively modest. The bridges are simple, and the palisades are of open-work construction with similar-looking gateways. The watchtowers are of single timbers with a flat platform at the top, and would be used for fire-watching in the *jinaimachi* as well as in case of attack. But when one crosses from the network of outer islands formed by these moats and natural streams, the picture changes. The well-defined inner moat, which encloses only the main temple area, frames a view that matches any samurai castle in both strength and appearance. The stone walls are high and intersect at precise angles. Along their top runs a plastered white wall protected from the weather by tiles. It is pierced by loopholes, and trees are planted along its length to shield the castle from prying eyes. Two-storey towers that look like miniature keeps stand at its four corners. There is an additional single-storey tower guarding the main east gate. The bridges across the inner moat are sturdy and supported on piers, each one terminating in a steep flight of steps that leads up to a fortified gatehouse with massive reinforced wooden doors. The progress of an attacker approaching these gates would be covered every inch of the way.

On entering the gatehouse, a visitor would find himself in the large temple courtyard that was covered in gravel with stone pathways linking the buildings. There is a bell tower and a drum tower, together with numerous other temple buildings that lie behind an additional low inner wall. If our visitor enters by the eastern gateway he has the finest view, which is of the *goeidō* hall linked to the *amidadō* by a covered corridor. Each is an imposing structure with large overhanging eaves and a covered staircase in front of the main doors of each. (The *goeidō* of Ishiyama Honganji is the subject of the scale model in the new Osaka City Museum of History across the road from Osaka Castle.) The gables are carved ornately with designs of peonies and a *komainu* (mythological Chinese dog), and the scale of the *raido* is very noticeable.

An indication of the large number of dwellings within the *jinaimachi* of Ishiyama Honganji is provided by documents relating to the rebuilding of the area after a fire in 1562. The conflagration, it was noted, had consumed 2,000

The Rurido (Lapis Lazuli Hall) on Hieizan, the only building to have survived Nobunaga's attack in 1571.

homes, while another fire destroyed 900 residences and some temple buildings in 1564. For its reconstruction we have the evidence of woodblock prints made many years later, and numerous comparisons from other medieval towns. One print shows the edge of the *jinaimachi* where it meets the moat leading up to the temple buildings. The street here is wide, but the quarter that begins at its entrance gate has narrow streets and tightly packed buildings. There are shops with bright divided curtains hanging in front, as well as gardens and trees.

This is the image presented by another exhibit in the Osaka Museum of History. It is a model of the streets of Osaka as they would have appeared under Toyotomi Hideyoshi, and the *jinaimachi* 20 years earlier cannot have looked very different. We see narrow streets in quarters divided from one another by gates and fences within an overall local perimeter of ditches and earthworks. Between the road and the fence is a drainage ditch. The buildings are simple one-storey houses, shops and craftsmen's establishments with shingled roofs. A framework of bamboo across the surface of the sloping roofs is held down by heavy stones to stop the panels blowing away. There are gardens and wells to the rear of the buildings.

THE *JINAIMACHI* OF TONDABAYASHI

Less than an hour's train journey from the site of Ishiyama Honganji brings us to a place that was once known simply by the name of *jinaimachi* and which still evokes the spirit of the temple town. It is known today as Tondabayashi and was

A model of the streets of Osaka as they would have appeared under Toyotomi Hideyoshi.

one of the temple towns that negotiated terms for its inhabitants that were similar to those of Ishiyama Honganji. Although none of the buildings in it date from before the Edo Period, it is worth studying for the light it shines on the idea of the *jinaimachi*. It was founded around the site of Koshoji, a Jōdo Shinshū establishment dating from about 1570. The foundation was originally part of the Yamashina Midō complex, destroyed in 1532. Determined to build the new temple, the priest Shoshu acquired a patch of uncultivated grassland on top of the Ishikawa River terrace. He requested eight *shoya* (village headmen), two each from four neighbouring villages, to co-operate with him in the building of the temple, the cultivation of the fields and the construction of a town.

Apart from Koshoji no other local building has a direct connection with the Ikkō-ikki, but Tondabayashi is also interesting because of its defensive location. An illustration from *Kawachi Meisho Zukai* (*Collection of Beautiful Places in Kawachi Province*) shows Koshoji dominating the town. Fences and foliage, particularly bamboo groves, protect it to the river's edge, where a series of very rudimentary bridges link it to the area across the river. For security purposes, visibility at intersections of roads was reduced by specially designing them so that they did not cross at right angles.

NEGORODERA – THE FORTRESS OF THE LAST OF THE *SŌHEI*

Negorodera provides a unique example of a warrior monk temple of the Shingon sect. Unlike the other temples mentioned in this book, its name is pronounced using the Japanese reading of the characters rather than the Chinese style, so the suffix for 'temple' is read as '-*dera*' rather than '-*ji*'. It is possible to reconstruct its appearance in about 1585 with a high likelihood of accuracy for two reasons. First, the site still exists in the same location and is still a Shingon temple. Second, several of the original buildings have survived. Only three of the buildings remain on the site itself, but the removal by Hideyoshi of the others to the Shingon temple of Daigoji near Kyoto has ensured their survival. There are also a considerable number of pictorial illustrations of Negorodera monks. This is largely because they were finally quelled by Toyotomi Hideyoshi, whose illustrated biographies furnish us with some fascinating details of the physical appearance of the last of the *sōhei*.

Negorodera owes its fame to the Buddhist priest Kakuban (1095–1143), known to posterity as Kogyo Daishi. He was regarded by his followers as a reformer and restorer of Shingon, much in the same way as Rennyō was viewed within Jōdo Shinshū. Kogyo Daishi was given the estate containing Negorodera by former Emperor Go-Toba in 1132, and grew to exercise great influence within Shingon. His views met with opposition from rivals on Koyasan, so that he was eventually driven out and retired to Negorodera. Kogyo Daishi's faction became known as the Shingi (which translates as 'new meaning') branch of the Shingon sect, but there was never the tragic split that other sects were to experience. Instead the monks of Negorodera channelled their energies against samurai. Just like the Ikkō-ikki, they were early converts to firearm technology, largely through the influence of the priest Suginobo Myosan. He was the brother of a certain Tsuda Katsunaga, who happened to visit the territories of the Shimazu *daimyō* in 1543, the same year that the Portuguese first arrived in Japan. Katsunaga was given an arquebus as a gift. Suginobo took it back to Negorodera, where a local smith copied it and began producing guns for the Negorodera *sōhei*.

The Negorodera complex was built in a naturally strong position on the southern slopes of the Katsuragi Mountains, the dense forested peaks of which protected it from the north. The site also made clever use of a number of minor rivers that merged into the Negorogawa having already created three moats for the fortified temple. To the west of the Rengedanigawa were two small lakes or large ponds, the Ote ike and the Shin ike, while a much larger lake lay further to the west again. The modern road follows the southern boundary of the temple north of the lower rivers. Here, where the ground still sloped away, were Negorodera's southern defences. A steep decline was left forested, except where the area was cleared immediately in front of gates and strongpoints to provide a clear field of fire. The artificial defence here was an earthen embankment topped by a palisade. Along its length were simple towers and one gateway, from which a path dropped away steeply. An open wooden watchtower was established at the western end. Behind the embankment were more trees; then came the natural moat of the Negorogawa and Bodaigawa. The actual temple compound lay just inside this line and was protected by a ditch and long plaster walls of modest height. On the steepest slopes were artificial gullies down which rocks could be rolled.

THE FORTIFIED TEMPLE AND ITS *JINAIMACHI*: ISHIYAMA HONGANJI 1580

The great fortified cathedral of Ishiyama Honganji with its attached *jinaimachi* (temple town) are shown here in their final developed form prior to their destruction by Oda Nobunaga in 1580. There is the usual pair of temple halls typical of Jōdo Shinshū, while the defences of the site match those of a contemporary castle, particularly through the inclusion of massive stone bases. This reconstruction is based on a scale model of Ishiyama Honganji in Namba Betsuin, Osaka. (Peter Dennis © Osprey Publishing Ltd)

A comparison between the layout of Negorodera and Ishiyama Honganji illustrates the difference between a Shingon establishment and a Jōdo Shinshū temple on one hand, and the constraints on building forced by the two very different locations of a wooded mountain and a swampy estuary on the other. The buildings of Negorodera extended over a vast area, and consist of a number of different compounds. The sheer extent of Negorodera was one reason why Hideyoshi's capture of it in 1585, which made much use of fire, did not destroy the whole compound but allowed Hideyoshi to salvage some choice pieces of architecture as loot. The mountain streams that acted as moats would also have been useful firebreaks.

The temple halls also have particular functions, as noted earlier, for the esoteric rituals of the Shingon sect, and much of the original layout survives to this day as separate compounds and courtyards. In the south-western corner, near to the Ote pond, was the Aizen-In, the residence of the monk Suginobo Myosan, who was largely responsible for the development of firearms. Its single-storey gatehouse still exists. Nearby is a very fine temple gateway, the Nishi Daimon (Western Great Gate) that was the main entrance to Negorodera from the west. The present structure is a replacement for the original, which is believed to have become the main gate at Daigoji.

In the centre of the complex lie a number of buildings dating from the Edo Period that replace others lost in the fire. One, the Honbo, the residence of the chief priest, includes beautiful Edo Period gardens. Similar gardens may well have been a feature of the original Negorodera. On the eastern extremity of the site the deity Fudo is the focus of attention, worshipped inside an octagonal Fudodo.

Negoroji's loveliest architectural treasure: the Daito or Great Pagoda. It was built in 1496 and is of a form known as the *tahoto* or 'pagoda of many treasures'.

Further up the mountain on the eastern side lies Negorodera's most important courtyard. It reaches to the mountain itself, and was spared the fire of 1585. Here is found Negorodera's loveliest architectural treasure: the Daito or Great Pagoda. It was built in 1496 and is of a form known as the *tahoto* ('pagoda of many treasures'). The style is associated particularly with the Tendai and Shingon sects, and is a variation on the Indian stupa, as transformed by Chinese culture. In China the cylindrical body of the stupa with its domed top was modified by giving it a roof. In Japan the dome was of plaster over a wooden framework, so to protect it from the weather the *tahoto* acquired an extra roof, thus providing its final appearance. Bullet holes from 1585 are the only embellishment to Negorodera's perfect specimen.

Next to the pagoda lies another building to have escaped Hideyoshi's fire: the Daishido, a small hall that encloses an image of Kobo Daishi, the founder of the Shingon sect. To its rear is Negoroji's *kondō*, built in 1801 to replace the original building that was moved to Daigoji after Hideyoshi's attack. The first *kondō*, now perfectly preserved, was constructed during the Kamakura Period (1185–1392). The central image inside is of Yakushi Nyorai, the Buddha of healing.

The Living Sites

The Social Structure Within a Fortified Temple

The *sōhei* temples were inhabited by warrior monks under the leadership of a *zasu* (chief priest). The 'warrior' element in the expression is fairly self-explanatory, but 'monk' is more difficult to pin down, because although the *sōhei* lived in monastic communities, not all of them were monks. Many had indeed taken the vows requisite upon becoming a member of the Buddhist clergy, of which the outward sign was a shaved head, but their armies also included many who had not been ordained. Their inhabitants included many who were not really monks at all, men who were more familiar with swords than with prayers, as well as monks who were poorly educated and uncommitted to their faith.

The social organization of the inhabitants of a fortified temple of the Ikkō-ikki involved a wide range of social classes, resulting from the sect's complex origins in which samurai played an important role. In the early Sengoku Jidai there was only a small distinction in practical terms between a low-ranking samurai of modest financial means and a wealthy farmer who might also be a village headman. The latter could not levy taxes, but collected rent from the peasantry and resisted 'real' samurai who attempted to collect taxes from him. The name *jizamurai* is often used for them. To some extent their duties and aspirations were very similar to those of the up-and-coming *daimyō*: they shared a common interest in defending their territory and collecting revenue from it in an efficient manner.

The difference between them occurred in the growth of internal structures. Whereas a *daimyō* aspired towards a vertical vassal structure in a hierarchy of which the *daimyō* was the apex, *jizamurai* had an alternative: the formation of an *ikki*, whereby potential allies joined forces in a mutual protection association. The Ikkō-ikki was the largest example of such a creation in Japanese history, but there were many others. For example, in 1485 samurai and 'peasants of all the province of Yamashiro' gathered for a meeting

三高天明神
八幡大神
月山大権現

A samurai serves *sake* to his lord before they leave for war. This is a display in the Nejo castle museum in Hachinohe, where a 14th-century castle has been partially reconstructed.

to agree to drive out the troops of the two *shugo* (provincial governors of the *shōgun* who had been battling over the area. The resulting Yamashiro *ikki* was under the leadership of local samurai, but the organizations of the villages sustained it.

Needless to say, *ikki* formation cut right across the vertical vassal structures that ambitious *daimyō* were trying everywhere to create. In some cases this caused considerable conflicts of interest, because some who were attracted to a *daimyō*'s service might have become accustomed to the horizontal structure of an *ikki* association. Others retained membership of their *ikki* even after they became vassals of a *daimyō*. Weaning them away from such ties was very difficult if the *ikki* involved staunch religious beliefs, such as those that were demanded by Jōdo Shinshū. A prime example was the situation that faced the young Tokugawa Ieyasu in the early 1560s. The Ikkō-ikki of Mikawa Province were among his greatest rivals, but several of his retainers embraced Jōdo Shinshū, so when issues of armed conflict arose such men were placed in a quandary. For example, in the *Mikawa Go Fudoki* account of the battle of Azukizaka in 1564 we read that:

> Tsuchiya Chokichi was of the *monto* faction, but when he saw his lord hard pressed he shouted to his companions, 'Our lord is in a critical position with his small band. I will not lift a spear against him, though I go to the most unpleasant sorts of hells!' and he turned against his own party and fought fiercely until he fell dead.

A detail from the screen in Osaka Castle depicting the battle of Shizugatake in 1583 and showing a typical stone castle base topped by plaster walls. There are two sorts of loophole – square ones for bows, round ones for arquebuses, from which the barrels of the guns protrude. Portable wooden shields of a type used for centuries in Japan provide extra defence.

Through their membership of *ikki*, samurai created alliances beyond their immediate kinship circles under the formal pledge of mutual loyalty. The structure of an *ikki* was therefore broadly democratic, and its rules stated explicitly that any conflict among its members should be resolved at a meeting where the majority decision would apply. Nowhere was this democratic structure more dramatically illustrated than in the ritual that marked the initial formation of an *ikki* or the resolution of a major problem such as a decision to go to war. The visible proof that an agreement had been reached would take the form of a document. Inscribed upon it was a set of written rules to which the members' signatures were added. The signatures were often written in a circle to show the equal status of each member and to avoid quarrels over precedence. Next, a ritual called *ichimi shinsui* ('one taste of the gods' water') was celebrated, when the document was ceremoniously burned. Its ashes were mixed with water and the resulting concoction was drunk by the members. The ritual was considered to symbolize the members' like-mindedness that was the outward sign of their solidarity.

Similarly democratic rules applied initially with the Jōdo Shinshū's Ikkō–ikki, where oaths were signed on a paper that bore an image of Amida Buddha. As it developed, however, the structure of their organization became more hierarchical, with the ruling Honganji on top of the pyramid, intermediate temples in the middle and the local *ko* at the bottom.

Contributions, which evolved into annual pledges, came from all levels in the hierarchy. Rennyō also placed his children at major temples and established the *ikkeshū* (family council). It consisted of Rennyō himself, his sons and his grandsons. The *ikkeshū* became the de facto ruling body of Jōdo Shinshū following Rennyō's retirement in 1489, and continued to serve in that capacity for at least two generations. During the decades following Rennyō's death the *ikkeshū* built up considerable power among the *monto*. To discipline his more unruly followers Rennyō insisted that the *monto* obey the established secular authorities wherever their temples were located. However, the other principle of defence of the faith was also important and, as we have seen, the two often came into conflict. Two formidable sanctions could be applied to miscreants. Excommunication was much feared within a religious-based community, and even execution could be threatened during times of war.

RELIGIOUS LIFE IN THE FORTIFIED TEMPLES

Jōdo Shinshū shifted the emphasis of Japanese Buddhism from a monastic-centred organization to the ordinary lives of ordinary people, whose fortified temples housed communities for whom the practice of their religion was a fundamental part of life. The basis of the beliefs of Jōdo Shinshū was a purposeful devotion to the worship of Amida, the Supreme Buddha of the Jōdo (Pure Land) in the west, who will welcome all his followers into the paradise of the Pure Land on their death. This teaching contrasted sharply with the insistence on attainment of enlightenment through study, work or asceticism stressed by the older sects. To a Tendai monk, Jōdo Shinshū belief was an illusory short cut to salvation, but Jōdo Shinshū welcomed all into its fold and did not insist upon meditation or any intellectual superiority. It also stressed the dire consequences of non-belief as set against the promise of salvation to believers, a dichotomy that led to the Jesuit missionaries dubbing Jōdo Shinshū 'the Devil's Christianity'.

Central to the daily life of the temple fortresses was the recital of the *nembutsu*. This brief prayer, Namu Amida Butsu (Hail to Amida Buddha), which could be repeated up to 60,000 times a day by devotees, became the motto of the Ikkō-ikki armies, who were Japan's 'holy warriors' par excellence. Its *monto* welcomed fighting because their faith promised that paradise was the immediate reward for death in battle, and nothing daunted them. The devotion associated with the practice only became really apparent when the Ikkō-ikki were about to go into battle and the sound of the mass *nembutsu* chilled the blood of their enemies, or when a special service was performed and the *goeidō* was packed with worshippers. Lamps twinkled on the pure-gold surfaces of the altar furnishings. The air was heavy with incense and seemed to throb with the responses from hundreds of voices. Just as Shinran intended, to a believer the scene stood as a promise of the western paradise guaranteed by Amida Buddha.

TRAINING FOR WAR

Apart from prayer and daily work, preparation for war in the form of military training was the other main activity in the fortified temple, as confirmed by the only description of *sōhei* by a Western writer. It comes from the European Jesuit missionary Father Caspar Vilela, who has left us a fascinating pen-picture of Negorodera's warrior monk army. He surmised that most of the *sōhei* he saw had taken no monastic vows, because they wore their hair long and were devoted to the practice of arms, their monastic rule placing less emphasis on

The gathering of the *monto* to defend Ishiyama Honganji, from *Ehon Shinchokoki*, an illustrated version of the life of Oda Nobunaga. Armour boxes and flags are seen. Note the shaven heads of some of the defenders.

prayer than on military preparation. Each member was required to make five or seven arrows per day, and to practise competitively with bow and arquebus once a week. Their helmets, armour and spears were of astonishing strength, and, to quote Vilela, 'their sharp swords could slice through a man in armour as easily as a butcher carves a tender steak!' Their practice combat with each other was fierce, and the death of one of their number in training was accepted without emotion. Fearless on the battlefield, they enjoyed life off it with none of the restrictions normally associated with the ascetic life.

DAILY LIFE IN TIMES OF WAR

When the fortified temple was threatened by an attack, the daily life of its community was placed on a war footing. Just as every member of Jōdo Shinshū shared fully in its peacetime activities, so did they share in the responsibilities when conflict loomed. Every man, woman and child became involved. All hands were needed, and certainly by the 1580s the experience of a century of war had taught them that if they lost to a samurai army then a massacre of every member of the community would follow.

The first requirement was to concentrate resources on defending that which was most defensible. This meant that outlying farms and fields might have to be abandoned, with the defensive line probably being drawn at the edge of the *jinaimachi*. This was likely to be defended already by some form of perimeter fence or wall, or by natural features such as a river, slope, forest or groves of impenetrable bamboo. There could then be a progressive withdrawal further inside the complex, until a last-ditch stand had to be made within the *hon maru*.

Regardless of the strength of any fortified place in Japan, whether it was a castle or a temple, additions could always be made to its defences when there was an immediate danger of attack. The archaeological research at Torigoe discussed above found large earthenware storage jars buried in the ground. There was also evidence that when the castle changed hands not only repairs but quite considerable alterations were made to the defences in preparation for a counter-attack. The altered features were no doubt based on the experience of the assault. Those sectors that its captors had found easiest to penetrate now had to be made difficult.

OPERATIONAL HISTORY

SŌHEI TEMPLES IN THE GEMPEI WARS (1180–85)

Sōhei were only involved in the first two years of the Gempei Wars. The *Heike Monogatari* gives a brief account of how the *sōhei* of Miidera tried to hold off the Taira samurai in 1180:

> At the monastery about a thousand soldier-monks, arming themselves, made a shield barrier, threw up a barricade of felled trees and awaited them. At the Hour of the Hare [6am] they began to draw their bows, and the battle continued the whole day, until when evening came on three hundred of the monks and their men had fallen. Then the fight went on in the darkness and the imperial forces forced their way into the monastery buildings and set them on fire.

The following year the Taira attacked Nara. The monks put up temporary defences and fought so well that Taira Shigehira was forced to risk using the dangerous weapon of fire. His resulting victory was achieved at the price of the almost total destruction of Kōfukuji and Tōdaiji, including the latter's Great Buddha, so that, in the words of *Heike Monogatari*, 'its full moon features fell to the pavement below, while its body melted into a shapeless mass'.

THE SIEGE OF ISHIYAMA HONGANJI (1570–80)

The events of Nobunaga's longest campaign veered between two extremes: grand strategy designed to isolate the Ishiyama Honganji from any outside help, and a few sporadic but intense periods of bitter hand-to-hand fighting across the fortified temple's walls. The main method of defence for Ishiyama Honganji was the mass use of firearms. In 1570, five years before Oda Nobunaga was to win his famous victory at Nagashino using volleys of arquebus fire, his army, preparing to assault Ishiyama Honganji, were subjected to a surprise night attack involving thousands of gunners. In 1576 Nobunaga

led another attack on Ishiyama Honganji that got as far as one of the inner gates. But again mass arquebus fire drove his men back, and Nobunaga was himself wounded in the leg. From that time on, strategic considerations dominated Nobunaga's thinking, and over the next four years Ishiyama Honganji was gradually starved of all resources. A decisive moment came with the defeat of the Mōri fleet at the sea battle of Kizugawaguchi in 1578. The Mōri had provided the main supply line to Ishiyama Honganji, and with this support cut off, and Nobunaga's programme of slowly destroying all of the Honganj's outlying forts, the great fortress cathedral stood alone. A conference was held between the Abbot Kosa and his colleagues, and in April 1580 an imperial messenger was sent with a letter from no less a person than the Emperor of Japan, suggesting an honourable surrender. Oda Nobunaga had of course prompted the letter, but it did the trick, and the fortress surrendered a few weeks later. The actual surrender terms were bloodless, and 11 years of bitter fighting eventually came to an end in August 1580.

NAGASHIMA (1571–74)

The position of Nagashima amid sea and swamp determined the ways in which it was defended against Oda Nobunaga's army, and his first attack was a disaster. His mounted samurai began to ford towards the first *waju* (dyked area), only to find that the river bottom was a deep sea of mud. The horses' legs quickly mired, and as the animals struggled many threw off their heavily armoured riders, who were met by a hail of arrows and bullets, causing severe

Although the captions reads 'The Ishiyama War', this woodblock print actually shows the attack on Negoroji in 1585 by Toyotomi Hideyoshi, who appears on the left. In the background is the Ote-ike, one of the ponds that provided defence for Negoroji on its western side.

casualties. The shoreline was covered by tall, dense reeds, and as the desperate and demoralized samurai crawled into the reed beds they discovered them to be swarming with more Ikkō-ikki arquebusiers and archers. When night fell, the defenders realized that the sole survivors of the Oda army were confined within the next *waju*, so the dyke was cut, rapidly flooding the low-lying land and catching the remaining samurai in an inrush of muddy water.

In 1573 Nobunaga, who had benefited from his experience at Ishiyama Honganji in 1570, led an attack on Nagashima spearheaded by thousands of firearms. Unfortunately, a sudden rainstorm rendered most of the weapons inoperable. The Ikkō-ikki kept their powder dry, and when they counter-attacked one bullet almost shot Nobunaga off his horse. Nagashima finally fell in 1574 when Nobunaga managed to isolate the sea approaches to it using his fleet. His capture of all the Ikkō-ikki outposts on the mainland further cut off Nagashima from help. Waiting until the weather was dry and a suitable wind was blowing, Nobunaga's men simply piled up brushwood against the outer buildings of the Nagashima complex and set fire to the entire place.

TORIGOE AND FUTOGE (1581–82)

The first attack upon the Ikkō-ikki fortified temples of Torigoe and Futoge was made by Shibata Katsuie in the third lunar month of 1581. He captured both and set up a garrison of 300 men, but before the month was out the

The Kuromon (Black Gate) of the Kan'eiji showing the numerous bullet holes from the battle of Ueno. The gate and fence are now preserved as a memorial to the battle in the Entsuji in Minowa in Tokyo.

Kaga Ikkō-ikki had recaptured them and slaughtered the unfortunate troops. The attack was part of a general uprising by the *monto* based at these places, as well as the fortresses of Matsuyama and Hinoya.

In the 11th month of 1581, Shibata Katsuie and Sakuma Morimasa returned to Kaga and crushed the resistance once again, killing all the *monto* involved. We read that on the 17th day of that month the heads of the ringleaders were sent to Nobunaga's castle of Azuchi and placed on public display. The chronicle names the Ikkō-ikki leaders as the father and son Suzuki Dewa no kami and Suzuki Ukyo no shin. Yet in spite of this setback Ikkō-ikki resistance continued, and elements of the organization recaptured Torigoe and Futoge once again during the second lunar month of 1582. The defences were rapidly strengthened to face an anticipated third attack by Oda Nobunaga's forces, which materialized on the first day of the third month. The temple castles were taken and destroyed, and this time no chance of resurgence was to be allowed. First, 300 men of the Ikkō-ikki were crucified on the river bed, and after this gruesome local display Sakuma Morimasa carried out further suppression with great severity. Over the next three years the inhabitants of the local villages of Yoshinodai and Oso were annihilated.

Ganshoji, the rebuilt temple at the heart of the Nagashima complex. A drum tower and a bell tower stand on either side of the gateway through a low but solid wall that make it look well defended. There is a fine *goeidō* inside the courtyard, and the whole ensemble is redolent of the idea of a fortified temple.

NEGORODERA AND OTA (1585)

The joint operation against Negorodera and Ota Castle was the last campaign ever conducted against warrior monks. On the tenth day of the third month of 1585, an army of 6,000 men under the command of Toyotomi Hidetsugu, Hideyoshi's nephew, and Hashiba Hidenaga, Hideyoshi's half-brother, entered

THE FORTIFIED TEMPLE AS *YAMASHIRO*: TORIGOE 1582

This plate shows the *hon maru* (inner bailey) and *ni no maru* (second bailey) of Torigoe as they would have appeared prior to Oda Nobunaga's final assault in 1582. It is a typical small isolated fortified temple that has all the characteristics of a *daimyō's yamashiro* (mountain castle). The fortifications are reconstructed based on the archaeological evidence and the reconstructed buildings on site, some of which make use of the limited stone that was available. The religious buildings within the *hon maru* are based on existing contemporary structures elsewhere, particularly Shorenji at Takayama, built in 1504. (Peter Dennis © Osprey Publishing Ltd)

Kii Province. They crushed four minor outposts, and on the 23rd day of the same month approached Negorodera from two separate directions. At that time the military strength of Negorodera was believed to be between 30,000 and 50,000 men, and their skills with firearms were still considerable, but many had already crossed the river and sought shelter in the more formidable walls of Ota Castle. Hideyoshi's army therefore put into operation the crudest, but often most effective, tactic in samurai warfare for use when the enemy are occupying a large complex of wooden buildings. Beginning with the priests' residences, the investing army systematically set fire to the Negorodera

THE BURNING OF NAGASHIMA: 1574

In this plate we see the culmination of Oda Nobunaga's long campaign against the Ikkō-ikki of Nagashima, who have been driven back into the heart of their defences in the river estuary of Ise Bay. Nagashima resembles Torigoe in all but its dramatically different location. Wooden piles have been driven into the muddy shore to build up a firm foundation against floods. But now the main defensive elements of swamps and reed beds have been breached, and flames from piled bundles of wood are starting to lick at the outer walls of Nagashima, which is shown as a predominantly wooden structure of palisades, fences and watchtowers. (Peter Dennis © Osprey Publishing Ltd)

complex, and cut down the *sōhei* as they escaped from the flames. Several acts of single combat occurred between Hideyoshi's samurai and the Negorodera defenders. Some sources tell of Hideyoshi targeting the temple's gunpowder stores with fire arrows, so that several explosions helped the process along. Mercifully, the fires were controlled so as to leave part of the temple intact.

Ota Castle was under the command of Ota Munemasa, whose garrison was now considerably increased at the expense of food supplies. In a re-run of his successful campaign against the castle of Takamatsu in 1582, Hideyoshi ordered the building of a dyke to divert the waters of the Kiigawa and flood the castle. A long palisade was begun at a distance of about 300m from the castle walls and packed with earth to make a dam. On the eastern side, which was the Kiigawa, the dyke was left open to allow the waters in. By the tenth day of the fourth lunar month, the waters of the Kiigawa were beginning to rise around the castle walls. Heavy rain helped the process along, isolating the garrison more completely from outside help.

Nevertheless, the defenders hung on, encouraged at one point by the partial collapse of a section of Hideyoshi's dyke, which caused the deaths of several besiegers as water poured out. Yet soon hunger began to take its toll, and on the 22nd day of the fourth month the garrison surrendered, although 50 men performed instead a defiant act of *hara-kiri*. The remaining soldiers, peasants, women and children who were found in the castle were disarmed of all swords and guns. Any samurai *monto* were executed out of hand, including 23 of the ringleaders, who were decapitated and had their severed heads displayed in Osaka. Their wives were crucified inside the castle grounds. Any farmers were sent back to their masters' fields, thus making the conclusion of the operation a forerunner of Hideyoshi's 'Sword Hunt' of 1588, whereby the non-samurai classes were disarmed and set to work in more fitting occupations.

The battle of Ueno in 1868 was fought round a temple that had received temporary defences. In this contemporary print we see the fierce fighting going on at the Kan'eiji, with the fence being knocked to one side.

THE BATTLE OF UENO (1868)

One of the most important battles at the time of the Meiji Restoration took place at a temple that, like the temples of Nara in 1181, had received temporary fortifications. This was the Kan'eiji in Ueno, where supporters of the ousted *shōgun* were attacked by the pro-imperialist army. The walls and fences of the Kan'eiji, reinforced by sandbags, became a defence line across which some savage fighting took place with swords and modern rifles. Almost the entire temple was burned to the ground during the battle, but the Kuromon, the 'Black Gate' that was one of the main entrances, was preserved, and now stands in the Entsuji temple in Minowa to the north-east of Ueno. It is riddled with bullet holes, a fitting memorial to the last battle in Japan to be conducted against a fortified temple.

Next page: The fighting here at Hara has been fierce and two headless female bodies lie against the palisade at the rear. Apart from these poignant details there is considerable information about the defences. The walls, seen here from the outside at the top, are again of solid planking anchored on to the bedrock of the hill, and have the addition of a firing platform in the form of planks laid across strong supports. One defender is kneeling on this rough walkway to loose an arrow over the wall. To his left lies a pile of rocks for dropping through the holes in the walls. A plank laid across a mound of earth gives access to a dropping hole at the left.

JAPANESE CASTLES 1540-1877

PART 3

INTRODUCTION

This reconstructed section of the walls of Shōryūji Castle shows the grassy bank, which in the later forms of castle was replaced by the massive stone bases. Here also is a simple corner tower with a stone-dropping port and very rudimentary stone reinforcements to the wall.

From about 1540 onwards, we see an important development taking place in Japanese castle design through the increasing use of stone as a building material. Stone had been used for centuries to provide secure foundations for temples and palaces, and its use in the design of the Sengoku *yamashiro* and *yashiki* was originally no more than this. But when castles that utilized mountains became anything more than just temporary structures, stone was found to be very useful for protecting the outer surfaces of the hillside that had been sculpted into the fortress. This resulted in the familiar form of the huge stone bases on which gateways, towers and keeps could safely be built.

The final development was the use of stone to create additional tower bases like artificial hills, either on top of the sculpted bases or adjacent to them.

Yet the Japanese castles as we see them today are not only the final products of the long evolutionary process described above, but also the evidence of a military revolution. In the latter half of the 16th century Japanese warfare was transformed. It changed from an activity characterized by the use of loosely organized troops wielding bows and arrows and defending largely wooden fortifications, to one that involved well-disciplined infantry units armed with guns, fighting from castles of stone. The similarities to the military revolution that was taking place in Europe at the same time are striking, but until the beginning of this period there had been no cultural contact between Japan and Europe.

Contact was made when a Portuguese ship was wrecked on the Japanese coast in 1543, and the two cultures soon began to realize how their widely separated worlds had been evolving in roughly similar ways. Both were experiencing warfare on a larger scale than ever before, which required the development of strong internal army organization and good discipline, and both were seeing a move towards a preference for fighting on foot. Guns were first used in battle in Japan in 1549. They were hand-held matchlock muskets or arquebuses, fired by dropping a smouldering match on to a touchhole. Larger-calibre guns existed, but siege cannon as understood by Western Europe did not really appear until the siege of Osaka in 1614/15. Instead the most common technique that developed in a siege situation was volley firing to clear the walls of a castle of its attackers.

The interior of a section of small wall at Sumpu (Shizuoka) Castle. We see the triangular gun ports and the rectangular arrow ports, the wooden supports inside the walls, over which planks could be laid to provide firing platforms, and the tiles which give weather protection.

Italian visitors to Oda Nobunaga's castle of Azuchi in 1579 compared it favourably with any contemporary European fortress, and remarked particularly on the richness of the decorations and the strength of the stone walls. As none of these early visitors were military men, rather merchants or priests, they cannot be expected to have commented upon Japanese castles from a position of technical knowledge of fortifications, but it is abundantly clear from the impression given to them by the walls of Azuchi, Osaka and Edo, all of which were enthusiastically described in contemporary Jesuit writings, that they were making comparisons with existing structures in Spain or Italy, where huge sloping stone walls had become a recognized and vital part of the townscape of a successful city. These walls were the defining features of the 'trace italienne', the fortification style characterized by the use of the arrow-shaped angle bastion, which was designed for artillery warfare. The walls of fortresses such as Osaka certainly had much in common with the European system, but what the visitors did not know was that these curiously similar structures had a completely different developmental history, were built in a completely different way, and were designed to withstand attacks of a completely different nature.

The last quarter of the 16th century was the age of the great *daimyō* whose territories covered entire Japanese provinces and eventually, with the triumph

Edo Castle, built to be the greatest castle in Japan by Tokugawa Ieyasu, is now the palace of the Emperor of Japan and lies at the heart of Tokyo. The immense area it covers has to be seen to be appreciated.

of Toyotomi Hideyoshi, the entire country. From the time of the building of Oda Nobunaga's Azuchi Castle in 1576, one of the characteristics of these 'super-*daimyō*' was a large and magnificent castle that acted as a palace, a symbol and as a military headquarters. Castles such as those at Odawara and Osaka also experienced siege warfare on an appropriately grand scale. When wars ceased under the Tokugawa, the castles became the centres of castle towns, until the fighting that attended the development of modern Japan in the late 19th century gave them a brief military role once again.

The fine detail of castle construction is provided by this exhibit at Odawara Castle. Note how the supporting beams for the protective roof have lengths of bamboo tied around them using rope. Plaster would be applied on top of this secure foundation.

Design and Development

THE INTRODUCTION OF STONE

The great weakness of the Sengoku *yamashiro* model described earlier was the inherent instability of the natural foundations created from a sculpted hillside, particularly where the forest cover had been removed. Three storeys was the absolute maximum height that could be risked for an enclosed tower with rooms in a *yamashiro*, and outlook towers tended to be mere skeletal structures. If stronger, and therefore heavier, structures such as keeps and gatehouses were to be added, then something more substantial than a grassy bank was needed as a castle base, and the solution to the problem was to provide the Japanese castle with its most enduring visual features. These were the great stone bases, a fundamental design element that can be identified in even the most ruined castle site.

To a large extent it is these stone bases that are the essence of 'Japanese castles' from the Sengoku Period onwards, because many never had elegant tower keeps, such as those at Himeji and Hikone, raised upon them. Simple wooden buildings and plastered walls were often enough to augment the stone bases. It is also with these stone bases, rather than any superstructure, that comparisons can be made with European bastions. However, as has already been stated, the evolution of the Japanese form was very different from that of Europe, especially with regard to construction techniques. A European bastion was built from scratch, either completely from stone or from earth (whether the earth was clad in stone or brick revetments or not), while a Japanese one tended to be carved as in the descriptions above and then clad in stone with other bases being created. The result in either case was the same – an immensely thick defensive wall.

It must not, however, be thought that the new style of stone castle immediately supplanted the earlier models. Apart from financial considerations, few *daimyō* relied on one castle alone, and instead maintained networks of 'satellite' castles as described above in the context of the Hōjō family. Some

The striking red bridge of Matsumoto sets off the beauty of the keep that lies behind it. Unlike most castles built on a hill, Matsumoto is a *hirajiro* – a castle on the plain, except that the immediate plain is beside the wide river that forms its moat. The complex we see today consists of the keep (1597) and an attached northern tower which balances it perfectly.

shijō would be miniature versions of the *honjō*, demonstrating a similar use of stone bases and wooden towers, but related to them would be another network of sub-satellite castles, which would probably be old-style Sengoku *yamashiro* with sculpted hillsides and plastered walls but little else in the way of elaboration. These little castles were not necessarily permanently garrisoned, but weapons would be stored there and part-time soldiers would take control of them on declaration of an emergency situation. The Hōjō's Gongenyama Castle, for example, had a strength of 252 men, so these castles were more than just lookout posts. As a result of the satellite system, therefore, even as late as the 1590s, it was possible to see examples from earlier stages of Japanese castle development still in use.

THE DEVELOPMENT OF THE TOWER

The introduction of stone as a building material not only combated the problem of soil erosion and weather damage, it also allowed castle designers to raise new structures that would previously have been thought impossible, leading to the Japanese castle as we know it today. Stone castle bases sloped dramatically outwards, as did European artillery bastions, but the geometrical reasoning behind them was very different. The horizontal geometry of a European bastion was primarily concerned with discovering the ideal angle for providing covering fire with no blind spots, and its vertical geometry was designed to keep to a minimum the amount of soil that would spill out after bombardment (thus affording a ramp to the enemy), and to provide a sufficient angle to make scaling ladders impossibly long. The Japanese considerations were more ones of strength, both to hold back the inner core (which in the case of a stone castle on a flat surface had to be artificially created) and to take the weight of a keep. There was also the constant threat of earthquakes, which occur frequently in Japan, and it was found that long and gently sloping stone walls absorbed earthquake shocks very well.

The foremost exponents of stone base construction were the masons of Anou in Omi Province. They had specialized for centuries in the building of stone bases for temple buildings and pagodas, and their clever use of trigonometry revolutionized Japanese castle design. Through the use of massive shaped stones the base could not only be sloped, but could also be given a curve. This ensured that the stresses could be directed very accurately to give the solid foundation that was sought. Towers were commonly located at the corners of walls. Utsunomiya Castle in Tochigi Prefecture, for example, had five towers and two gate-towers around its perimeter wall that sheltered the completely undefended residential and administrative buildings within. None of these uniformly sized towers could be described as a keep, thus making Utsunomiya look as if it was a European-style 'concentric castle'.

Hirosaki Castle in Aomori Prefecture, however, did have a keep, although this was little more than a multi-storeyed corner tower. Hirosaki's remoteness helped ensure the survival of its keep, although the domestic buildings beside it no longer exist. As in so many cases, the *daimyō* lived in this single-storey *yashiki* complex, leaving the keep and other towers as purely military structures. In terms of survival the opposite has happened at Nijo Castle in Kyoto, where the keep was demolished but the palatial *yashiki* has been preserved.

The Anou masons who made these developments possible appear to have come on to the scene in 1577, by which time several multi-storey towers had already been experimented with. The *daimyō* Matsunaga Hisahide is credited with the first tower keep at his castle of Tamon in 1567, but nothing of it has survived. Maruoka's keep was built in 1576 and survived almost intact until 1948 when it was levelled by an earthquake, but has since been reconstructed using the original materials. The oldest original keep is probably the beautiful Matsumoto, which can be reliably dated to 1597. Older keeps exist, but they have all been relocated to their present sites. Hikone's fine keep, for example, started life as Otsu Castle in 1575 and was moved to its present location in 1606. Of castles in existence in situ prior to the siege of Osaka in 1615, Inuyama, which looks down dramatically on the Kiso River, dates from 1600, Matsue, on the coast of the Sea of Japan, from 1611, and the peerless Himeji was built between 1601 and 1610.

KAKEGAWA CASTLE, GROUND PLAN, ELEVATION AND CROSS SECTION
OF THE KEEP: 1610

A welcome trend in recent years has been the rebuilding of Japanese castle keeps using the correct materials and based on the plans which the *daimyō* was required by law to keep. This plate is of the outstanding example provided by Kakegawa Castle. Total floor space: 304.96m². Height above ground: 19.78m. (Peter Dennis © Osprey Publishing Ltd)

The keep of Hikone Castle, first erected at Otsu in 1575. It is one of the finest of the original keeps left in Japan. It has a characteristic stone base, and the windows of its upper storey are finished in *kato mado* style, with an external balcony. It was the seat of the Ii family.

All these examples, therefore, date from a time when wars were still continuing, so the popular view that consigns Japan's extant castles to a time when wars had ceased is far from the truth. Quite elaborate structures existed during the age of samurai warfare, and this can be confirmed by pictorial sources, in particular the painted screens produced to commemorate famous battles in which their patrons took place. One important source is the Nagashino Screen in the Tokugawa Art Museum in Nagoya, because in the right-hand corner there is a representation of Nagashino Castle. One other very important source is the screen of the Summer Campaign of Osaka, 1615. Here the representation of the keep tallies very well with what is known of its contemporary appearance.

Far from being a product of the peaceful Edo Period, therefore, the elaborate tower keep, designed as much to impress an enemy by a display of the *daimyō*'s wealth as for military considerations, was an integral part of Japanese castle design almost as soon as the techniques were developed to allow it to be built and anyone had the resources to create one. In fact one of the most spectacular keeps of all was one of the earliest. This was Oda Nobunaga's glorious castle of

Azuchi, burned by rebels at the time of Nobunaga's murder in 1582. Nothing remains of Azuchi above its stone base, but enough illustrations and descriptions of it have survived to allow its appearance to be reconstructed with some confidence. One feature of Azuchi, never repeated anywhere else, was the building of an octagonal tower as the uppermost of its seven storeys.

In 1586 Toyotomi Hideyoshi, who succeeded Nobunaga, commissioned Osaka Castle, which was to add its own chapter to the history of Japanese castle-building. It was built on the 'great slope' (*o-saka*) that had formerly housed the fortified cathedral of Ishiyama Honganji. The solid base, although of modest height, lay in the midst of a bewildering maze of rivers, reed beds and ever-changing islands that made up the estuary of the Kiso River where it entered Osaka Bay. This topography, the classic *hirajiro* situation, was cleverly exploited in the construction of Osaka. Concentric rings of huge stone walls built around earth cores provided multiple layers of defence with little height advantage until one moved closer to the central keep, which was of such a size as to dominate its surroundings completely. Osaka's keep was therefore an example of a structure that lay right at the heart of a complex defensive arrangement. Tokugawa Ieyasu's Edo Castle was realized on a similarly grand scale, and as it is now the imperial palace in Tokyo most of its outer baileys still exist, allowing the visitor an opportunity to appreciate fully the sheer scale of the venture.

The years between the battle of Sekigahara in 1600 and the siege of Osaka in 1615 witnessed the most furious spate of castle-building and redevelopment in Japanese history. This was the beginning of what would become two and a half centuries of peace under the iron rule of the Tokugawa. One major element in their polity was the *baku-han* system, whereby national government was provided by the *bakufu* or shogunate, and local government by the *daimyō*'s fiefs or *han*. Like everything else in Tokugawa Japan, there were regulations governing the *daimyō*'s castles, which became the focal point for local administration. Yet along with the rebuilding and redevelopment of provincial castles, many were destroyed under the policy of 'one province – one castle'. The result was that the mighty fortresses we see today became the centre of a *daimyō*'s territory in a more decisive and defined way than ever before.

THE USE OF EARTHWORKS

There is a considerable body of evidence to suggest that walls of earth formed part of some Japanese castle designs. As in the European context, earth bastions had the advantage of speed and economy, although they were always a temporary solution. Earthworks formed the main element of the barbican built out to the south of Osaka Castle to strengthen its defences prior to the great siege of 1614–15. It was named the Sanada-maru after the castle commander, Sanada Yukimura, and saw much action in the winter of 1614. On top of the earth bastion a simple but effective two-storey wooden wall with firing platforms was constructed.

THE MAZE OF WALLS AND GATES THAT MAKE UP THE DEFENCES
OF HIMEJI CASTLE: 1611

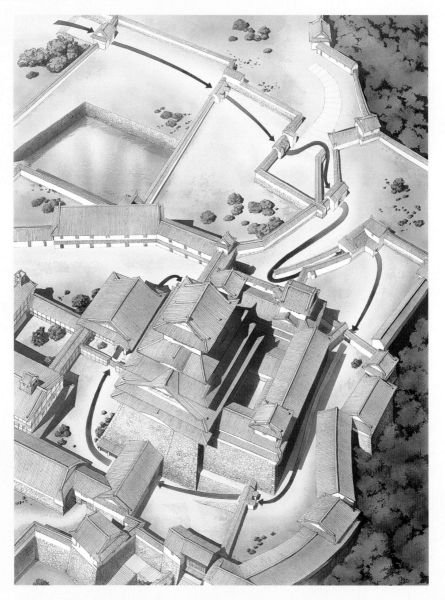

One of the most important defensive elements in the developed style of castle was the need to make the approach to
the keep as difficult as possible. The ultimate example is the maze created by the succession of walls, gates and baileys,
at Himeji, which can still be enjoyed today. The successive gates are labelled in the Japanese alphabetical system of
'i, ro, ha, ni, ho, he...', although some of the final Water Gates no longer exist. (Peter Dennis © Osprey Publishing Ltd)

Inuyama Castle holds a dramatic and romantic position above the Kiso River. It is still owned by the same family who owned it in the 17th century. Here we see it in the early morning with the keep reflected from the water's surface.

One of the most prominent earthwork defensive walls was built round Kyoto in 1591. The Odoi (Great Rampart) was an earthen wall about 3m high and 9m wide, which extended 22.5km round the outside of the city. The wall was partly moated and bamboo was planted along the top. It was completed within five months, but could not compare defensively to the mighty stone walls that already surrounded many Japanese castles, and seems to have been built largely to control individual malefactors. A diarist wrote that if a suspicious character appeared, a bell was rung and the wall's ten gates were rapidly closed so that no one could go in or out without a pass. Yet no army would have been deterred by the Odoi, which resembled the failed attempt to enclose the capital several centuries earlier. Indeed its resemblance to a Chinese city wall may well have been a major factor in Hideyoshi's decision to build it. He was planning to conquer China and may have wished to create a monument to impress ambassadors from the Ming court.

The Sanada-maru was essentially a temporary structure to meet the demands of the moment, and was not copied elsewhere, nor did the Odoi last long. Instead the final flourish in Japanese castle design went to the other extreme, and by the time of the fall of Osaka in 1615 the keeps that now grace the Japanese landscape had all been completed. Like so many other things in Japanese military history, with the establishment of the Tokugawa Peace developments in castle architecture came to an end. The castles might be rebuilt after fires or earthquakes, but until the coming of Europeans in the 19th century forced a reaction, the Japanese castle remained as the most visible and attractive symbol of past military glory.

THE CASTLE TOWN

Around these fine castles developed the castle towns of the Edo Period, but in the vast majority of cases the *daimyō* who ruled their territories from these

THE DEFENCE OF THE EARTHWORK SANADA BARBICAN AT OSAKA: 1614

Primitive-looking earthworks and wooden palisades formed the main element of the barbican built out to the south of Osaka Castle to strengthen its defences prior to the great siege of 1614–15. (Peter Dennis © Osprey Publishing Ltd)

splendid castles and towns had no family connection with the immediate area. Following the battle of Sekigahara in 1600 Tokugawa Ieyasu, the first Tokugawa *shōgun*, commenced a drastic policy of relocation. The *fudai daimyō*, those who had a long tradition of service to the Tokugawa, were allocated rich fiefs in strategic locations where they could keep an eye on the *tozama daimyō* or 'outer lords', those who had been on the losing side at Sekigahara, or whose loyalty was less than fully trustworthy. Thus Tokugawa Yorifusa, the ninth son of Tokugawa Ieyasu, was transferred in 1609 to the 350,000-*koku* fief of Mito in Hitachi Province, which was vacated by Satake Yoshinobu. Yoshinobu, who had ruled all of Hitachi province, had fought on the losing side at Sekigahara, and went from a 540,000-*koku* fief to one of less than half that size in distant Akita in Dewa Province.

This policy of settling potential rebels in distance fiefs with loyal *daimyō* to watch over them was enhanced by a development of the long Japanese tradition of taking hostages for good behaviour. So while all the *daimyō* lived in their castle towns from where they governed their provinces, their wives and children were required to live in Edo, right under the eyes of the *shōgun*. The wisdom of this move was seen in 1638 when the Shimabara Rebellion broke out. It started as a peasant revolt and drew in dispossessed samurai, but none of the *daimyō* broke ranks to join them. The final refinement of the system was to require the *daimyō* to make regular visits to Edo to pay their respects to the *shōgun*, accompanied by a large and ruinously expensive retinue.

It is often possible to identify the original layout of a castle town even from modern maps. At the heart lies the castle with its successive rings of defensive walls. Even where these walls have disappeared, a hill usually survives. Below these walls would have been the *buke-yashiki*, the residences of the *daimyō*'s samurai retainers. Some individual *buke-yashiki* buildings have survived, and may be visited in cities such as Kanazawa, Shiroishi and Hirosaki. In a few rare examples such as Kakunodate there are still entire streets of 'the samurai quarter'.

One particular defensive policy adopted by many *daimyō* was the forcible relocation of Buddhist temples from outlying towns and villages to a defined area within the castle town, known as the *teramachi* or temple town. Many *teramachi* still survive, and although the temples may have been rebuilt, they still stand surprisingly close to each other. This was for purely military reasons, so that the temples provided an outer line of defence for the castle town. Good examples of a *teramachi* layout may be found in Akita and Inuyama.

This situation continued throughout the Edo Period, so that by the time of the Meiji Restoration in 1868 the *daimyō*'s *han* was defined by his castle at the

Left: It is rare to have a view of the roof of a Japanese castle's keep from above, but this is provided here by the reconstructed Fushimi Momoyama Castle near Kyoto, which has now been demolished.

Right: Built up on top of the stone bases were the small white walls pierced with triangular gun ports and rectangular arrow ports, as shown here at Fukuyama.

The black and white 'long wall' of Kumamoto Castle is the finest example of the small wall, and provides an outstanding architectural feature to this superb castle.

heart of his castle town, and even the most modest of *han* in financial terms might include a very splendid stronghold. A good example is the tiny fief of Kameda, in what is now Akita Prefecture. The *daimyō* Iwaki Takakuni lived in some state in Amasaki Castle, a place that would have done justice to a *daimyō* with ten times his income. Sadly, Amasaki was one of the castles that was destroyed during the Boshin War, the civil war that attended the Meiji Restoration. Iwaki Takakuni changed sides halfway through the Boshin War, and during the fighting that followed his grand edifice was reduced to ashes.

The unique star-shaped fort of Goryōkaku in Hakodate on Hokkaidō, the site of the last battle of the Boshin War in 1869.

The best-preserved of the artillery fortresses erected in Tokyo Bay is this one, the 'Third Battery', viewed from the Rainbow Bridge that connects central Tokyo with the new developments shown in the distance. In the Edo Period this would have just been open sea.

COASTAL DEFENCES

One important factor that brought about the Meiji Restoration and the emergence of modern Japan was the increasing attempt by foreign nations to force Tokugawa Japan to end its policy of isolation, a scheme that succeeded with the arrival of Commodore Matthew Perry of the US Navy in 1854. This resulted in a paradoxical approach to foreign military technology, whereby its ideas were embraced enthusiastically as a means of providing defences against these same foreigners, or even, in the minds of diehard Japanese traditionalists, as a way of forcing them out of Japan for good. Among these innovations was the creation of a handful of European-style forts that added a new but short chapter to the history of Japanese castle development.

Japan's first and only star-shaped fort was built between 1857 and 1864 on Hokkaidō. This was the Goryōkaku, which replicated the ideal shape of the European angle bastion in that it had no blind spots for artillery defence. It was designed by Takeda Ayasaburō, who based it on illustrations he had studied in European books of angle bastions. Vauban's fortress in Lille was the model he chose for Goryōkaku. He also built Benten Daiba, a pentagonal artillery fort in Hakodate Bay. The pointed star created by the stone walls was repeated outside a wet moat by earth embankments, and there was one detached ravelin within the moat itself. As it was Japan's first attempt at building to such an unfamiliar design it had certain technical deficiencies, and a shortage of both materials and labour meant that no use was made of the small packing stones used in Japanese castle wall construction to hold the large stones in place. The Goryōkaku therefore needed frequent repair work and was not as resistant to earthquakes as a conventional stone base. Nevertheless it was an outstanding achievement in the dying days of the Tokugawa shogunate. Takeda Ayasaburō's artillery fort of Benten Daiba was a much simpler affair shaped like a pentagon. Of very similar design were a number of other artillery forts that were built in Edo (Tokyo) Bay.

ELEMENTS
AND FEATURES

THE OVERALL LAYOUT

All castles of the 'developed' style (those with stone bases and a complex of buildings) had certain design elements in common. The first feature found in all the Japanese castle sites was an overall style whereby the keep (if one was included) lay at the highest point of the area enclosed by the castle and was surrounded by a series of interlocking baileys. The general term for the numerous courtyards and enclosed areas formed by this kind of layout was *kuruwa*. Some were on the same level, paths and staircases linked others, and the way in which the *kuruwa* related to each other was one of the first points to be taken into consideration by the castle designer. He adopted a method of planning known as *nawabari*, which literally meant 'marking with ropes'. As the term implies, this referred to the very practical first step in designing a castle, which was to mark out the future extent of a castle using ropes pegged into the ground.

One of the most important considerations for a castle's defensive system was how these *kuruwa* would provide an overall defensive pattern for the castle, a matter that was often determined by the local topography. Rivers, mountains and the sea all set limits on the scope of a design. Nagashino Castle, site of the famous siege and battle of 1575, was built on a triangular rock where two rivers joined. Takamatsu and Karatsu used the sea as their moats, while Takashima and Zeze used Lake Suwa and Lake Biwa respectively to provide water defences in a style sometimes called *fujō*, or 'floating castles'. Inuyama utilizes a river and a high mountain as two natural defensive elements, while Bitchū–Matsuyama gazes down from the highest castle hill in Japan.

The central area of the *kuruwa*, which is frequently all that has survived in many castles, was the most important in terms both of defence and display. Its core was called the *hon maru* (main or innermost bailey) and contained the keep and any other residential buildings for the *daimyō*'s use. The second

courtyard was called the *ni no maru* (second bailey) and the third was the *san no maru* (third bailey). The expression '*maru*' has survived to this day in the form of addresses in old castle towns. Many have an area of the city called Marunouchi, in other words 'the area inside the *maru*'. Tokyo's Marunouchi district, for example, lies between the imperial palace and Tokyo Station.

In many cases an existing castle's outer works have disappeared under modern development, and the ground plans of earlier castles are sometimes all we have to go on when it comes to determining the layout that a castle once possessed. Archaeology and field observation can give further clues, and the resulting layout designs may be classified as follows:

1. *Rinkaku* style
   The *rinkaku* style has the *hon maru* in the centre and the *ni no maru* and the *san no maru* arranged in concentric rings around it. Although this may seem to be the ideal style for the defence of the *hon maru*, there are surprisingly few examples of this type of castle. There are two possible reasons for this. Firstly, the moats and stone walls of such a castle had to be extremely long compared to the small area on which the *hon maru* was built. Secondly, such defence works were very labour intensive and therefore very costly. The ruined Shizuoka and Tanaka castles follow this style, while mighty Osaka is the nearest surviving approximation of it.

Fukue Castle on the Goto islands provides an unusual example of a stone bridge. It leads to a simple castle gate.

The bridge of Yamagata Castle, a recent reconstruction done entirely in accordance with the original design.

2. *Renkaku* style
    The *renkaku* style has the *hon maru* in the centre with the *ni no maru* and the *san no maru* on either side. When building a castle of this style, it was necessary to provide extra protection for the more exposed *hon maru*. Mito and Sendai are examples of the *renkaku* style.

3. *Hashigokaku* style
    In the *hashigokaku* style, which can only apply to a *yamashiro* setting, the *hon maru* forms the apex of the castle while the *ni no maru* and the *san no maru* descend in steps like a staircase. As the *hon maru* is exposed on one side, it needs to back onto a lake, river or cliff. Aizu-Wakamatsu, site of fierce resistance during the Meiji Restoration, is an example of *hashigokaku* style, while Inuyama on the Kiso has a dramatic cliff on the *hon maru* side.

In the case of a larger castle, the three *maru* would in turn be encircled by two or three outlying *kuruwa*, referred to as *sotoguruwa* or *soguruwa* (the outer courts). Each of these successive areas was so arranged that any line of defence captured by an enemy could readily be recaptured from the area inside it. The ultimate result was a maze of interlocking walls and gates that would confuse an enemy and allow him to be observed for every inch of his way up to the keep. Himeji, with its 21 gates and labyrinthine walkways that literally turn back on themselves, shows this principle to perfection, and was described earlier (see p.144). Even the simpler *yamashiro* utilized this feature of successive twists and turns. The excavated and restored sections of the Hōjō castle of Hachiōji in Musashi Province shows this feature to very good effect.

The *tamon yagura* at Hikone, showing the finest example of the *tamon* style of tower, which combined the functions of tower, outbuilding and wall in one.

THE CASTLE WALL

The successive *kuruwa* and *maru* were divided from one another by moats, ditches and two sorts of walls, the smaller ones on top of the stone bases and the massive bases themselves, which presented a wall-like outer surface of roughly hewn and partly dressed stone. No mortar was used, making them the world's greatest dry stone walls. At first sight the walls look as if the stones have been placed haphazardly, but in fact they followed a very careful geometric arrangement whereby the stones settled into a compact solidness through their own weight. The outward curve, if any, is concave in shape, resulting from the stones being placed with their smaller sides outwards and their larger sides inwards, although earlier examples tend to be straighter.

Behind these large stones, and rarely seen, are two layers of pebbles that were settled into the excavated earth core of the wall and base. Smaller stones were also used to fill up gaps in the outer wall surface and to bind the large stones together. In cross section a castle's stone base is wedge-shaped, and some reach a height of 40m. What made up a castle's foundations, therefore, was a series of these stone bases, holding up towers and gateways linked by other sections that only housed low walls of plaster on top of them. Nevertheless, all these stone bases were of a similarly formidable thickness, and their outer surface projected in and out to give well-constructed and overlapping defences.

The small walls of plaster and ground rock on top of the bases were surprisingly solid, and would be pierced with openings – triangular for guns, rectangular for arrows. These walls add greatly to the aesthetic appeal of the castle. The white walls of Himeji are quite splendid, and the black 'long wall' of Kumamoto is a tremendous architectural feature. As they were small, these minor walls were frequently buttressed using wood or stone. Behind the small walls a row of trees, usually pines, would be planted. These would act as a shield from arrows and bullets, but could also provide timber in the case of a prolonged siege, and added greatly to the decorative effect that was in any case part of the overall plan. Within the outer walls, trees were also planted to veil the movements of soldiers within the defences and to provide a food source.

BRIDGES AND GATES

Roadways were provided to give access to the castle complex from outside. Sometimes these were conveyed across bridges, otherwise through a smaller version of the stone bases described above. The entrance at the front of the castle was usually called the *ote* (meeting place), while the gate it led to was known as the *ōtemon*. The passage on the postern was called the *karamete*, meaning 'the place where prisoners will be captured', because postern gates were used as sally ports for surprise attacks.

Bridges came in many different styles. They were usually of wood, although Fukue Castle on the Goto islands provides an unusual example of a stone bridge. Of the fixed wooden bridges, most tended to be of cantilevered construction and could be very graceful. The bridge at Hachiōji is straight. The ones at Hikone, Yamagata and Matsumoto are particularly pleasing examples of curved bridges. No actual drawbridges appear to have survived anywhere in Japan, but we know they existed from drawings and descriptions, although they were very rare. A variation on the conventional European drawbridge was also found in Japan. This was a removable bridge that could be rolled out on wheels across a gap along very narrow horizontal supports.

Not all castles had keeps. This model at Utsunomiya, based on a contemporary map, shows how the walls, towers and gatehouses enclosed an inner bailey in which there were only one-storey domestic and administrative buildings.

Of the buildings that were part of a castle's superstructure, the ones that a visitor first encountered were the gatehouses. A castle gatehouse would make up quite a complex micro-system of defence. A pair of gateways would cover entrances. The first was directly open onto the roadway, and sometimes had small roofs projecting outwards on the forward support of the gate. The second, inner, gate would be set at right angles to the first so that an attacker would have to make an abrupt turn. In the case of castles built on a hill, the second gate would often be positioned so that it was higher than the first, a feature shown very well at Hikone. Whatever the arrangement, there was always a roughly rectangular-shaped area between the gates that was fully enclosed and overlooked from all points. This space was called the *masugata*, from the shape of the measuring vessel (*masu*) commonly used for liquids and grain. Another meaning of the term derives from the fact that a castle commander could assemble his men in sections in this area and thereby count them. Small, so-called *uzumi* or 'secret gates' also appear in concealed places along the walls. The actual gates that were hung in the gatehouses were of heavy timber on massive iron hinges, and were reinforced with iron plates and spikes.

CASTLE TOWERS

Gatehouses that were built in the form of a tower were called *watari yagura*, meaning 'the tower that bridges both sides'. *Yagura* was in fact the generic name for a tower; the word literally means 'arrow store', which was one of their original functions. However, *yagura* in a Japanese castle could take many different forms apart from the conventional Western understanding of the word 'tower'. One common variety was the *tamon* or *tamon yagura*, which was a long one-storey building set on top of a stone base acting as a defensive wall, a lookout post and a utility building all in one. The name may derive from Tamon Castle, which was built by Matsunaga Hisahide and where such a structure was effectively the first Japanese castle keep. The fine *tamon yagura* at Hikone was used by the maidservants as living quarters.

At the corners of the walls may be seen other towers of two or three storeys. Known simply as *sumi yagura* (corner towers), they comprised an important element in the overall castle design. Corner towers were often fitted with *ishi otoshi* (stone droppers), which were the Japanese equivalent of machicolations. The Inui tower of Osaka Castle, which lies at the northwest corner of the complex, has the unusual feature of having two storeys of equal size. Matsumoto Castle has a subsidiary tower that is open on the eastern and southern sides. Called the Tsukimi tower, it was not designed as a military structure but was rather for moon-viewing. In many cases the stone base on which the corner tower is built projects out into the wet moat or dry ditch. This gives the tower a very formidable appearance, and would also allow some flanking fire to be delivered against attackers. The Uto tower of Kumamoto Castle is a good example.

THE CASTLE KEEP

The largest tower of all in a Japanese castle is the *tenshu kaku* or keep. Its name means 'high heavenly protector' and height is usually the first characteristic that is noticed. In many cases, in fact, the keep will have caught the visitor's eye long before he or she appreciates the gates or corner towers, because the keep is almost invariably the highest point of the entire structure and may be visible for miles. In some cases only the keeps of Japanese castles have survived, which can give a misleading impression of the original design of the fortress.

A typical keep would be of at least three storeys, maybe even as many as seven, but frequently their outward appearance did not correspond exactly to their actual interior structure and design because there were often underground cellars built deep inside the stone core of the base, and the number of floors above ground was often not discernible from the apparent number visible from outside. The purposes of a keep included the following key functions:

1. To provide a vantage point
2. To act as the final line of defence
3. To symbolize the *daimyō*'s power
4. To provide secure storage.

As the Portuguese Jesuit Joao Rodrigues put it:

> They keep their treasure here and it is here that they assemble their wives in time of siege. When they can no longer hold out, they kill their women

In this model at Hyogo Prefectural Museum, a huge stone to be incorporated in the walls of a castle, ornamented with Hideyoshi's flags, is floated down river on a raft.

and children to prevent them falling into the hands of the enemy; then after setting fire to the tower with gunpowder and other materials so that not even their bones or anything else may survive, they cut their bellies.

The first tower keeps (including the original one at Himeji, demolished in 1601) were less ornate structures, resembling larger versions of the simpler corner towers. However, when embellished to the extent revealed by many surviving examples, they made dramatic statements of a *daimyō*'s power. Unlike almost anywhere else in the castle, the windows, roofs and gables of the keep were arranged in subtle and intricate patterns. The shape of the keep's roof was almost without exception in the ornate style that had been used for centuries for the most palatial residences, and the use of two contrasting styles of gable on the same elevation of a keep was also a frequently noticed aesthetic element. The first style, *chidori hafu*, was triangular in shape. The second, *kara hafu*, was curved, with the apex flowing into the line provided by the cornice. This style of architecture can be seen to good effect at Himeji.

The windows of a keep were generally square, though the uppermost storey was often provided with ornate windows in the shape known as *kato mado*, and usually had an exterior balcony. Roofs were almost always tiled with thick blue-grey Japanese tiles, though in the early days some castles had thatched roofs, and old photographs of Iwakuni Castle confirm that it was once roofed with wooden shingles. The ridge of the topmost roof of the keep was often decorated with *shachi* (dolphins) made of metal or tile. These striking ornaments in the shape of fish are supposed to be charms against evil spirits and fire. They are sometimes gilded, and there is a charming story told

This model at Nagahama Castle shows several of the stages that went into the building of a castle, from the cladding of the excavated hillside in stone to the raising of the keep. Note the workmen on their cradle platform, and the big stone being wheeled up on a cart.

AZUCHI CASTLE: 1576

Only a stone base remains of the great Azuchi Castle, raised by Oda Nobunaga in 1576 as one of the wonders of Japan. It was Japan's first great tower keep, and was burned to the ground when Nobunaga was assassinated only six years later. For this reason no one can be sure for certain what Azuchi actually looked like, but the consensus of opinion is that this revolutionary building had seven storeys, of which the uppermost one was octagonal, and was richly decorated. Military corridors inside surrounded domestic areas. (Peter Dennis © Osprey Publishing Ltd)

about the *shachi* on the roof of Nagoya Castle, which were made from a core of cypress wood covered in lead and copper, and finally coated with pure gold. A thief had himself floated up by means of a kite to steal the gold scales from the fish!

The external colour of surviving keeps is usually white; however, this was not necessarily their original colour. Both Azuchi and Osaka are known to have sported bright colours and designs of tigers and dragons on their exterior surfaces. The exceptions are the so-called 'black castles' such as Kumamoto, Matsue and Okayama, where the predominant colour comes from the black wood that dominates the white plaster around it, with only the *mon* (family crest) of the *daimyō* carved on the apex of the gable ends for decoration.

In some cases topographical considerations led to the construction of keeps of unusual shapes. The ideal shape for a stone base was rectangular, but this was not always achievable, especially when the base had to be built round the core of an extinct volcano, as is the case with Wakayama Castle. In spite of intensive cutting away of the hill top, the resulting area was so limited that the keep had to be rhombic in plan with all corners of the building curved, while the small tower adjacent to the keep was built on an irregular pentagonal first storey. At Kumamoto Castle the first storey actually overhangs the stone base so as to give a rectangular shape, and the extra space created was used to provide an area for dropping stones. At Bitchū-Matsuyama a long climb provides the reward of seeing stone walls integrated superbly with the natural rock, inside which the complex housing the keep makes the best possible use of the restricted space available.

BUILDING A CASTLE

The building of a pre-stone Sengoku *yamashiro* has been adequately described above, but the construction of a developed stone-clad model complete with tower keep was an altogether different process.

Firstly, the chosen site was surveyed, and the architect designed on paper the best style of castle layout commensurate with the constraints of the site. Before any actual building began, however, there would be a religious ceremony conducted by a Shintō priest. This consisted of ritually cutting the first sod within a sacred enclosure formed by fastening four ropes to four green bamboo poles. From the ropes paper *gohei* (streamers) would be hung. With the *daimyō* and his representatives watching, a ceremonial offering of rice and salt would then be made.

After this the labourers took over, and under the guidance of supervisors, who would work from the architect's plans and sometimes even from a relief model, the colossal and labour-intensive business of carving up a mountain would begin. After some preliminary ground-breaking, a nearly vertical groove would be dug into the hillside to provide the first guideline. The actual line that the outer surface of the final stone wall would follow was provided

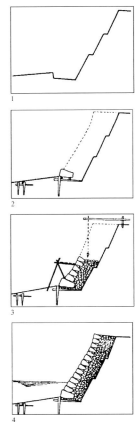

The stages of building the stone base of a castle.
1. The hillside is carefully carved away, staggered for safety. 2. The vital *ne ishi* (root stones) are laid in the precise position determined by wooden supports.
3. While wooden scaffolding and walkways allow the workmen to operate in safety, the curve of the wall is followed, with pebbles being rammed behind the line of the outer stone surface. 4. The wall is completed, and the moat is filled.

by a long length of timber projecting parallel to the earth line and about a metre away from it, secured into the position by projecting wooden stakes. About 10m further along a similar guideline would be erected. Excavation would then continue between the two markers, which would be joined by other poles horizontal to the ground when the shape was complete. The result would be that one section of the castle was beginning to take its roughly final shape, surrounded by this guidance frame that looked like open wooden scaffolding. In the case of high wall sections, different horizontal levels would be staggered. Great care was taken to produce as near perfect an outer surface as was possible, and if there was any danger of collapse the earth surface would be sheathed in wood.

The labourers who worked on the excavation had two main tools, one for digging, an implement resembling an adze, and baskets slung on a pole between the shoulders of two men for carrying away the soil. Because of the danger of rain bringing the fresh excavations down, the next stage – that of adding the stone – was begun before all the site had been carved, so a developing castle site would have shown nearly every successive process in action at any moment.

The delivery to the site of the ordinary building stones (as distinct from the 'ceremonial' donated ones described below) was accomplished by various means depending on their size. Two men would carry smaller ones slung from a pole. Bigger ones would be taken on a two-wheeled cart with two men pushing and two others pulling. Oxen would pull carts for even larger varieties.

When the stones began to be added to the carved surface, the guide poles mentioned above came into their own to provide the target line for the finished product. Careful preparation began at the base of the section under construction. A timber base provided the exact angle for laying the bottom line of stones. The crucial one was the extra-large *ne ishi* or root stone. This would have its top and bottom surfaces precisely worked to launch the correct angle for the chosen slope – the higher the wall, the lower the angle. Behind the root stone was a layer of compacted smaller stones, and behind them a layer of pebbles pressed into the shaped earth core. From then on wall-building was a matter of adding height to this sandwich of stones and pebbles until the top of the wall was reached. Particular care was taken over external corners, where the specially shaped corner stones 'dovetailed'.

As the wall progressed upwards, structures were put in place for delivering materials to the builders, either by wooden ramps from below, or by lowering baskets of stone from above. The workmen toiled on top of wooden platforms laid along the ever-increasing upper surface of the wall. The smaller stones were pounded into a compact mass using wooden drivers.

The placing of the outer layer of stones required much effort and great precision, particularly when the largest stones were added. One colourful feature of the process of building the largest and most prestigious edifices concerned the transportation to the site of huge individual stones that were to be incorporated into the walls. In cases such as the building of Hideyoshi's Osaka Castle, the *daimyō* vied with each other as to who could donate the largest stone. The arrival of these monsters at the site was always a source of celebration, and numerous contemporary illustrations depict some massive piece of rock being dragged on a sledge, or towed along on a barge. The stone would be festooned with banners and religious objects as if it were a portable shrine in a religious festival. The labourers heaved on the ropes while small boys balanced on top of the stone waved fans and led the rhythmic chanting. One colossal stone at Nagoya Castle has an outside surface area of 6m², and was donated by Katō Kiyomasa. The huge stones of Osaka are still a

A clever stone-dropping opening built into the corner of a keep is shown here. This example is at Hamamatsu.

tourist attraction today, but recent excavations have revealed that some of these giants are not all that they appear to be. One, which is 10m long and 3m high, turns out to be less than a metre thick!

In addition to carving away a hillside and cladding it in stone, other walls would be created by constructing an artificial hill. Once again the resulting wall had a sloping outer surface of large stone blocks. Inside it was a firmly rammed core.

Once the stone base was complete, a very different building process would begin to raise the superstructure of the small walls, the gatehouses, side towers and above all the keep. Here the key material was wood, and the amazing skills of the Japanese carpenter who could build pagodas and temples came into their own. Within scaffolding constructed from long wooden poles, a huge timber framework would take shape. The vertical sections were sunk deep into the untouched core of the original hill, where they rested upon massive rocks placed there as foundations. Plaster was applied to the coarse framework between the pillars to give the outer surface to the buildings in a similar way to the building of the low plaster walls already described. Alternatively, in the case of the 'black castles' of Kumamoto and Matsue, the external surface would be of painted wood. Tiling, decoration and gilding, topped off with the traditional golden *shachi*, were the final stages used to produce the external appearance of the mighty edifice. Such were the human and financial resources available to a *daimyō* that the whole process from excavation to completion could take a surprisingly short space of time. Nagoya Castle, for example, was completed for the Tokugawa *shōgun* after only two years.

THE PRINCIPLES OF DEFENCE

Whatever their aesthetic appeal, Japanese castles were primarily fortresses, and the Japanese castle represented a sophisticated defence system, even if the way this operated is not always directly apparent. At first sight the graceful superstructures look flimsy and very vulnerable to fire, but they were in fact highly fire resistant, and the Japanese also lacked the means for effective artillery bombardment until quite late in their history.

One obvious disadvantage provided by the gently sloping and curved walls of the typical castle stone base was the ease with which attackers could climb them, and the way in which the unmortared blocks of stone fitted together also provided numerous handholds. One solution was the incorporation into the design of towers of the stone-dropping holes noted above which were akin to European machicolations. Unlike machicolations, however, the *ishi otoshi* were closed by hinged doors. An additional deterrent to would-be climbers were rows of spikes pointing downwards from certain horizontal surfaces, such as those seen on the keep at Kumamoto Castle and the small walls at Nagoya.

Whereas the primary consideration behind the European angle bastion was protection against artillery fire, this was only one factor taken into consideration in Japan, even though the two styles look superficially similar. In Japan an infantry attack or mining were far more likely to occur than an artillery bombardment, and it is only at the siege of Osaka in 1614–15 that

The 'gallant youths' of Nihonmatsu defend the castle during the Boshin War of 1868. In the background we see the reconstructed gatehouse.

anything resembling a European cannon bombardment becomes a major feature. In this case guns of European manufacture supplied the bombardment, so for this reason alone no Japanese castle can be regarded as an artillery fortress by design. There are no gun emplacements or casemates as such, and there would be few places inside Himeji, for example, where cannon could be mounted successfully. Instead the most common gunpowder weapons would be thousands of arquebuses with which an attacker or defender would sweep his opponent's lines. This was the technique that won the Korean castles for the invaders of 1592, an invasion army, incidentally, that took almost nothing in the way of an artillery train with it.

MINING AND COUNTERMINING

A few attacks on a castle by mining will be illustrated in the 'operational history' section that follows, but there appears to be no evidence of permanent counter-mining measures being introduced, as was often the case in Europe. Attacks by flooding were also something that could not be adequately prepared for, apart from choosing high ground on which to build one's castle. The great flooding sieges of Japan, Takamatsu, Ota and Oshi, all made use of very large-scale civil engineering works to create dykes and divert rivers, followed by immense patience as the waters rose, and there was little the defenders could do other than attack the workmen. Many castles would have had moats wide enough to cope with rising water levels, however, although whether the threat of flooding was the reason they were built is hard to discern.

MISSILE WEAPONS

As noted earlier, bombardment from gunpowder weapons was never a major factor in Japanese sieges until Osaka in 1614, so little consideration was given to cannon fire in defensive planning for a Japanese castle until the very end of the period under discussion. If castle towers were ever set on fire from a distance it was by the use of fire arrows, and treachery among the defenders was a far more common reason for a castle burning down. Crossbows passed out of use late in the 12th century. The catapults used were Chinese-style traction trebuchets, and in fact the best account of their use, which dates from 1468, describes them throwing soft-cased exploding bombs not against a *yamashiro*'s castle walls but against the samurai defending the rudimentary palisades set up during the Onin War. Traction trebuchets appear in a clearly defensive role for a castle when the Mōri family attacked Takiyama Castle and were met by smooth river stones loosed from catapults. As late as 1614 traction trebuchets armed with soft-cased bombs were to be found on the walls of Osaka Castle. Otherwise volleys from thousands of arquebuses would cut a path for an infantry assault by samurai armed with spears and swords, a pattern that worked very well in Korea in 1592.

THE LIVING SITES

DAILY LIFE IN THE CASTLE IN PEACETIME

The castle was the centre of a *daimyō*'s territory in more ways than one. The population may have depended upon the castle for its defence during wartime, but during peacetime the *daimyō* depended upon the population to grow food for the army, for providing a supply of recruits who would act as part-time soldiers summoned in times of emergency, and also for castle maintenance. Apart from agricultural work, this was probably the greatest contribution made in peacetime by an individual peasant to the *daimyō*'s cause.

Big or small, all castles had to be maintained and many fascinating records have survived of the process. For example, in 1587 Hōjō Ujikuni ordered a certain Chichibu Magojiro, the commander of a company associated with Hachigata Castle, to maintain a 174-*ken* stretch of walls, plus one tower and three gates in that section. At four labourers per *ken*, the Chichibu contingent had to supply about 700 men to work on the walls of Hachigata. The rules were strict. If the man was a part-time soldier who was away on campaign, his wife and maidservants had to come and make repairs. When the damage was due to a typhoon, they had to move immediately to make the repairs, and if the damage was to the gates, tower or embankments of the castle, they had to repair the castle first, even if their own homes had been destroyed. The *daimyō*'s needs always came first.

As well as repair, walls also had to be monitored as to their condition, and the area allocated to a particular company had to be policed and inspected once a month. The rope joints on the walls had to be fixed and frayed knots repaired during the last four days of every month, a time set aside specifically for this purpose. When the work was completed, it had to be reported to Hōjō Ujikuni, and if he was away from the castle for any reason, it had to be reported to the appointed official. If a single person failed to perform his duty, a punishment was imposed on the whole company. Care had to be taken regarding the materials used for castle repair, and the members of the company itself had to make sure that any additional labourers they brought along with them used the right materials and were not negligent.

The beautiful keep of Himeji Castle seen among cherry blossom. This view shows several important features, such as the use of two styles of gables. The first style, *chidori hafu*, is roughly triangular in shape. The second, *kara hafu*, is curved, with the apex flowing into the line provided by the cornice. Himeji is the most visited castle in Japan.

The villagers thus impressed worked from the drum of dawn to the bell of evening, both signals being given from the castle tower. An earlier note, from 1563, spells out in more detail the schedule of repair. Barring typhoons, the walls were to be repaired every five years, at four persons per *ken* per day. The villagers had to bring with them at their own expense five large posts, 15 small posts, ten bamboo poles, ten bundles of bamboo, 30 coils of rope, and 20 bundles of reed. The instructions were as follows. At intervals of one ken on top of the earthworks the labourers had to drive in the large wooden posts, place two bamboo poles sideways between them, and arrange four bundles of bamboo on top using the small posts. These were fastened by six coils of rope and then thatched with the reeds.

The defence of a castle, of course, relied on more than stout, well-maintained walls. The men of the garrison were vital. Depending upon the size of the castle, the garrison could be permanent, rotated, or kept as a skeleton force. For example, the Arakawa company, located a few miles from Hachigata Castle, were ordered to run to the castle when they heard the conch shell trumpet sounding an attack. An order from 1564 relating to Hachigata has been preserved, which requires the leaders of 'company number 3', consisting of 13 horsemen and 38 on foot, to relieve 'company number 2' and serve 15 days' garrison duty.

Garrison life in a samurai castle was a matter of constant readiness, with its own, sometimes boring routine. The Hōjō had a strict system for the samurai of mighty Odawara. In 1575 they were required to muster at their designated wall prior to morning reveille. When the drum beat indicated the dawn, they would open the gates in their sector to the town outside. Guard duty lasted for six hours during the day, with a two-hour break. The gates would be closed at dusk when the evening bell tolled. Guards were mounted at night, and had strict instructions not to trample on the earth walls. When off duty their armour and weapons were stored at their duty stations, but guards were posted in the towers day and night, and the utmost care was taken at night to prevent fires and to guard against night attack. Troops were not allowed to leave the castle for unauthorized reasons, and if someone did leave, he would probably be executed and the person in charge severely punished.

THE CASTLE AS PALACE

In the discussion above relating to the design elements of the typical Japanese castle a brief reference was made to those parts of the castle set aside for ceremonial and administrative functions. This was a role every bit as important as defence, and there are many records of castles being used to entertain ambassadors and for high-level meetings. In this context, possibly the most elevated use of a castle as palace was when Toyotomi Hideyoshi entertained the Emperor of Japan with a tea ceremony in the gold-plated tea room of Fushimi Castle.

In only very few cases were the 'palatial' areas of the castle located in the keep. For example, when Oda Nobunaga moved his capital to Gifu in 1568, all his domestic and administrative buildings were located at the foot of the high mountain upon which the purely military keep was located. With the building of Azuchi in 1576, however, the military and the civic function of the castle merged, so that Azuchi showed Nobunaga as both general and prince at the same time. This principle was emulated by Hideyoshi at Osaka, but at Osaka there were in addition some splendid reception rooms in the grounds. Few other places were able to follow these examples, and the keep stayed as a military building with the main domestic architecture to be found within the large courtyards.

Uniquely in Japan, at Nijo Castle in Kyoto it is the military keep that has disappeared while the palace has survived. In other places we know about the design of the greatest *yashiki* because rooms from other castles have been removed and preserved elsewhere. Fushimi Castle had outstanding reception rooms, some of which may now be found in the Nishi Honganji temple in Kyoto. Otherwise we can glean much information about *yashiki*, and reception rooms in castles generally, from the descriptions of European visitors, who were received in these surroundings by great men such as Nobunaga and Hideyoshi. For example, Luis Frois visited Gifu and wrote that 'of all the palaces and houses I have seen in Portugal, India and Japan, there has been nothing to compare with this as regards luxury, wealth and cleanliness'. The long description that follows lists the reception rooms and gardens that made up Nobunaga's palace at the foot of the mountain on which sat the purely military keep. When Frois visited in turn Azuchi Castle, he was able to see the same degree of ostentation within a castle keep. He mentions the lavish use of gold, and the whole thing was 'beautiful, excellent and brilliant'. He also did not fail to notice the strength of the stone bases, and, like other visitors to Edo and Osaka, was most impressed by the strength of the gates.

Rodrigo de Vivero y Velsaco had an audience with Tokugawa Hidetada, the second Tokugawa *shōgun*, at Edo Castle in 1609, and described the first room he entered as follows:

> On the floor they have what is called *tatami*, a sort of beautiful matting trimmed with cloth of gold, satin and velvet, embroidered with many gold flowers. These mats are square like a small table and fit together so well that their appearance is most pleasing. The walls and ceiling are covered with

Interiors of a keep are difficult to photograph adequately, but this corner inside Matsumoto shows several typical features. Note how there is a corridor running round the edge. The floor in the centre would be fitted with interlocking *tatami* mats. There are two gun ports at the apex of the corner, and two rectangular windows.

wooden panelling and decorated with various paintings of hunting scenes, done in gold, silver and other colours, so that the wood itself is not visible.

Lesser *daimyō's* rooms would of course have been simpler, but all would have reflected the economy of style of traditional Japanese architecture, characterized by the use of *tatami* mats, *shoji* (sliding screens) to divide a large area into rooms, and a *tokonoma* or alcove.

THE CASTLE UNDER SIEGE

When war began, the daily lives of its garrison and the local population changed rapidly as the castle was converted into an active military headquarters. The state of a castle's food supplies was crucial when it was about to be besieged, or when such a prospect seemed likely following an enemy incursion. In 1587 Hōjō Ujikuni ordered the village of Kitadani in Kozuke Province to collect and deposit all grain from the autumn harvest in his satellite castle of Minowa. The value placed on provisions is also given dramatic illustration by another order from Ujikuni issued in 1568, the same year that Takeda Shingen invaded western Kantō, that no supplies were to be moved without a document bearing the seal of the Hōjō. Should anything be moved without the seal then the offender would be crucified. Such draconian measures were justified because the threat of starvation could seal a castle's fate. After a 200-day siege in 1581, the defenders of Tottori were almost reduced to cannibalism. The strangest device for combating starvation may be found at Kato Kiyomasa's Kumamoto Castle. Not only did he plant nut trees within the baileys, but the straw *tatami* mats that are to be found in every Japanese dwelling were stuffed not with rice straw but with dried vegetable stalks, so that if the garrison were really desperate they could even eat the floor mats.

A reliable water supply was also vital during a siege, and if a besieging army could locate the source of a garrison's water supply and destroy it they acquired a tremendous advantage. In 1570 Chokoji Castle was fed by a complex wooden aqueduct that Shibata Katsuie kept closely guarded. The besieging Rokkaku troops, however, succeeded in smashing the aqueduct and waited for the 400 men of the garrison to die of thirst or to surrender. To fool the enemy, and to keep up morale within the castle, Katsuie kept sending out troops to make attacks and then withdraw, but one samurai was captured during a raid and cried out for water. The enemy then knew that the water must be very close to running out, so they prepared for a final assault. That night Shibata Katsuie gathered all his men into the inner courtyard of the castle and showed them the three remaining water jars, which between them held only enough water for one more day. Then, in full view of his army, Katsuie took his spear and with the iron butt end smashed the sides of the jars, allowing all the precious water to run away. With the words, 'Sooner a quick death in battle than a slow death from thirst!' he led the Shibata samurai out in a wild impetuous charge. So vigorously did they fight with nothing to lose that they carried all before them. The Rokkaku pulled back, completely routed, and the castle was saved.

In three of the Takeda campaigns, the water supply played a crucial role. At Futamata in 1572 the castle obtained its water by lowering buckets from a wooden tower built high above the neighbouring river. Takeda Katsuyori constructed heavy wooden rafts and floated them downstream to crash into the supports of the tower, which eventually collapsed. At Noda in 1573 miners tunnelled into the side of the castle's moat and drained off all its water. A popular anecdote concerning the fall of Katsurayama in 1557 tells how the castle's greatest weakness was its lack of a water supply. There was no spring on top of the mountain, so all drinking water had to be carried up from a source near the Joshoji temple on the mountain's lower slopes. This fact was initially unknown to the besieging Takeda troops, and as water was always a crucial factor in a siege the garrison decided to fool the besiegers into thinking that they had ample supplies. As they had plenty of rice, the Ochiai soldiers chose a place that was easily visible from the Takeda lines and poured out the white rice in a torrent that looked like a waterfall. It boldly proclaimed the message that this desperately defended castle would be able to hold out until relief came.

Unfortunately for the Ochiai, the chief priest of Joshoji betrayed their clever scheme. He passed on to the Takeda the secret information that their only source of water supply in fact lay down beside the temple. Baba Nobuharu's men rushed to occupy the spring and then attacked the castle with renewed confidence. This time they managed to set fire to the castle buildings and the brave castle commander was killed in the attack that followed. There followed a mass suicide by the wives, women and children of the castle, who flung themselves to their deaths from the crags. The castle burned to ashes, so that 'even now when the site is dug, baked rice may be found'.

The mass suicide by the women of Katsurayama Castle shows that during a siege everyone inside the castle was fully involved in its defence. When Suemori Castle was attacked by Sasa Narimasa in 1584 Okamura Sukie'mon was ably assisted by his wife in its defence. She walked the walls and inspired the men until Maeda Toshiie rode to its relief. Among the tasks traditionally performed by the women within a castle in a war situation were casting bullets, treatment of

The water tower at Futamata, from which buckets were lowered to obtain water from the river. This reconstruction may be seen at the nearby Seiryōji temple in Futamata.

the wounded and the preparation of enemy heads for the head-viewing ceremony. There is a rare eyewitness account that was recorded by the daughter of a samurai living in Ogaki Castle during the siege of 1600. The young girl, later known as Oan, was the daughter of the samurai Yamada Kyoreki. The women gradually got used to the roar of the guns, and helped to cast bullets in the keep. Severed heads taken by the garrison were brought together in the keep for Oan and the other women to prepare. They attached a tag to each head in order to identify them properly, then they repeatedly blackened the teeth – the ancient sign of a distinguished man – by applying a generous coat of dental dye to any heads with white teeth. At night Oan would sleep next to piles of severed heads. One day, a samurai tried to calm the women by telling them that the enemy had retreated, but just at that moment Oan's brother was hit by a bullet before her eyes, yet because of the privation she had already experienced in the besieged castle she was too numb to cry.

Death was the likely fate for the defenders of a doomed castle, but as the absence of fortified towns meant that Japanese sieges were conducted against almost purely military installations, civilian casualties outside the walls would probably be limited to the swathe of destruction cut by the army passing through. When Takeda Shingen was repulsed before Odawara Castle in 1569, he burned the town of Odawara before retiring, but when Toyotomi Hideyoshi took Kagoshima in 1587 and Odawara in 1590 there was nothing that remotely resembled the sack of a European town. In one strange incident, when Otsu was besieged in 1600 the local people took their picnic boxes along to a nearby hillside to watch the fun!

Fear of death was nevertheless an important factor, so that the number of people within a castle would be swelled by farmers and others moving in for safety when an attack was imminent, and this could stretch the garrison's resources and provisions to their limits. When Takeda Shingen invaded the Kantō in 1569 the local people flocked to Odawara, causing severe pressure on resources. During Hideyoshi's invasion of the Hōjō territories a much larger movement of population took place, and the garrisons of nearly all the Hōjō satellite castles were stripped to the bare minimum while most troops were packed into Odawara. Hōjō Ujiteru's Hachiōji Castle and Ujikuni's Hachigata Castle were exceptions, and came under concerted attack. Hideyoshi's support forces under Uesugi Kagekatsu and Maeda Toshiie spread 35,000 troops round Hachigata, and after a month-long siege Ujikuni surrendered, thus providing a foretaste of what was to come at Odawara. Starvation was but one of the weapons Hideyoshi employed at Odawara, and to drive the point home the besiegers created a town of their own around the walls, where they feasted loudly within sight of the defenders.

While the garrison of a castle was preparing for a siege, the attacker would be similarly organizing his forces and engaging in political negotiations that could result in a bloodless victory. This was far from uncommon, and a good

The keep of Bitchū-Matsuyama Castle under snow. This is the highest-situated castle keep in Japan.

example occurs during Toyotomi Hideyoshi's campaign against the Mōri family on behalf of Oda Nobunaga. The first castle Hideyoshi had to face was Himeji. The castellan was a certain Kodera Yoshitaka, whose loyalties were somewhat unsure, and in fact Kodera was persuaded to surrender Himeji without a shot being fired. With Himeji as a base, Hideyoshi could then concentrate on capturing Miki Castle, which was also in Harima Province. It was held by Bessho Nagaharu, whom Hideyoshi wished to spare so that he might join the Toyotomi side as well. Not all the elements of Hideyoshi's carefully considered plans worked. He won Miki Castle, but Bessho Nagaharu preferred to commit suicide.

OPERATIONAL HISTORY

The operational history of the later Japanese castles is the story of the interplay between constantly improving methods of assault and new means of defence to counter them. This can be seen as siege warfare moves from fire arrows against wood in the 1540s to the artillery bombardment of the stone walls of Osaka in 1615. The final military challenge came with the Boshin War in 1868 and the destruction wrought by modern artillery.

THE INTRODUCTION OF FIREARMS

From 1549 onwards firearms began to be used in operations against castles, yet with a few notable exceptions these weapons were handheld arquebuses, not cannon. Rather than battering down walls, gunpowder weapons cleared those same walls of defenders, allowing an assault to take place. The technique for doing this may be credited to Oda Nobunaga when he attacked Muraki Castle in 1554. The account in Nobunaga's biography tells us that he set up his position on the very edge of the castle moat, and ordered three successive volleys against the loopholes in the castle defences. The arquebusiers appear to have been organized in squads that fired in succession, confirming Nobunaga's sophisticated battlefield control.

But even the new arquebuses were not infallible, and the castle of Moji, which occupied a prominent vantage point overlooking the straits of Shimonoseki, changed hands five times between 1557 and 1561 in spite of gunfire, amphibious assault and even a bombardment from Portuguese ships. This was a unique event in Japanese history, and so dramatic was the illustration of the devastating effects of cannon balls against a predominantly wooden fortress that it is surprising that there was so little future development in this direction. Otherwise sieges were more conventional. At Musashi-Matsuyama in 1563 Takeda Shingen used miners to collapse its walls. In 1567 Inabayama fell, but only as a result of a classic infantry assault up its steep hill.

THE SIEGE OF HACHIŌJI (1590)

For an excellent example of a siege against a late *yamashiro* we need look no further than Hachiōji in Musashi Province, which was one of the most important satellite castles in the Hōjō's strategic defence system. Whereas mighty Odawara, the Hōjō's *honjō*, was clad in stone like Osaka, Hachiōji stayed as a *yamashiro* built predominately out of wood but with some good use of stone cladding, particularly for small towers and the sides of walkways that twisted and turned up the mountain on which Hachiōji was built. The keeper of Hachiōji was Hōjō Ujiteru, the second son of Hōjō Ujiyasu. In 1590 Toyotomi Hideyoshi commenced operations against the Hōjō. The siege of Odawara itself was long-lasting but saw little bloodshed. By contrast the sieges of the Hōjō's satellite castles were very violent affairs. Ujiteru was not present in Hachiōji when Hideyoshi attacked it. He was in Odawara, where it was

The keep of Aizu-Wakamatsu Castle viewed under snow. In 1868 this became the site of one of the last and most violent battles to be conducted against a Japanese castle.

The reconstructed gate, stairway and fence of Hachiōji Castle, defended to the death by the samurai of Hōjō Ujiteru in 1590.

believed that he was most needed, and Ujiteru reckoned that Hachiōji's topography would enable it to withstand an attack.

The castle was indeed well situated, with the main approach being along a narrow valley through which rushed a river. The paths up to Hachiōji's *hon maru* on the summit of Shiroyama (460.5m) made their way across a high bridge over a gorge and through a succession of leveled areas connected with one another by walkways reinforced with sloping stone walls that kept turning through 90 degrees. Hideyoshi overcame these obstacles by the application of overwhelming force. Fifty thousand men attacked Hachiōji's garrison of only 1,300. It is often hyperbole to say that the river ran red with the blood of the slain, but in the case of Hachiōji it is probably literally true if the corpses fell into the narrow mountain stream. Ghost stories are included in contemporary accounts of the slaughter at Hachiōji, with tales of the sounds of hoof-beats and fighting being heard long after the battle had finished. The women of the castle jumped to their deaths from the towers rather than be captured by the Toyotomi forces, and on the anniversary of the battle, 23 June, according to legend, the waters of the river turn red once again. One tradition that was maintained by local families was the cooking of blood-red *azukimeshi* (red beans and rice) on the anniversary day in memory of the slain.

Hōjō Ujiteru, of course, was safe in Odawara, where Hideyoshi was conducting the most theatrical siege in Japanese history. The siege lines became a town in their own right, where the besiegers loudly proclaimed their wealth of wine, women and song to the miserable Hōjō defenders cooped up inside. Ujiteru thus avoided the immolation of his garrison in Hachiōji, but when Odawara surrendered he was one of the Hōjō leaders who was required to commit suicide.

OPERATIONS AGAINST FIELD FORTIFICATIONS

In 1575 Nagashino Castle withstood several ingenious attempts to capture it, and was eventually relieved by the famous victory at the battle of Nagashino. This involved the mass use of arquebuses firing from behind field fortifications. Instead of simply falling on to the rear of Katsuyori's army Oda Nobunaga took up a planned position a few kilometres away at Shidarahara, where the topography enabled him to restrict enemy cavalry movement. Bounded by mountains to the north and a river to the south, Nobunaga's position was not susceptible to outflanking manoeuvres. He erected a loose palisade of lashed timber that provided protection to his army while allowing some gaps through which a counter-attack might be launched. Behind this fence stood massed ranks of arquebusiers.

The popular view of Nobunaga's victory at Nagashino is that it came about entirely as a result of the third of these factors. The reality of the situation is somewhat less dramatic, yet it detracts nothing from Nobunaga's generalship on the day. At Nagashino Nobunaga did not possess the resources to mimic machine guns. Many of the arquebusiers he arranged behind the palisades were not his own troops but had been supplied by allies and subordinates a few days before the battle took place. There was therefore no time to drill them. Alternate volleys were certainly delivered, but should be understood as a response to the successive waves of attack launched by the Takeda cavalry under the iron discipline of the men whom Nobunaga had placed in command of the squads. When the charge was broken the spears and swords of the samurai came into their own.

Although the precise situation of Nagashino was never repeated, its influence can be seen in the temporary earthworks raised by both sides during the Komaki campaign of 1584. Ieyasu built a military road to connect Komaki Castle with a series of forts out to the south-east. This was almost certainly fortified, at least as far as Hachimanzuka, a conclusion drawn from his rival Hideyoshi's response to it. A reconnaissance of Ieyasu's position showed that both of Hideyoshi's own two front-line forts of Iwasakiyama and Futaebori were on ground lower than Komaki. Hideyoshi therefore ordered the construction of a long rampart to join the two together via the fort of Tanaka. The resulting earthwork, probably strengthened with wood, was completed overnight. It was over 2km long, 3m high and 2m thick, and was pierced with several gates to allow a counter-attack. The slope of the rampart also allowed for the provision of firing positions. Hideyoshi set up his headquarters to the rear at Gakuden, which was linked to Tanaka by a series of communications forts. From behind their lines both commanders waited, fearing to launch a frontal attack and meet the fate of Takeda Katsuyori at Nagashino. The result was stalemate, as neither side wished to repeat the mistake of Nagashino, and in fact the battle of Nagakute was fought several miles from the Komaki lines as much as a result of boredom as anything else.

The 'trench system' of Komaki was never seen again in Japanese history as it just did not fit in with the samurai ethos, and the only use of earthworks in future was to augment a castle's stone walls. The best example is the barbican at Osaka in 1614 called the Sanada-maru. With rivers or canals at three points of the compass, only the southern side lay open to attack. It was accordingly decided to cut a ditch between the Nekomagawa and the Ikutama canal. It does not seem to have been a wet moat, because there was not enough time for the extra engineering that this would have required. Instead it was a wide, dry ditch, reinforced with palisades. A wall of earth and stone was constructed on its inner side, with gateways protected by angled walls at the points where major roads left the castle. At the eastern end of the new ditch a barbican was constructed. Named the Sanada-maru after the illustrious Sanada Yukimura, it consisted of a half-moon-shaped earthwork with wooden walls.

Every new siege made fresh demands upon the ingenuity of both besiegers and besieged, and the early 1580s saw two very different actions against castles. In 1581 at Tottori, a *yamashiro* with formidable stone walls, the weapon of starvation was used on an unprecedented scale. Kikkawa Tsuneie held out for 200 days, and surrendered only to save his men from having to eat each other. At Shizugatake in 1583, however, the situation was totally different. Shizugatake was one of a chain of Sengoku *yamashiro* raised north of Lake Biwa by Toyotomi Hideyoshi to protect his communications with Kyoto, and the means of attack adopted by Sakuma Morimasa show a very good understanding of the layout of a Sengoku *yamashiro* complex, because instead of making a frontal assault on the most forward of the castles, he made his way along the connecting ridge to the rear, capturing one castle at a time and then using it as a base for the next attack. The strategy would have succeeded had Hideyoshi not mounted a surprise rescue operation by night, catching Morimasa unprepared. Several sieges were involved in Hideyoshi's invasion of Kyūshū in 1587; the weapons used ranged from infantry assault to bribery and trickery, but a siege of the Shimazu headquarters of Kagoshima was avoided when surrender was negotiated.

CASTLES IN THE TŌHOKU SEKIGAHARA CAMPAIGN

The preliminary moves to the battle of Sekigahara in 1600 saw several castles change hands as both sides tried to establish fortified lines of communication. Gifu, Otsu and Fushimi experienced fierce fighting. Less well known are the sieges of the Tōhoku Sekigahara campaign, which is a convenient way of referring to the actions in the north-east of Japan (Tōhoku) fought in 1600 between supporters of Tokugawa Ieyasu and Ishida Mitsunari while these two leaders were engaging each other at Sekigahara.

The key player on the Ishida side in Tōhoku was Uesugi Kagekatsu (1555–1623) who controlled a domain worth 1,200,000 *koku* based round

THE ATTACK ON FUSHIMI CASTLE: 1600

This plate shows the famous defence of Fushimi Castle in 1600 by Torii Mototada. We see the influence that Azuchi had on 'ordinary' castles, approached from the point of view of defensive needs. The graceful superstructures look flimsy and very vulnerable to fire, but are in fact highly fire resistant, and the Japanese also lacked the means for effective artillery bombardment until quite late in their history. There are therefore no gun emplacements or casemates as such, and there would be few places inside Himeji, for example, where cannon could be mounted successfully. Instead the most common gunpowder weapons would be thousands of arquebuses with which an attacker or defender would sweep his opponent's lines. This would be followed by a massive infantry assault. One obvious disadvantage provided by the huge but gently sloping and curved walls of the typical castle stone base was the ease with which attackers could climb them, and the way in which the unmortared blocks of stone fitted together also provided numerous handholds. One solution was the incorporation into the design of towers of the stone-dropping holes noted above that were akin to European machicolations. Unlike machicolations, however, the *ishi otoshi* were closed by hinged doors. An additional deterrent to would-be climbers were rows of spikes pointing downwards from certain horizontal surfaces. (Peter Dennis © Osprey Publishing Ltd

Wakamatsu Castle (now modern Aizu-Wakamatsu). Uesugi Kagekatsu's retainers held several strongpoints to the north and east. The most important among these was Yonezawa, owned by Naoe Kanetsugu.

The keep of Matsue Castle, one of the best preserved of Japan's 'black castles'. Note in particular the extension of the stone base to form the walls of the entrance.

Kagekatsu's territory posed a close and substantial threat to Tokugawa Ieyasu's own power base in the Kantō. As Ishida Mitsunari was gathering forces in central Japan Ieyasu was faced with war on two fronts. His response was to delegate the control of Kagekatsu to Date Masamune and Mogami Yoshiaki. The first move of the campaign was made by Date Masamune, who attacked Shiroishi, the first castle in Uesugi territory. A period of calm followed during which each commander tried to discover the plans of his rival. The stalemate was finally broken when Naoe Kanetsugu moved against Mogami Yoshiaki's castle of Yamagata. In a brilliant display of co-ordination of his forces, Kanetsugu organized three separate armies to move against it. His main body of 20,000 men circled round to approach from the west, while his second division of 4,000 men under Hommura Chikamori headed straight towards Yamagata, a move that directed them first against the castle of Kaminoyama to the south of Yamagata, held by Satomi Minbu. Meanwhile a third army approached from Shonai to the north of Yamagata. This was under the command of Shima Yoshitada and consisted of 3,000 men.

Naoe Kanetsugu's main body first attacked the castle of Hataya, defended by the redoubtable Eguchi Gohei, as described in *Ou Eikei Gunki*:

> When he heard of the treacherous gathering at Aizu, he immediately replastered the wall and deepened the ditch, piled up palisades, arrows and rice, and waited for the attack … The vanguard were under the command of Kurogane Sonza'emonnojo, with 200–300 horsemen. He sounded the conch

and the bell to signal the assault. As those in Hataya were approached by the enemy they attacked them vigorously with bows and guns. Seventy of the enemy were killed in one go, and many were wounded. The deaths led to a change of plan, and the army who had tried to take the castle came to a halt.

Morale was helped during the attack when a ninja infiltrated the Naoe camp and brought back a battle flag, which was then flown in mocking triumph from the main gate. Naoe Kanetsugu eventually won owing to sheer weight of numbers, because Eguchi's garrison was only 300 strong. A short march eastwards the following day placed the Naoe army in a position from which they could besiege Hasedo, the last Mogami outpost before Yamagata. Kanetsugu was however unaware that the Mogami and Date forces had been shadowing his moves, and were almost ready to close in.

Hasedo was commanded by Mogami Yoshiaki's retainer Shimura Takaharu, who was determined to follow the fine example of loyalty shown at Hataya. Over the following 15 days he did just that, buying time for Date and Mogami as he waged a war of attrition against the besiegers. On learning of the approach of a relieving army Naoe Kanetsugu ordered an all-out attack on Hasedo Castle. His vanguard under Kasuga Mototada fought bravely but was stopped at the castle's outer defences by fierce arquebus fire. Kanetsugu then ordered a tactical withdrawal, but while this was happening a sortie was made from the castle and caught them in the rear.

Naoe Kanetsugu then apparently decided to discontinue the siege of Hasedo and attack Yamagata instead, but a very serious development occurred as he was on his way, because the news was brought to him of the defeat of the coalition forces at a place called Sekigahara. The cause was lost. The messenger ordered Naoe Kanetsugu to retreat to Yonezawa and safety.

Naoe Kanetsugu's rearguard was harassed as he moved south, eventually arriving at Uesugi Kagekatsu's castle of Wakamatsu. Throughout the whole of the Tōhoku Sekigahara campaign, Uesugi Kagekatsu, the great northern *daimyō* on whose behalf the campaign had been waged, had never left the safety of his own fortress. But if Kagekatsu thought that sitting idly by would endear him to the victorious Tokugawa then he was sadly wrong. In the redistribution of fiefs he lost Wakamatsu and was given Naoe Kanetsugu's fief of Yonezawa, his revenues being reduced by 900,000 *koku*.

OSAKA (1614) AND EUROPEAN ARTILLERY

During the Winter Campaign of Osaka in 1614–15, the Tokugawa made use of long-range artillery weapons acquired from European ships and bombarded Osaka's walls and keep. Toyotomi Hideyori had no comparable weapons and simply dispersed his cannon round the walls, but even the biggest ones were out of range of the Tokugawa lines. The first bombardment was carried out for three consecutive days at ten o'clock at night and at dawn. A nobleman

Above: Yokote Castle in Akita Prefecture was one of several castles burned to the ground during the Boshin War of 1868. Its keep has been rebuilt and provides a picturesque backdrop to the cherry blossoms.

in Kyoto noted in his diary that the sound of firing could be heard from there, and the psychological effects on the defenders of the castle soon proved to be far more important than any actual structural damage. The range of the European cannon meant that the domestic buildings, normally untouched until the final assault on a castle, could be attacked from the Tokugawa lines. One cannon, deliberately targeted on to the apartments used by Hideyori's mother Yodogimi, succeeded in dropping a cannon ball on to the tea cabinet she was using at the time. A later bombardment took out a wooden pillar, which crushed to death two of her ladies in waiting. Yodogimi was terrified, and as she exerted a considerable influence over her son the most decisive result of the Tokugawa bombardment was to bring the Toyotomi side to the negotiation table.

The fall of Osaka was decisive in bringing about the Tokugawa peace, and only one other serious rebellion involving a castle occurred during the next two centuries. This was the Shimabara Rebellion of 1638, where an army led by a Christian fanatic defied the *shōgun* for several months from the castle of Hara. There was some limited use made of artillery at Hara, including a rather reluctant bombardment from Dutch ships, but Hara eventually fell when starvation reduced the garrison's ability to fight. In the Akizuki Museum there is displayed the contemporary Shimabara Battle Screen, where we see in minute detail a 'citizens' army' defending the castle. Their activities are remarkably similar to those we read about in accounts of the Ikkō-ikki, with full participation from men, women and even children.

THE LAST SIEGES OF JAPANESE CASTLES

The short but bloody Boshin War of 1868-69 and the Satsuma Rebellion of 1877 not only saw the last ever sieges to be conducted against Japanese castles, but also resulted in the destruction of many of them.

The Boshin War ('the War of the Year of the Dragon') began when several diehard supporters of the Tokugawa *shōgun* refused to accept the fact that he had resigned and handed over his power to the new Meiji Emperor. They joined forces in the Ouetsu Reppan Domei (Northern Alliance), and much of the fighting pitted the Northern Alliance against the handful of *daimyō* in northern Japan who had chosen the imperial side. Foremost among these were the *han* that lay in what is now Akita Prefecture. Their armies were reinforced by soldiers from the *tozama han* such as Satsuma and Chōshū, and it was the operations against them that resulted in the destruction of many fine castles.

One of the first places to suffer as a result of the Northern Alliance assault was Shinjō Castle, which was burned to the ground after a brief attack. The Akita army retreated to Yokote, a castle protected in part by a river. Believing that Yokote could not be held, the Akita army soon abandoned it to the disgust of its young commander Tomura Daigaku, aged 19, who resolved to defend his castle with only the 280 men he had left against the Northern Alliance army of 3,000 men. Like a samurai of old, Tomura Daigaku personally killed two men before the castle fell. Most of the garrison escaped to the north, but Yokote Castle was destroyed.

Honjō Castle was the next to be wiped from the map, but in the case of Honjō the destruction was brought about by the retreating Akita army against the wishes of its *daimyō* the 20-year-old Rokugo Masaakira. On the day Honjō was burned the Kameda *han* further up the valley surrendered to the Northern Alliance. Its *daimyō*, Iwaki Takakuni, did not flee like the other *daimyō* but instead changed sides, yet this was not

Surely the finest combination of stone base and corner tower is the dramatic juxtaposition of the wall and the Uto tower at Kumamoto, which soars up from the dry moat. Kumamoto experienced the last major siege of a Japanese castle during the Satsuma Rebellion of 1877.

enough to save his magnificent Amasaki Castle. The Northern Alliance advance north was finally stalled at the Omonogawa, the wide river that provides a natural moat for Akita. Moves were made across it, but all were beaten back, while from out at the sea the Northern Alliance army was bombarded by the heavy guns of a Satsuma battleship, a foretaste of modern warfare.

The other main action of the Boshin War consisted of imperial forces moving against Northern Alliance armies in the Sendai and Aizu-Wakamatsu areas. The siege of Nihonmatsu saw a brave but futile resistance by a group of youths who found themselves in the position of being the only garrison the castle had left. At Aizu-Wakamatsu there occurred the famous suicide of the 'White Tiger Corps', another group of heroic young samurai, who watched helplessly as the castle burned. No fewer than 230 non-combatants committed suicide when Aizu-Wakamatsu Castle fell, including the entire family of Saigo Tanomo, a senior retainer of the Aizu *han*, whose mother, wife, five daughters and two sisters killed themselves.

The final resistance of the pro-Tokugawa forces was led by Hijikata Toshizō, the former leader of the Shinsengumi, the Tokugawa *shōgun*'s special force, who had recently faced an imperial attack at Utsunomiya Castle. During the course of the fighting Hijikata cut down one of his own men who attempted to flee and then took a bullet in his shoulder. He was carried from the battlefield as a wounded hero, but his injuries prevented him from fighting at Aizu-Wakamatsu.

When the Sendai *han* pledged allegiance to the Meiji government (an act Hijikata Toshizō regarded a the final betrayal), he and the remaining pro-Tokugawa army of 2,300 men headed for Hokkaidō, which was then called Ezo. Their destination was Japan's most modern castle – the pentagonal bastion of Goryōkaku near Hakodate. The fortress was officially in the

A frequent end to a siege of a castle would be the suicide of the wives and families of the defenders. In this life-sized diorama in the Aizu Buke-Yashiki in Aizu-Wakamatsu we see the tragic end of the family of Saigo Tanomo, a leading retainer of the *daimyō* of Aizu in 1868. His family made ready to kill themselves, and this tableau shows the moment when they were discovered by an officer from the Tosa *han*, wearing the bizarre red wig headdress that was Tosa's strange headgear. Saigo's wife begged him to kill her out of mercy, even though he was an enemy.

hands of the new Meiji government, but Hijikata's army easily defeated them and in December 1868 set up a Tokugawa 'government in exile' on Hokkaidō, which they called the Ezo Republic.

One of the first acts of the Ezo Republic was to demand the surrender of the castle of Matsumae. When this was refused Hijikata Toshizō led a force of about 800 men, who destroyed the castle with its recently reinforced walls using the modern weapons at their disposal in less than one day. But even more powerful weapons were to bring about the end of the Ezo Republic. This happened in 1869 in the shape of a formidable ironclad battleship called *Stonewall Jackson*, which the *shōgun* had once purchased from America. It had

lain at anchor off Yokohama until the foreign powers were satisfied that the new Meiji regime was the appropriate customer. The stage was then set for the most bizarre display of the art of the samurai swordsman in the whole of Japanese history, as Hijikata Toshizō prepared to capture a battleship. A large number of determined samurai managed to get on board but were mown down by gunfire, and the *Stonewall Jackson* sailed on at the head of the imperial navy, ready to land troops on Hokkaidō. The last stand of these remnants of the pro-Tokugawa army took place at Hakodate, where Hijikata Toshizō led sword charges against the besiegers' camp. With the city surrounded on all sides, Hijikata left the Goryōkaku fortress after composing a farewell poem, and was shot dead while on horseback as he led his troops into battle.

The last siege of any castle in Japan occurred during the Satsuma Rebellion of 1877, when Saigō Takamori's army attempted to capture Kumamoto. The first move against it was heralded by the rather quaint action of firing 'arrow letters' into the castle calling upon the defenders to surrender. The exhortations produced no response, so for the next two days furious attacks were carried out on the castle ramparts. The Satsuma samurai, their ancestral swords in hand, clambered up the walls like suicide squads to be shot down by the rifle fire from General Tani's imperial army. The siege developed into a war of attrition, and casualties mounted on both sides of Kumamoto's walls until the fortress was relieved.

Kumamoto had been built centuries earlier by Katō Kiyomasa, who had personal experience of a long siege in Korea and had built into Kumamoto's design several features to sustain the garrison should it ever be attacked. General Tani's brave defence of Kumamoto fully justified the confidence Katō Kiyomasa had placed in his great stronghold.

The walls of Kagoshima's Tsurumaru Castle, pock-marked with holes from rifle bullets, are a suitable memorial of the final operation to be conducted against any Japanese castle. This was where Saigō Takamori made his last stand in 1877 and committed suicide in the battle of Shiroyama.

JAPANESE CASTLES IN KOREA 1592-98

PART 4

INTRODUCTION: THE VERY SHORT HISTORY OF THE *WAJŌ*

Previous page: The siege
of Ulsan, as depicted on a
painted screen owned by
Saga Prefectural Museum
of History. It shows the
inner castle consisting of
four areas on the same level,
subdivided by walls and
gates. There are five corner
towers but no keep. The
towers are simple structures
with a wooden frame
and tiled roofs. The long
parapet walls topped
with tiles are pierced with
square loopholes. Within
the walls are simple wooden
buildings, some of which
are thatched. Use is also
made of *maku* (field
curtains) ornamented
with Katō Kiyomasa's *mon*.
Dead bodies lie everywhere,
and within one courtyard
the defenders are eating a
dead horse. Thousands of
Chinese soldiers are flinging
themselves at the walls.

The invasions of Korea in 1592 and 1597, the attempt at occupation between those two dates and the desperate rearguard action late in 1598 together make up a military operation unique in Japanese history. Apart from numerous pirate raids on China and Korea, some of which were very large in scope, and the annexation of Ryukyu (modern Okinawa Prefecture) by the Shimazu clan in 1609, the Korean expedition remains the only occasion within a period of a thousand years during which the destructive energies of the samurai were expended on a foreign country.

Japan's Korean expedition – known to Koreans as the Imjin War – was also the last military campaign to be set in motion by Toyotomi Hideyoshi, and was to prove a disastrous end to the glorious military career of a brilliant general who is regarded as Japan's equivalent of Napoleon Bonaparte. Having risen from the lowest ranks through a mixture of skill and opportunistic cunning, Hideyoshi was adored by his subordinates, who served him with a keen loyalty to a 'soldiers' general' that transcended the legendary fidelity expected of samurai. In this Hideyoshi had set them a fine example when he served as the most loyal and talented member of the inner circle of generals under Japan's first unifier, Oda Nobunaga. Nobunaga, an early enthusiast for the firearms introduced from Europe in 1543, had transformed Japanese warfare, and had taken the first steps towards reuniting the country from the patchwork of competing petty *daimyō*.

When Nobunaga was murdered in 1582, Toyotomi Hideyoshi became his avenger, and by a series of rapid offensives overcame his fellow generals to inherit Nobunaga's former domains. Three massive campaigns followed: the invasion of the island of Shikoku in 1585; the conquest of the island of Kyūshū in 1587; and the defeat of the powerful Hōjō family near modern Tokyo in 1590. Within a year all the other *daimyō* had submitted to him, so that by 1591 Japan was reunited under the son of a peasant.

186

The site of the *wajō* of Ulsan today, looking across the river from the south. The Japanese-style stone walls are obscured by the dense foliage. Ulsan marked the eastern end of the line and was incomplete when attacked by the Ming in 1598.

If Hideyoshi had been content to stop there, his place in Japanese history would have been assured. His campaigns of the 1580s had involved the successful deployment of armies numbered in many tens of thousands and their safe transport by sea. By 1591 everything looked possible to him, even the conquest of China, a dream that he had entertained for several years. Geography, if nothing else, suggested that to carry out such an outrageous scheme – which would have to be aimed at Beijing, the capital of the Ming dynasty – a Japanese invasion would have to proceed via the Korean Peninsula. When the Korean king refused to allow the Japanese unimpeded progress through his country, the planned Chinese war became a Korean war.

The invasion of Korea took place in May 1592 and involved an uninterrupted crossing of the sea via the islands of Iki and Tsushima. The first shots of the campaign were fired against the fortress guarding the harbour of Busan, a castle that would one day become one of the most important Japanese *wajō*. From here the First Division under Konishi Yukinaga proceeded northwards, taking two other future *wajō* at Dongnae and Yangsan. The Second Division under Katō Kiyomasa followed them along this route, while Kuroda Nagamasa's Third Division landed further to the west across Busan's great natural moat of the Nakdong River and captured Gimhae, another site that was to become a Japanese strongpoint.

A rapid advance followed, and within a few days Seoul, the Korean capital, had fallen to the Japanese. A delay at the Imjin River allowed the Korean king to escape to the Chinese border, but not long afterwards Konishi Yukinaga occupied Pyongyang, while Katō Kiyomasa set off on a campaign to pacify the north-east and to cross into Manchuria. The successful conquest of Korea was reported back to a satisfied Toyotomi Hideyoshi (who never left Japan during the entire campaign), and plans were rapidly drawn up for the occupation of Korea, the allocation of territory, the drafting of tax rolls and its inhabitants' incorporation under Hideyoshi's hegemony in much the same way that the Japanese *daimyō* had submitted to him in 1591.

WAJŌ IN SOUTH KOREA: 1593–98

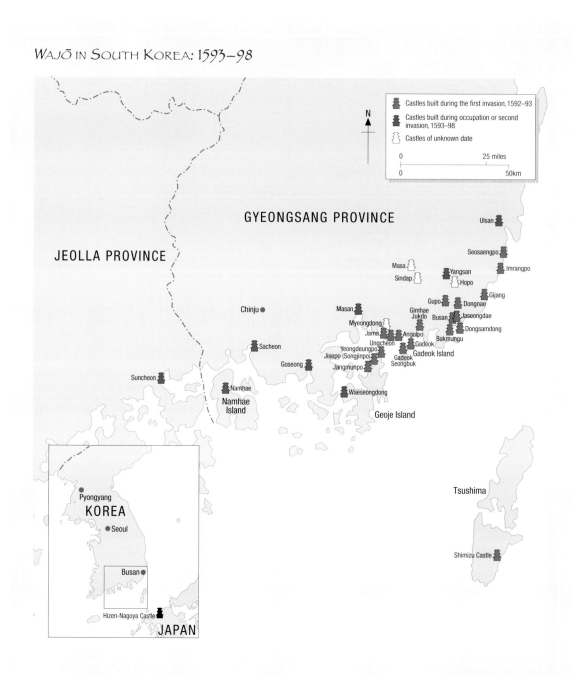

It was at that point that the counter-attack began, and Pyongyang, captured so easily by Konishi Yukinaga, was destined to be Japan's last outpost on the road to China. Three developments were to thwart Hideyoshi's dream of conquest. The first was the activity of Korean guerrillas, who were drawn from the shattered remnants of the army and fought under newly inspired leaders.

The *wajō* of Yangsan as viewed from the modern bridge over the Nakdong River, near the foot of the hill on which was built the *wajō* of Hopo. Hopo shared with Yangsan the defence of the Nakdong above Busan. Yangsan *wajō* was built along the ridge of the two prominent hills in the middle distance.

The second was the series of naval victories won by the renowned Admiral Yi Sunsin, whose heavily armed 'turtle ships' destroyed many Japanese vessels and disrupted communications with Japan. The third, and ultimately the most important development, was the intervention of Ming China. In a battle that was to prove the major turning point in the war Pyongyang was recaptured in February 1593. From this moment on the Japanese were involved in a fighting retreat. By the autumn of 1593 their invading armies had evacuated Korea, leaving behind a handful of garrisons to 'occupy' their remaining toehold on Korea's south coast. The fortresses from which this defiant illusion was to be maintained for the next five years were the first of the *wajō*.

A second invasion of Korea was launched in 1597. The main attacks were carried out to the west of the existing *wajō*, and the Japanese armies initially enjoyed a similar success to 1592. But this time the reverse was much swifter in coming, and the Japanese were to be on the defensive for most of the second campaign. A decisive intervention from China soon forced the Japanese back to the *wajō* line, which was extended westwards to Suncheon and eastwards to Ulsan. Ulsan was Japan's last *wajō* to be built, and was still unfinished when a Ming army attacked it in an epic siege early in 1598. Three other Chinese attacks followed later in the year. Two were launched against the *wajō* of Sacheon and Suncheon while another attempt was made against Ulsan, but before these operations were even under way Toyotomi Hideyoshi died peacefully in his sleep. The governing council that was to rule Japan during the minority of his son Hideyori decided to make a final withdrawal from Korea, but this did not happen before massive Chinese assaults were beaten off from these three key *wajō*. Almost the last Japanese contingent to leave Korea turned out to be the one under the command of Konishi Yukinaga, who had led the first assault in 1592. He first rescued some soldiers and sailors isolated in the *wajō* of Namhae by Korea's last naval victory at Noryang, and then supervised the evacuation of Busan. The last members of the invading army arrived back in Japan to hear the stunning news that their great leader was dead. Hideyoshi's dreams of conquest had died with him, leaving behind a devastated land and a line of abandoned castles, which were to become the monuments of a lost empire.

Design and
Development

THE KOREAN FORTIFICATION TRADITION
AND ITS SHORTCOMINGS

The *wajō* were castles built entirely in the Japanese style, a way of constructing fortresses – unique to that country – that was labour intensive, time consuming and architecturally demanding. The decision to reject the simpler native Korean style, which would have been easier and quicker to construct, was made by the invading generals based upon their experience of two years of warfare in Korea and their observations of the Korean fortresses that they had overcome.

There was certainly no shortage of examples for them to study, because the land that the Japanese invaded in 1592 was a country of fortresses. They fell into two categories. Like China and unlike Japan, Korean towns and cities had walls round them. These enclosed areas were called *eupseong*, and some had been built as a response to the Japanese *wako* (pirate) raids. Also, many mountain tops sported isolated mountain castles called *sanseong*, written using the same Chinese characters as the Japanese *yamashiro*.

It was the latter type of fortification that formed the main plank of the Korean government's defensive plan when the Japanese invasion appeared imminent. When danger threatened, the principle was to be 'strengthen the walls and clear the countryside'. It was a curious policy decision that dated from the time of the *wako* and did not mean that the peasants would simply move within the nearest *eupseong*. Instead they were to head for the distant *sanseong*. Anyone who failed to comply would be liable for arrest and execution on the grounds of collaboration with the Japanese. What happened was that because the *sanseong* were so far away, when a raid began the peasants buried everything in the nearby hills and waited in their villages for the Japanese to arrive, plunder and depart.

This bizarre situation had produced one unfortunate outcome even before the war started, because the peasants were so suspicious of the *sanseong* they failed to respond to commands to repair and maintain them. Men were

frequently called out for ten weeks of work, but their lack of skills meant that their efforts began to collapse almost as soon as they left. As a result the neglected and crumbling *sanseong* became even less attractive as a refuge, and when the 1592 invasion began the rapid Japanese advance caught the peasants undefended. Because the Korean army largely abandoned the towns for the *sanseong* the important population centres were lightly defended, leaving the main communication routes through Korea virtually unprotected. And this time, of course, the Japanese robbers did not simply plunder and withdraw.

This is not to say that the Korean *sanseong* suffered only from bad workmanship. They also had built-in design faults of which the Koreans themselves were acutely aware. The statesman Yu Seongnyong greatly admired the work of Qi Jiguang, the Chinese general who had fought the *wako* and then gone on to be the chief architect of the Great Wall of China. Yu despaired when he compared his own countrymen's pathetic efforts to Qi's magnificent creation for the Ming emperors. Instead of thinking about the best location for their walls, the Korean builders just followed the shape of the mountains and mountain paths to create a pastiche of the Great Wall where the turrets were too low to provide cover for their defenders, who had to crouch or lie down to move from place to place. There were no proper gun emplacements, the gaps in the parapet were wide enough to let an attacker climb in with ease, and there was no provision for crossfire and no loopholes. The stonework was also poor, leaving the walls prone to collapse or to destruction by an attacker.

Yu's pessimism about the weakness of traditional Korean military architecture was borne out within minutes of the Japanese landfall in Busan.

The hill of Jaseongdae as seen from the roof of the Kukje Hotel, looking south. Part of the inner harbour of Busan lies behind.

Busan Castle, an extension of the city wall on the edge of the sea, was in fact one of the best examples of a Korean fortress, but the Japanese were under the command of So Yoshitoshi, whose connections with Korea, facilitated by the location of his fief on Tsushima Island, must have given him an inside knowledge of the weakness of Korean castles and how to exploit them. The Japanese filled the moat with rocks and timber and climbed up scaling ladders under cover of a hail of bullets from thousands of arquebuses. When Kuroda Nagamasa attacked Gimhae shortly afterwards he filled the moat with bundles of cut barley. Dongnae, a *sanseong* a few kilometres to the north of Busan, proved no safer than Busan's *eupseong*, and when the Japanese reached Yangsan a few volleys from the massed arquebuses were enough to cause the defenders to flee. To Hideyoshi's men, the Korean fortress network looked like a pushover.

ADOPT, ADAPT, IMPROVE – THE FIRST JAPANESE CASTLES IN KOREA

As the Japanese raced for the capital the Korean fortresses fell before them like houses of cards, and in the optimistic climate that followed the fall of Seoul, Ukita Hideie, the 'Supreme Commander of Japanese Forces in Korea', established a line of communication forts between Busan and Pyongyang. For speed and convenience he did this by placing Japanese garrisons inside the captured Korean fortresses. The new occupiers of Korea were so confident of their continued success that the tactical weaknesses of the castles that their own armies had so recently exposed gave them no immediate cause for concern. The castle commanders were even allowed to have concubines with them, and a Korean attack on the castle of Yongin seemed only to confirm this optimistic view when Wakizaka Yasuharu led a contingent out of the gate and frightened the attackers away.

Yet as the months went by two ominous developments threatened their sense of security. First, Admiral Yi Sunsin's naval victories meant that the Japanese advance north of Pyongyang was stalled partly owing to a lack of support by sea. Although these battles happened far from the inland communication castles, the news inevitably reached their commanders, but of more immediate concern to the castle garrisons were the attacks they were now experiencing from guerrilla bands. In spite of the Japanese superiority with handheld firearms, these sudden raids vividly exposed the inherent weaknesses of the Korean fortresses, and the Korean guerrillas began to knock holes in the Japanese land communications as efficiently as Admiral Yi was disrupting their communications by sea.

One operation is of particular interest. This was the action conducted against the fortress of Mugye, which lay where the Japanese line actually crossed the Nakdong to the west of Daegu. The interesting point is that Mugye was not a former Korean possession, but a castle newly built by the Japanese commander Mōri Terumoto. In this sense Mugye was technically the first *wajō*, and was built at about the time of Japan's first defeat on land at

GUPO: BUILDING A CASTLE FOR RIVER DEFENCE

The castle of Gupo was built to support the larger fortress of Gimhae Jukdo further downstream on the Nakdong River. It provided defence for the Busan area from the north. This plate shows the site of Gupo being prepared in traditional Japanese style whereby the existing hillside was carved away and clad in stone. No superstructure has as yet been added, but the site is a hive of activity with labour being provided by Korean captives and press-ganged Japanese peasants. Under normal conditions in Japan the whole site would be cleared before the stone is added, but these are not normal conditions, and every day counts. (Peter Dennis © Osprey Publishing Ltd)

the battle of Euryeong, although we do not know whether or not Mugye was built in the Japanese style. Its garrison held off one assault by Korean volunteers soon after it was completed, but several months later Mugye was abandoned in the face of another Korean attack.

It would, however, be incorrect to conclude that the subsequent creation of the *wajō* in a purely Japanese style was solely due to the bruising experiences in attack and defence that the Japanese had been through in 1592. Certainly the Korean fortresses had fallen easily to Japanese firepower. Certainly some Japanese-occupied Korean fortresses had then fallen or been abandoned to the

Koreans, but there were several instances when Korean fortresses had resisted massive Japanese attacks. The classic example is the first siege of Jinju, with its high walls and strong gates, which was defended successfully in Korea's greatest land victory of the war. The conclusion might therefore have been reached that Korean castles could be strong enough for Japanese purposes provided they were properly defended. But that was not the conclusion that was drawn, and this came about because of what happened during the first few days of 1593.

On 5 January 1593 the vanguard of the Ming army crossed the Yalu River with a mission to liberate Korea. The winter was regarded as an ideal time for campaigning because the frozen ground allowed the Chinese to transport their artillery with ease. The Koreans warned them of the reverses they had suffered from the Japanese firearms, but the Chinese general Li Rusong replied, 'Japanese weapons have a range of a few hundred paces while my great cannon have a range of five or six *li* (about 2.5km). How can we not be victorious?' It was a prophetic statement, because the liberation of Pyongyang by the Ming was the turning point in the Korean invasion, and set in motion a Japanese retreat interrupted by a handful of rearguard victories. The *wajō* line was essentially a response to the Chinese advance, and provided the last refuge for the occupying troops. The new fortresses may have had roles concerned with communications and harbour defence, but the principle underlying their creation was that of providing a final toehold on the Korean Peninsula.

THE CREATION OF THE *WAJŌ*

In the furious building programme that established the *wajō* line, some castles were created by rebuilding Korean fortresses that already enjoyed an important strategic location. Others were completely new projects, such as Ungcheon, which was built on a mountain overlooking the harbour about a kilometre from the weak Ungcheon *eupseong*. Admiral Yi was particularly impressed by Ungcheon, and noted that: 'The enemy had built long walls on the eastern and western mountainsides where he took up positions planted with multi-coloured war banners, and rained gunfire towards us in a haughty manner.' Yi Sunsin in fact raided Ungcheon four times, but as his ship-to-shore bombardment was not supported by land operations no real damage was done either to the Japanese soldiers or to their building programme. 'The enemy battalions hide themselves in fortifications and will not come out', wrote Yi, thereby summing up the Japanese High Command's current strategic mentality for the entire fortified line.

Yi Sunsin also recorded a great deal of activity round the ports, but misunderstood its purpose. He thought that what he was witnessing was an operation designed to cover a complete Japanese withdrawal, and accordingly held back from any major attack until the transports began to sail back to Japan. He would then engage them at sea and inflict huge damage. But intelligence brought to him by a number of escaped Korean prisoners of war painted a very

The dramatic promontory on which the *wajō* of Ungcheon was built, viewed from across the strategic harbour that the *wajō* defended so well. The mouth of the harbour has now been partially closed owing to the extensive land reclamation works around Ungcheon.

different picture and finally convinced him. 'The enemy is increasing in number and he is building bunkers and spreading tents twice as much as before', reported one man. Another noted the transport of 'war provisions and clothing from Japan'. Yi sadly concluded that 'he is going to spend another winter in our country, to our great mortification'. The loyal admiral was correct in his conclusion, but would have been even more mortified had he known that it was not one more year that the Japanese would stay, but five.

By the end of 1593 at least 18 out of the final 30 *wajō* had been created to secure the Japanese gains. The castle that lay furthest to the east was mighty Seosaengpo, with two other coastal forts, Imrangpo and Gijang, lying back towards Busan, where four *wajō* defended Busan harbour and the strategic Dongnae, built over a Korean site, lay just inland. Gimhae Jukdo and its dramatically situated subsidiary Gupo covered the Nakdong River just above Busan. The important waterway between Geoje Island and the mainland, a sea area plagued by Admiral Yi, was defended by three *wajō* on Geoje Island, two on Gadeok Island and four (Ungcheon, Myeongdong, Jama and Angolpo) on the mainland. These, with the addition of a few minor support castles, sufficed for the time of the Japanese occupation between 1593 and 1597.

The second invasion of Korea in 1597 was launched with the help of the existing *wajō* bases, and was directed at the 'virgin territory' of Jeolla Province. The capture of Namweon gave the Japanese a foothold in a part of Korea that had been relatively untouched during the first invasion. To consolidate their new gains the *wajō* of Suncheon, Sacheon, Goseong and Namhae, together with a replacement *wajō* on Geoje Island and a new castle at Masan, enhanced Japan's coastal defences west of Ungcheon. Two other *wajō* were built at Yangsan and Hopo to extend the defences up the Nakdong River, while Ulsan, to the north of Seosaengpo, literally became the end of the line. Over the next 18 months the *wajō* line experienced the full range of furious military activity from construction or rebuilding to siege and eventual abandonment.

STRUCTURAL AND ARCHITECTURAL FEATURES OF THE *WAJŌ*

Wherever they were built, and regardless of what existing Korean structures they were replacing, the *wajō* represented the transfer of Japanese castle styles into the continental environment. By the time of the Korean invasion the basic features of Japanese castle design had become well established, and had been used so often in Japan itself that when a new site for a castle was chosen the requirements for its construction could be assessed very rapidly. This was very important in the Korean context where the danger of attack was imminent.

In Japan there was only a very limited tradition of fortifying towns by building walls round them. Contemporary Kyoto was defended by its Odoi of earthworks and palisades, but had nothing resembling a 'city wall'. Instead the process of urbanization tended to happen in reverse. A successful fortified structure, chosen for strategic reasons, offered security and economic promise, so towns tended to develop around the castles as a defended community. The growth of the *jinaimachi* or temple towns associated with the self-governing communities of Jōdo Shinshū and defended by their Ikkō-ikki armies provides the best example.

A similar development of castle towns would eventually occur around some of the *wajō* sites in Korea, but the initial considerations behind building them were purely military. The process began with the selection and rapid survey of a mountain or large hill, but instead of then building snake-like stone walls in the Korean style, the main tool used in Japanese castle construction was the spade. By digging out soil and piling it up elsewhere the mountain was almost literally carved up like a gigantic sculpture to produce a system of interlocking baileys on different levels. The excavated soil and stones would be used to create extra lines outside the central castle area that followed the overall pattern of walls and ditches, or to build up carved sections and give even greater height. Many weird and wonderful combinations were created to hinder and trap an

The 'proto-*wajō*' of Shimizu above the port of Izuhara on the island of Tsushima. Shimizu, which consists of three baileys on very high ground, was the last friendly base before Korea, and served as a prototype for the *wajō*.

attacker. One favourite was the 'tiger's mouth', a defended gateway involving a 90-degree turn. Surviving examples in Korea are at Seosaengpo and Ungcheon.

The well-established techniques of castle construction described above, in particular the use of huge sloping stone bases, produced a style of fortress instantly recognizable as a 'Japanese castle'. It was so different from Korean and Chinese models that Yu Seongnyong refers to the unfamiliar appearance of the *wajō* twice in *Chingbirok* (*The Book of Corrections*), his account of why Korea failed:

> The enemy built clay walls with holes on top of their fortress, which looked like a beehive. They fired their muskets through those holes as much as they could, and as a result, a number of Chinese soldiers were wounded.

And elsewhere:

> As I observed, the stronghold of the enemy was very quiet, and I could hardly see any activity. They did not build battlements on top of their fortress; instead, they made a long corridor all around [the fortress walls]. The guards of the enemy stayed inside that corridor and from there discharged their muskets whenever their opponents approached, pouring down bullets. Every day this kind of battle was repeated, and the bodies of Chinese soldiers and our own began to pile up under the walls of the fortress.

An escaped Korean prisoner of war observed the construction of the three *wajō* on Geoje Island. The information he fed back to Admiral Yi Sunsin confirms the techniques the Japanese used:

Arriving at Yeongdeungpo on Geoje Island I saw about 200 houses newly built at three places on the archery grounds on the shore and under [Mount] Bukbong. They felled trees on Bukbong and levelled the ground to build a wide circular mud wall, inside which houses were being built. ... In Jangmunpo and Songjinpo also they levelled the mountains and built mud-walls and houses there, with their large and medium boats moored under the rocky cliffs.

Being designed for coastal defence, a typical *wajō* consisted of an inner castle built on a hill overlooking a harbour, with most of its structures having been created by carving up the hill and cladding it in stone in classic Japanese fashion, although if there was extensive bedrock this would be built into the structure. Nearly all the *wajō* had keeps and towers, and the larger *wajō* such as Seosaengpo and Suncheon would have looked no different from the castles the samurai had left behind in Japan. Most also had very extensive outer works, particularly where harbour defence was needed. To have built these with stone was too expensive in terms of time alone, so stone-based outer walls are only found in the most elaborate models such as Seosaengpo. Ditches and embankments built without stone were otherwise created. Long white plastered walls along the mounds would have been built wherever possible, but otherwise simple wooden fences and palisades would have had to suffice. These simpler walls would have had wooden observation towers built along the line, while many other wooden buildings for use as barracks, stables and storage would have been dotted about inside. In this the outer works of the *wajō* were little different from wartime extensions to Japanese castles back home. When the defences of Osaka were enhanced in preparation for the great siege of 1614–15 similar time constraints meant that the new outer walls were largely earthworks with ditches and wooden palisades. The typical *wajō*, therefore, was a Japanese castle that may have been as palatial in its inner quarters as a *daimyō*'s own fortress, but was defended on its outer perimeter by simpler structures reminiscent of castles of the early 16th century before stone was used extensively.

Because of their primary location at harbours the *wajō* most resembled Japanese castles that had a similar seaside location, although we do not find elaborate seawater moats in Korea. One feature found at some *wajō* was the existence of a 'mother' castle linked by a walkway of some kind to a smaller 'child' castle. This may have been done simply because of

The *tora no guchi* (tiger's mouth) gateway that passes through one of the inner walls of Ungcheon. This lies almost at the top of the main hill on which Ungcheon was built.

the proximity of two hills, but it also provided an extra form of defence for the harbour. Gijang provides an excellent surviving example.

All these techniques needed time and manpower. The Japanese were short of the former, but had the latter in great abundance: either from captured Korean civilians or Japanese peasants brought over as labourers and treated every bit as badly as their Korean counterparts. This was one reason why the *wajō* were built in a comparatively short space of time, but another factor was the long experience that the Japanese architects and designers brought to the task. In terms of concept and overall design, if not in actual structure, the *wajō* were therefore 'prefabricated buildings', and it was only through the use of the local lie of the land that any was a 'one off'.

An interesting link between the design of native Japanese castles and the *wajō* that replicated them may be traced through the castles built in Kyūshū and on the islands of Iki and Tsushima to support the invasion. Hizen-Nagoya Castle (as distinct from the other Nagoya Castle built a decade later in central Japan by the Tokugawa family) was the base from which the invasion was launched and the principal staging post from which reinforcements and supplies were channelled to Korea. It was built in a remarkably short space of time on a hill overlooking the port of Yobuko near Karatsu. The complete Hizen-Nagoya consisted of an enormous Japanese castle surrounded by the camps – effectively villages – that were used by the various *daimyō* who supplied men for the invasion. In the months leading up to the 1592 operation tens of thousands of men from all over Japan were housed there.

Less well known are the castles built on Iki and Tsushima for the same purpose of supporting the invasion. Both were like prototype *wajō*. The castle on Iki was on a mountain overlooking the harbour of Katsumoto at the island's northernmost point. There was probably some form of fortification already there when Hideyoshi ordered the building of a castle, which followed the usual Japanese pattern of a sculpted core clad in stone. The 'prototype' of Shimizu on Tsushima guards the harbour of Izuhara. The Sō family, who had important connections with Korea (both legal and piratical), ruled Tsushima from their existing castle of Kaneishi, which was probably a low-lying fortress designed for harbour defence, backed up by a number of lookout posts high on the mountains behind Izuhara. Kaneishi had been sufficient for Sō Yoshitoshi's own purposes, but in 1592 Tsushima became the final jumping-off point for the Korea invasion, so more was needed. The lookout tower on the mountain immediately adjacent to the harbour was replaced by a three-bailey, stone-clad castle, which was given the name of Shimizu. It would have been connected to newly strengthened harbour defences. In this it anticipated the pattern of the rapid utilization of strategic high ground for coastal defence that would become the norm in Korea.

THE *WAJŌ* AS A DEFENSIVE SYSTEM

Once established as a defensive toehold in 1593, the strategic role of the *wajō* was fivefold:

1. To provide communication with Japan to safeguard the inflow of reinforcements and supplies.

2. To deny harbours and moorings to the Korean Navy.

3. To provide a limited policing role during the occupation of Korea.

4. To provide the means for a rapid advance once the armies had landed (in the second invasion).

5. Finally, to provide a refuge against Chinese attacks, and then some security for the evacuation.

SAFE HARBOURS AND SECURE MOORINGS

Besides any communications role, the sheer existence of the *wajō* denied territory to the enemy on rivers, islands and coasts, and even though that territory was very small in area it was strategically very important to Korea, whose greatest strength was its navy. The Japanese had learned the hard way that if Admiral Yi caught them in the open sea, as he did in the decisive battle of Hansando in 1592, then they would be annihilated. Several of Yi's earlier victories involved his turtle ships luring the Japanese fleet out into open water and attacking them. From the Japanese point of view a turning point in the struggle was the use of coastal defences during Yi's attack on Busan harbour in September 1592. This time the Japanese did not sail out in pursuit, but counter-attacked from the fortifications they had created out of the castles

The site of the *wajō* of Suncheon looking from the sea, a view made possible by the recent land reclamation project. The promontory on which Suncheon was built is very noticeable from this angle.

they had captured during the first landing. Yi failed to make any impression on the defences.

In spite of all the individual firepower possessed by its ships, the Korean navy was limited in what it could do because of its need for night-time moorings. Once they realized this, the Japanese generals concluded that if they secured the coast of Gyeongsang Province with their *wajō* then Yi would not be able to base himself near enough to the major communication routes with Japan to threaten the Japanese ships. The raids on Ungcheon provided a good illustration of the Korean dilemma, because in spite of several attacks from the sea Yi was unable to control this vital harbour, and therefore did not dare advance into the waters to the east of Ungcheon, let alone launch another attack on Busan. Had he been able to destroy Busan, the partial Japanese evacuation of 1593 would have been as complete and as final as the one of 1598. Instead Busan continued to act as the main Japanese base in Korea with little fear of disruption.

The view from the magnificent ruins of Seosaengpo, looking towards the sea. Seosaengpo was the most important Japanese castle on the east coast of Korea. Fragments of the stone wall of the inner bailey appear in the foreground.

POLICING AND DEFENCE

During the occupation a policing role developed along with the denial of harbours, but when the Japanese invaded again in 1597 they found that they had even less to worry about from the Korean navy. Because of political intrigue at court, Yi had been temporarily suspended from his post. The inept Weon Gyun took his role as Korea's naval commander. When the second invasion happened the Korean fleet wandered round the seas off Korea's southern coast doing very little, and then Weon Gyun lost his life and much of the Korean navy in a battle in the straits to the north of Geoje Island. Meanwhile the Japanese used the *wajō* as splendid 'jumping-off points'.

By the time Admiral Yi was reinstated the *wajō* line had been extended to provide further bases from which Japanese attacks could be directed. But the situation soon changed, and any 'offensive' role envisaged for the new *wajō* was flung suddenly into reverse. Their garrisons now had to face the prospect of attacks from Chinese armies on a much more massive scale than the operations that had caused the evacuation in 1593, and the Ming army was now supported by a revitalized Korean navy. The *wajō* therefore had to be able to withstand attack from the land as well from the sea, so their defensive role became paramount, until, at the very end of the war, they served only as last-ditch structures from which the Japanese troops could be safely taken home.

Within this overall strategic role it is possible to further classify the 30 *wajō* by dividing them into four general categories according to their individual functions:

JAPANESE HEADQUARTERS
After the evacuation of Seoul, Busan became the base for all Japanese operations in Korea. The four *wajō* round the harbour may be regarded as a unity, with links to Dongnae, the coastal forts and the Nakdong garrisons. The Busan 'complex' was the only part of the *wajō* system to fall into this category.

THE DEFENSIVE MODEL
Here the emphasis was on providing a safe anchorage for Japanese ships. The accent was totally defensive, with strong walls around the *wajō*, extending to the harbour with no reduction in defensive capability. Seosaengpo, which dates from the first invasion, is the best example. Its walls reached right down to the rocky cliffs beside the harbour from a powerful castle defended on the landward side by a cliff.

THE SPEARHEAD MODEL
These were the *wajō* designed to provide safe anchorage but with a more pronounced accent on the offensive. From *wajō* such as these attacks could be launched with ease, but a base was available into which the raiding parties could withdraw. Suncheon is the best example.

Certain of the smaller *wajō*, particularly those not built on coasts or estuaries, were designed to provide support to a major fortress or to act as communication links. Sindap and Masa, which supported Gimhae Jukdo; and Jama, which supported Ungcheon, are good examples. Most of these *wajō* were arranged in groups that could provide mutual support. The Nakdong River line and the Ungcheon/Geoje/Gadeok group are good examples of such a relationship.

COMMANDERS AND GARRISONS

One vital factor in defending a *wajō* was the size and quality of its garrison, and throughout the war we find the names of Japan's most experienced generals in command of *wajō*. They would be in charge of troops drawn from their own domains, whose flags bore that commander's *mon*. No commands stayed the same for the whole of the six years. Nor, for that matter, did the number of the *wajō* or their locations. As circumstances changed so did the number of *wajō* in the line. Some were abandoned, others newly built.

By the end of June 1593, 17 *wajō* had been created. This was quite a large number, but the main reason for spreading the occupying forces between 17 forts was to allow for more successful foraging. It was a lesson that had been learned the hard way, because when the Japanese retreated from Seoul their supplies had quickly run out. The initial disposition of the command for these *wajō* was as follows:

WAJŌ	COMMANDER
Seosaengpo	Katō Kiyomasa
Imrangpo	Mōri Yoshinari, Shimazu Tadatoyo, Ito Yubei, Takahashi Mototane, Akizuki Tanenaga
Gijang	Kuroda Nagamasa
Dongnae	Kikkawa Hiroie
Busan group	Mōri Terumoto
Gimhae Jukdo	Nabeshima Naoshige
Gadeok Island group	Kobayakawa Takakage, Tachibana Muneshige and others
Angolpo	Wakizaka Yasuharu, Kuki Yoshitaka, Kato Yoshiaki and others
Ungcheon	Konishi Yukinaga
Myeongdong	Matsuura Shigenobu
Jama	Sō Yoshitomo
Yeongdeungpo	Shimazu Yoshihiro
Jangmunpo	Fukushima Masanori, Toda Katsukata, Chosokabe Motochika
Jisepo	Hachisuka Iemasa, Ikoma Chikamasa

SUNCHEON: THE SPEARHEAD STYLE

The castle of Suncheon is the best example of the so-called 'spearhead model' that was intended to provide a base for further penetration into Korea rather than just defensive purposes. For this reason it is a very extensive and confident building, and resembles a fully developed castle in Japan. The insert shows the principle behind the spearhead.
(Peter Dennis © Osprey Publishing Ltd)

In August 1593 a review was carried out of the size of garrisons to be stationed at each *wajō*, and it was decided to place 5,000 men in the larger castles and between 2,000 and 3,000 men in the smaller ones, making a grand total for the occupying forces of about 43,000 men, all of whom were based inside *wajō*.

A rotation system was in operation for the garrisons, as revealed in September 1593 by an escaped Korean prisoner of war who gave Admiral Yi a concise account of the garrison plan of the *wajō* and the rotation

An old photograph of Jaseongdae *wajō*, the 'child castle' of Busan.

mechanism. 'Half of their numbers defend their fortified walls and half returned home', he said. 'Those who defend the walls will also go home in the third moon of next year on arrival of their reliefs.' In a Memorial to Court dated 8 January 1594 Admiral Yi reported to the king on his own up-to-date observations of the *wajō* situation:

> The retreating Japanese robbers still occupy the southern coastal area without the least sign of evacuation. Judging from their movements no one can tell their unfathomable strategic plans. The increasing Japanese robbers on Geoje Island dig more dens, with their vessels moored deep in the ports as their boats busily ply up and down the sea entrances, threatening to come out with surprise attacks at any moment.

A month later Yi received a report which recorded active building work taking place on Geoje Island, by 'hundreds of Japanese taking positions in

A reconstructed gate and wall section of the Hōjō fortress of Hachigata. Very similar structures would have been seen in Korea.

barracks outside Jisepo and Okpo, pitching tents in fours and fives in never ending lines at strategic points in the fields'. The Japanese were also seen 'moving about in scattered companies in the daytime and signalling to each other with torches at night'. A separate report from Weon Gyun supported the observations that the barracks construction was in full swing 'amid the booming of guns'.

These arrangements continued throughout the occupation, but towards the end of the period many Japanese troops were withdrawn from Korea to assure the Ming peace negotiators that Japan was in good faith about reaching a negotiated settlement. The garrison strengths then shrunk considerably, but peaceful intentions were quickly forgotten in the months immediately preceding the second invasion, when the number of troops in Korea was increased to 20,390 to facilitate a rapid advance. Kobayakawa Hideaki, the adopted son of Kobayakawa Takakage, who had died in 1596, now commanded the main garrison of 10,390 men in Busan. Hideaki was then only 15 years old and owed his early promotion to the fact that he was the nephew of Hideyoshi. The other 10,000 left 'holding the fort' in preparation for a new advance were:

WAJŌ	COMMANDER	TROOPS
Angolpo	Tachibana Munetora	5,000
Gadeok Island	Takahashi Saburo	1,000
Seosaengpo	Asano Chokei	3,000
Gimhae Jukdo	Kobayakawa Hidekane	1,000

These *wajō* provided easy landings in Korea for the extra 121,100 men who invaded Korea for the second time in March 1597. Kobayakawa Hideaki was assisted by the 18-year-old Mōri Hidemoto, who replaced his cousin Terumoto. The veteran Katō Kiyomasa came ashore with his troops at Gimhae Jukdo. Konishi Yukinaga landed at Busan and headed west to the *wajō* of Angolpo, which was to be the main naval base during the second invasion.

The reversal to Japanese fortunes at the hands of Admiral Yi and a new Ming invasion came surprisingly soon after the landings, and led to an urgent reappraisal of the *wajō* line. Once again the line was changed to a new system consisting of only 14 fortresses. They were, however, spread out further than ever, and stretched as far west as Suncheon to encompass Namhae, Sacheon, Goseong, Waeseongdong, Masan, Gimhae Jukdo, Busan, Yangsan and Seosaengpo. The final *wajō*, that of Ulsan, was begun at this time. Waeseongdong was a new *wajō* on Geoje Island. It was built overlooking the strategic Gyonnaerang Strait and replaced the other three *wajō* on Geoje.

Busan and its support castles initially held 40,000 men under Mōri Hidemoto and Ukita Hideie. There was little activity for a few months after the epic winter siege of Ulsan, so on 26 June 1598 Hideyoshi recalled roughly half of his troops to Japan, including those men led by Ukita Hideie, Mōri Hidemoto and Hachisuka Iemasa. Kobayakawa Hideaki was also recalled, leaving the *wajō* line in its final form as:

WAJŌ	COMMANDER	TROOPS
Ulsan	Katō Kiyomasa	10,000
Seosaengpo	Kuroda Nagamasa	5,000
Busan	Mōri Yoshinari	5,000
Gimhae Jukdo and Masan	Nabeshima Naoshige and Katsushige	12,000
Waeseongdong	Yanagawa Tsunanobu	1,000
Goseong	Tachibana Muneshige	7,000
Sacheon	Shimazu Yoshihiro	10,000
Namhae	Sō Yoshitomo	1,000
	Total	61,000

THE *WAJŌ*'S DEFENSIVE ARMAMENTS

Handheld firearms in the form of matchlock arquebuses were the main means of defence of the *wajō*, just as they had been the main means of attack on the Korean fortresses in 1592. In contrast to the popular myth that the samurai regarded gunpowder weapons as dishonourable, the pragmatic generals used volleys of thousands of bullets to clear the walls of a castle to allow the sword-wielding samurai to scale the parapets and engage in hand-to-hand combat. The latter could not have been undertaken without the former, and a letter home from Korea sent by Shimazu Yoshihiro in November 1592 makes the position abundantly clear. 'Please arrange to send us guns and ammunition', he wrote; 'there is absolutely no use for spears.'

Siege cannon, either on a large European scale or on a smaller Chinese scale, were both unknown and unnecessary in the Japanese context. The stone bases that constituted Japanese castles were not the sort of walls that cannon could batter down, so Hideyoshi's army took nothing resembling a siege train with it, and it was therefore fortunate for the Japanese that the easily scalable walls were not able to withstand a Japanese assault with arquebuses. Strangely enough, cannon did not defend the Korean castles, even though heavy cannon were mounted on Korean ships, whose broadsides created havoc on the heavily laden Japanese transports. Not surprisingly, Yi fired on the walls of

Seosaengpo, the greatest of the early *wajō*, has this long wall that enclosed its inner bailey. It is the largest surviving fragment of any *wajō*.

the *wajō* from his ships, but was then surprised to find his fire being returned. What the Japanese had done was to mount captured Korean cannon on the *wajō*. From this time on cannon played a role in *wajō* defence, and there exists a fascinating diagram for Ulsan that sets out the angles and range of fire that could be brought to bear both from Ulsan and against it.

Apart from firearms and bows, the main means of defence of a *wajō* was through the use of cold steel, either in the form of the famous samurai sword, the long spear (*yari*), or the curved-bladed spear called a *naginata*. Ingenious use was also made of broken or discarded swords, including the Chinese blades that were considered so inferior, to create a sharp barrier as part of the defences. Records exist of the breakdown of weaponry in the two grades of *wajō* at the start of the occupation, as shown in the following table:

	LARGE *WAJŌ*	SMALL *WAJŌ*
Garrison size	5,000	2,000
Firearms (including)	200	100
Large caliber	1	1
50 *monme*	10	10
30 *monme*	10	5
20 *monme*	10	5
13 *monme*	4	2
6 *monme*	10	10
2.5 *monme*	150	72
Saltpetre	450 kin	400 kin
Gunpowder	800 kin	400 kin
Bullets	4,500	4,000
Lead	450 kin	400 kin
Sulphur	45 kin	40 kin
Bows	300	100
Arrows	6,000	2,000
Swords	450	400
Suits of armour	17	15
Helmets	10	7
Spears	200	100

One *monme* is 3.75g while 1 *kin* is 160 *monme*, or 0.6kg

On his visit to Pyongyang Yu Seongnyong noted that: 'The spears and swords that the Japanese had set up on the battlements, pointed at the Chinese soldiers, looked like the needles of a porcupine.' We encounter this means of augmenting defences again at Ulsan. Yoshimi Hiroyuki, aged 15 in one account and 18 in another, who 'excelled in the way of bow and arrow', ordered his *ashigaru* to draw the enemy on but not to waste their arrows, and led an impetuous charge that covered the retreat:

> After a short while Yoshimi returned to the safety of the castle, and seeing that the gateway of the section of the defence works for which he was responsible was looking in a poor state, he ordered his retainers to construct a low wall by using the various large and small swords that had been collected, thus producing a rampart of spikes.

THE *WAJŌ* FROM END TO END

The following gazetteer of all the *wajō* sites is based upon the excavation reports carried out by the Wajō Kenkyu Kai and other organizations, together with my own fieldwork observations. The name of the *wajō* as it appears in contemporary Japanese chronicles, where known, is in brackets after the *wajō* name. Further details may be found in the captions to the illustrations.

THE BUSAN HARBOUR DEFENCES

Busan was the nerve centre of the support system for the invasion of Korea from the moment of its capture, and the headquarters for the entire operation once Seoul was abandoned in 1593.

BUSAN *WAJŌ* (FUSANKAI)
Sadly, less survives of Busan *wajō* than of any other major Japanese fortress, which is largely due to the development of South Korea's most important harbour city. As most of the area is now built over, excavation has been very limited, so any conclusions about the appearance of the historic castle are based on old maps and the fragments of the walls that still survive in what is now a public park. Busan *wajō* consisted of three baileys, with a keep at the western corner of the inner bailey. A long stone wall ran down the hill towards the sea at the southern end. It is probable that Busan *wajō* was built on the site of a Korean *sanseong*, which may have been physically connected to the city walls beside the harbour itself.

JASEONGDAE
As shown in the accompanying map from 1919 (see p.212), to the east of Busan *wajō* lay another hill right at the water's edge, and this was to provide the location for Busan's secondary castle now known as Jaseongdae. The name means 'the child castle' as distinct from the 'mother castle' of Busan *wajō*.

THE *WAJŌ* FROM END TO END

The perfectly preserved base of the keep of Suncheon, from which a tree now grows in place of the graceful white superstructure that would have dominated the site.

Jaseongdae was created out of the fortress captured by Sō Yoshitoshi during the first assault. At that time its walls were lapped by the sea, and formed a continuation of the *eupseong* that defended Busan. The Japanese demolished the Korean fortress and the *wajō* was erected in its place. Again we see three baileys, but on a much smaller scale than the 'mother castle'. Almost the whole of the elevated area where the castle stood remains intact, although it is covered with trees and only small sections of the *wajō* walls remain. The flat upper surface of the inner bailey is still there. Jaseongdae originally had four gates, two of which have been restored in Korean style, which would have been the appearance they had when the Japanese attacked. These gates may well have been retained when the Korean castle was converted into a *wajō*.

BAKMUNGU

The 'mother' and 'child' castles of Busan protected the inner harbour, but to reach that area any attack from the sea would have had to pass Yeong Island, which is dominated by Mount Bongnae (395m). The small *wajō* of Bakmungu was built on the mainland directly across the strait from Yeong Island at its narrowest point. It has since completely disappeared.

DONGSAMDONG

Dongsamdong, otherwise known as Yeongdo from the island on which it lay, occupied a hill on the water's edge on the eastern shore of Yeong Island. Together with Bakmungu all shipping entering Busan harbour could be monitored. There is almost nothing left of the buildings, but the promontory on which it was built has so far escaped being built upon.

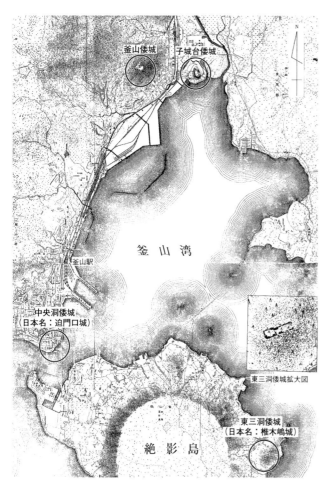

釜山倭城
子城台倭城

釜山湾

釜山駅

中央洞倭城
(日本名：迫門口城)

東三洞倭城拡大図

東三洞倭城
(日本名：椎木嶋城)

絶影島

A map from 1919 showing
the relationship between the
four *wajō* of Busan harbour.
In the north we have the
'mother and child' castles
of Busan and Jaseongdae.
Bakmungu lies at the tip
of the mainland, while
the eastern coast of Yeong
Island is protected by
Dongsamdong.

DONGNAE (TOKUNEKI)

Dongnae was an important *sanseong* on the road north out of Busan, which was captured by the Japanese soon after the fall of Busan. The mountains on which Dongnae was built command the area, and its walls were strengthened against Japanese pirate attack in 1381. It is not surprising that this too was taken over by the Japanese and converted into a *wajō*. When the Japanese left the site was re-used by the Korean army and nearly all the Japanese structures were demolished in favour of a new fortress in the Korean style. All that remains of any Japanese fortifications on Dongnae is a stretch of the long wall running down the hill, at the foot of which is the shrine built in memory of the Korean defenders of Dongnae in 1592.

THE *WAJŌ* ON THE NAKDONG RIVER

The Nakdong River provides a western moat for the Busan area, and indeed was used in that precise capacity by UN forces during the Korean War as part of the famous 'Pusan Perimeter'.

GIMHAE JUKDO (KINMUI)

The *wajō* of Gimhae Jukdo was built on the western bank of the Nakdong River near to the Korean *eupseong* of Gimhae that was captured by Kuroda Nagamasa during the first invasion. Its site, of which only a small section of wall survives, lies quite close to Busan's Gimhae Airport and has been excavated in recent years. Land reclamation has obscured its likely original setting, which probably saw half the *wajō* on an island (Jukdo) and the other on the riverbank. The two were probably connected by a bridge, and would have controlled river traffic very effectively. Following the 1597 invasion Gimhae Jukdo passed under the jurisdiction of Nabeshima Naoshige and had a garrison of 12,000 men.

SINDAP (TOKUHASHI)

Gimhae Jukdo was supported from a little way inland by the tiny communications fort of Sindap, probably built on the site of a Korean *sanseong*.

MASA

Upstream from Gimhae Jukdo a branch of the Nakdong River called the West Nakdong River flows west and then south beside the modern city of Gimhae. On its southern bank lies the site of a small *wajō* called Masa. Excavations in 1994 revealed a simple layout whereby two adjacent hills were levelled to make two baileys with a slope between them.

GUPO (KATOKAI)

Gupo, built to support the much larger Gimhae Jukdo, is one of the most accessible and rewarding *wajō* sites to visit. It occupies a dramatic position on the eastern bank of the Nakdong upstream from Gimhae Jukdo, the site of which can be seen from Gupo's well-preserved inner bailey. Excavations have revealed an elaborate use of the technique of hill shaping to produce a complex terraced structure. Nine separate levels in all have been identified. Three make up the inner, middle and outer baileys of the castle with a fourth on the northern side. A fifth lay below the castle gate to the south, while three more overlooked the river. A separate terrace projected into the river to guard the harbour, allowing boats to moor directly under the castle walls.

HOPO

Tiny Hopo lies further upstream. A few fragments of wall are all that remain.

YANGSAN (RYAKKUSAN)

Yangsan is the final *wajō* on the Nakdong River line, and dates from 1597. It lies within sight of Hopo on a hill across a minor tributary. The castle had an

金海竹島倭城
釜山広域市江西区鴨洛海竹林里
1998年4月30日～5月2日調査
高田　微作図

Map of the site of Gimhae Jukdo showing the two sections of the castle. It may well be the case that the outer castle was on an island in the Nakdong River.

BUSAN: DEFENDING A HARBOUR AGAINST ATTACK

This plate shows the attack on Busan harbour by Admiral Yi in 1592. The old Korean defences of the harbour have been augmented by Japanese construction, some of it quite rudimentary. We also see the characteristic curtained area called *maku* used on a Japanese battlefield. The Japanese defenders have mounted captured Korean cannon on makeshift gun carriages and await the onslaught. (Peter Dennis © Osprey Publishing Ltd)

unusual shape, being long and thin, having had a succession of baileys cut out of the very top of the mountain. A Korean fortress here was abandoned by its defenders in 1592 when the Japanese army opened fire.

THE EAST COAST

GIJANG (KUCHAN)

Kuroda Nagamasa was first associated with Gijang, and was there during the occupation, after which he moved to Yangsan. Otherwise known in Korea as Jukseongri, Gijang was one of the most important *wajō* during the first invasion. The ruins are well preserved and show better than any other *wajō* the relationship between a castle and the harbour it guarded, because the harbour area is still remarkably undeveloped and there has been little land reclamation.

Gijang also illustrates the model of a 'mother' and 'child' castle, each of which consists of a multi-bailey set of excavated terraces.

IMRANGPO (SEIGUHAN OR SEIGAN)
Very little remains of this east coast fortress that together with Gijang provided a link between Busan and Seosaengpo. It appears to have consisted of two sites on adjacent hilltops linked by a zigzag footpath.

SEOSAENGPO (SEKKAI)
Until the building of Ulsan late in 1597 mighty Seosaengpo lay at the eastern extremity of the *wajō* line. This very important fortress provides a classic example of the 'defensive' model of *wajō*. Built on a steep hill set back from the sea, Seosaengpo was defended on its eastern side by cliffs whose natural features were augmented with well-constructed stone-clad walls. Tiger's mouth gateways and secondary walls provided a number of twists and turns for an attacker, but even to reach the stage of attacking the inner castle he would have had to break through the two strong and almost parallel walls that ran down to enclose the harbour. At the water's edge these walls met a further castle mound that covered the entrance and exit of ships beside a number of jagged rocks that still protrude from the ground, even though the sea is now a couple of miles away. Seosaengpo was under the command of Katō Kiyomasa, and it was from Seosaengpo that Kiyomasa sailed to the relief of Ulsan. The destruction of Seosaengpo remained an important objective of the allied forces throughout the war, but it was so strong that no attack was launched on Seosaengpo until the very end of the war.

A view of Yeong Island from Busan tower, showing the site of Bakmungu on the mainland. Bakmungu was built on the small flat area of derelict land near the modern bridge.

ULSAN (URUSAN)

Ulsan was the last *wajō* to be built, and came under attack before it was finished in an epic siege in January and February 1598. The hill on which the inner bailey was built is still preserved, and in 1597 lay between two streams that fed the river estuary. Ulsan is illustrated on a remarkable painted screen made originally for the Nabeshima family. It shows the inner castle consisting of four areas on the same level, subdivided by walls and gates, which tallies with archaeological investigation in all but the actual shape. There are five corner towers but no keep. The towers are simple structures with a wooden frame and tiled roofs. The long parapet walls are pierced with square loopholes. Within the walls are simple wooden buildings, some of which are thatched. Use is also made of *maku* (field curtains) ornamented with Katō Kiyomasa's *mon* (family crest).

One weakness of Ulsan was the fact that it could be bombarded by the Chinese heavy artillery from a hill immediately to the north, although this does not appear to have been done very often during the siege, perhaps to avoid casualties to the human wave attacks that characterized the assault on Ulsan.

UNGCHEON AND THE ISLANDS

UNGCHEON (KOMAGAI)

Ungcheon, which was supported by Myeongdong and Jama, was the most important *wajō* after Busan during the first invasion and the occupation. Although Ungcheon possessed an *eupseong*, remains of which still exist, the invaders rejected it in favour of the nearby hill that projects out into the sea with cliffs on its southern side. The northern side provided excellent protection for a natural harbour, which is still used by fishermen and pleasure craft. A long wall ran from the summit down the hillside to the harbour, where there were some fortifications to protect the 'castle town' that grew up around it. There were also some fortified buildings on the eastern side, again linked to the summit by a long wall, but the most important part of Ungcheon *wajō* lay along the ridge at the very top of the hill. Here was a magnificent Japanese castle defended by stone walls and tiger's mouth gateways. Ungcheon is one of the best *wajō* to visit. The approach is up a mountain path that parallels the course of the northern wall as far as a saddle, from where a steep climb takes one up to the top.

MYEONGDONG (KOYAMA)

Essentially a support castle on the other side of the headland to the west of Ungcheon, the few remains of Myeongdong are to be found on four hilltops overlooking the small harbour area.

JAMA

This was also a support castle for Ungcheon and lies some distance inland beyond the Ungcheon *eupseong*. So little remains that until comparatively recently it was not thought to be a *wajō* site at all.

ANGOLPO (ANKAURAI)

Three Japanese admirals are associated with Angolpo, where a fierce naval battle took place in 1592. The *wajō*, which was to act as an important Japanese naval base during the 1597 invasion, occupied an interesting position along the ridge of a narrow peninsula that enclosed the harbour to the north. Two lines of fortifications ran down to the harbour area to enclose it very securely. Much of the site is still intact, but a great deal of the western end of the peninsula has been cut away as part of the massive harbour-building programme currently under way.

MASAN (CHAWAN)

Also called Changwon, Masan was one of the *wajō* created during 1597 to advance Japanese interests west of Ungcheon. It was the nearest to the Ungcheon area, and guarded the inlet of Jinhae Bay.

GADEOK (KATOKU)

Gadeok Island lies between the large Geoje Island and the area of Busan harbour, so was always of great strategic interest. The Gadeok *wajō* was one of the first to be built, and lay not on Gadeok itself but on a tiny island off its northern tip called Nulcha. Very little has survived of what was once a large castle.

GADEOK SEONGBUK

Gadeok Seongbuk was a support castle built on Gadeok Island itself within sight of Gadeok *wajō*. Again it appears to be a very simple *wajō* built on one hill.

YEONGDEUNGPO

Geoje Island, which became notorious during the Korean War for its POW camp, is the largest island in the waterway adjacent to the Korean coast. It is very irregularly shaped, and will soon be physically joined to Busan by a suspension bridge via Gadeok Island. Yeongdeungpo was the first *wajō* to be established on Geoje and was located at the island's most northerly point, where it commanded a harbour from a prominent hill. The castle was long, thin and L-shaped and overlooked the site of a Korean fortress that was considered insufficient for Japanese needs. The castles on Geoje Island acquired considerable significance during the first invasion following the naval battles of Hansando and Angolpo that happened nearby, but were abandoned towards the end of the occupation.

JANGMUNPO

Jangmunpo and Jisepo commanded a position in the north-west of Geoje Island. Each was built on a promontory that enclosed a harbour within a sheltered sea area protected to the west by Chilcheon Island. Jangmunpo to the south was the larger of the two. It consisted of a narrow L-shaped castle that followed the ridge with a separate castle below. Three walls ran down to the sea in a similar way to Ungcheon.

JISEPO
Also called Songjinpo, Jisepo lay to the north of Jangmunpo. It had a 'mother' and 'child' layout and was smaller overall than Jangmunpo.

WAESEONGDONG
Waeseongdong replaced the abandoned Geoje fortifications in 1597. It covered the strategic Gyonnaerang straits to the west that provided access to the seas around Hansando, the site of the epic battle of 1592. The site of Waeseongdong lies close to the modern Geoje Bridge that connects the island to the mainland at its western edge. Unlike the other *wajō* on Geoje Island, Waeseongdong utilized only one modest hill to the north of a river, and therefore had a simple and regular layout similar to Gadeok Seongbuk.

THE WESTERN *WAJŌ*

The *wajō* at the western end of the line initially owed their existence to the mood of optimism following the fall of Namweon in 1597. Although originally intended to act as bases for further conquest, the Chinese counter-attack meant that they were to see most of the defensive action in the closing days of the war.

GOSEONG (KOSAN OR KOSEO)
Goseong lies on the mainland near the gulf of Danghangpo, the site of one of Admiral Yi's celebrated victories. A few stone walls are all that remain.

SACHEON (SOSAN OR SOTEN)
At the very end of the war Shimazu Yoshihiro suffered a massive Chinese attack at Sacheon. The site had been in use throughout the campaign in one form or another, and is mentioned in reports of the naval battle fought there by Admiral Yi. This was the first occasion on which a turtle ship was used, and Yi's description also indicates that the Japanese were building one of their first fortified positions here as early as July 1592:

> Beyond the wharf at Sacheon along the coast stood a rocky crest above undulating ridges extending seven or eight *li*. On the hazy crest about four hundred Japanese were seen building a serpentine position with red and white flags planted confusedly in order to bewilder the eyes of the onlookers. There was a tent [probably open field curtains] pitched on the summit, where the Japanese hurried to and fro as if listening to instructions from their commanding officer.

The final version of Sacheon *wajō* that withstood the siege of 1598 was by all accounts a magnificent structure in a very strong position on cliffs overlooking the sea. Its inner baileys with separate domestic buildings and a fine keep rivalled Suncheon and Seosaengpo, and there were extensive outer works.

The long 'hog's back' hill in the far distance of this picture is the site of the *wajō* of Suncheon. The extant stone base of the keep may be identified.

NAMHAE (NAMUHAI)

Isolated on an island, Namhae provided the last refuge for Japanese troops retreating to Busan by sea after the final battle at Noryang. Its site, a modest hill on the eastern shore of Namhae Island, involved the now-familiar model of a castle on a promontory.

SUNCHEON

Suncheon held the western end of the line in Jeolla Province, and was therefore the only *wajō* not to be built in Gyeongsang Province. Its site is very well preserved and can be seen from miles away. The main castle sat on top of a rocky cliff that sloped gently down on the landward side. There was a keep, the base of which has survived intact. A Ming painting of the siege of Suncheon shows the castle with a moat across the headland, but this is not borne out by the archaeological evidence. As the classic example of the 'spearhead' *wajō*, Suncheon was designed to allow the Japanese to take the fight to the enemy while preserving the security of its two harbour areas. The outer walls were modest in size, but withstood the Ming siege engines in 1598.

THE LIVING SITES

THE REALM OF THE BEASTS: BUILDING THE WAJŌ

The *wajō* owed their rapid creation to the labour of thousands of unwilling workmen who would have been forgotten by history had it not been for the sympathetic observations of their plight made by a monk called Keinen, who accompanied the second invasion in 1597 in the capacity of Buddhist chaplain to the minor *daimyō* Ota Kazuyoshi. Keinen kept a diary in which he recorded the nightmare experience of the building and defence of Ulsan. Using language drawn from Buddhist concepts, he likened the scene to the lowest of the realms of transmigration of souls. In their brutality men had entered the 'realm of the beasts', the lowest but one state that existed. As the cruelty grew Keinen despaired even more, and concluded that the lowest realm of all had been reached. 'Hell,' he wrote, 'could not be anywhere but here.' It was the constant noise of building work that first gave him cause for concern:

> From all around comes the sound of the hammers of the blacksmiths and the workmen, and the swish and scraping of the adze. With the dawn it grows more and more terrible, but if it means we will not be defeated I can put up with the banging I am being subjected to even in the middle of the night.

The constant labour was hard and unremitting, and was imposed particularly cruelly on the shoulders of the press-ganged peasants drafted from samurai estates in Japan, who were forced to work alongside Korean captives. 'To prevent carelessness heads are cut off,' he writes, 'but blame is not shared equally, and to the sorrow of the peasants it is their heads that they cut off and stick up at the crossroads.' In the intense pressure to have the walls of Ulsan finished before the Chinese army arrived, these labourers were clearly regarded as expendable, and were worked until they dropped. One day Keinen looked across the fields white with snow and thought he saw packhorses, but instead it was the labourers trudging through the snow with their painfully heavy burdens.

The peasants whom the samurai were flogging were men who would be expected to till the lands of these overlords when they returned to Japan, but in

The well-preserved site of Gijang harbour, looking down from the hill on which the *wajō* was built.

the unreal atmosphere of the Korean campaign there was no thought for the future other than the immediate short-term goal of completing the *wajō*'s defences. 'With no distinction being made between day and night,' writes Keinen, 'men are made to exceed their personal limits. There are beatings for the slightest mistake in performing a task such as tying knots. In many cases I have witnessed, this is the last ever occasion on which the person gets into trouble.'

To add to the misery caused by overwork, the labourers also had to suffer attacks from the Chinese patrols that were beginning to appear in the vicinity. Keinen writes of a group of peasants left in the forest to trim the branches off the newly felled trees. A Chinese unit came upon them and beheaded them all. 'Brought here from thousands of miles away,' he writes, 'they are tortured for even one single moment of carelessness. I do not see these as actions which human beings could devise.'

In a vivid metaphor, prompted by seeing the labourers staggering under the weight of the supplies unloaded from the ships, Keinen writes:

> Yet even amidst all this, the carrying of heavy loads piled up like a *horai* [the 'treasure mountain' of Chinese mythology] between the harbour and the rear lines is an exceptionally terrible thing. They drag them along to [shouts of] 'Come on!', but when they reach the wooden palisade these dumb oxen are of no use anymore, and are slaughtered, their hides are flayed, and they are eaten. 'Is this not the realm of beasts?' thought I.

Keinen, of course, does not mean us to take literally his words about the 'dumb oxen', which the peasants have become, being 'flayed and eaten', but the reality of the situation is almost as terrible. When food supplies became a problem, the peasants 'were not given their rations, but were driven away up into the mountains and abandoned. I saw how this was done with my own eyes.'

FROM PRAYING TO RAIDING – DAILY LIFE IN THE *WAJŌ*

A very different eyewitness account of life in the *wajō* comes from Father Gregorio de Cespedes SJ, who went to Korea in the winter of 1594–95 in the capacity of visiting chaplain to the Christians among the Japanese troops. He was first based at Ungcheon, which he describes in the first of two letters sent from Korea:

> The fortress of Komangai is impregnable, and great defensive works have been erected there, which are admirable, considering the short time in which they were completed. They have built high walls, watchtowers and strong bastions, at the foot of which all the nobles and soldiers of Augustin [Konishi Yukinaga], his subjects and allies are encamped. For all there are well built and spacious. Houses with stone walls are built for the chiefs.

In his second letter he adds that Ungcheon is built 'on a very high and craggy slope. When I have to go down for some confessions at night, it gives me much work, and when I go back I ride a horse and rest many times on the way.' The solidity of the *wajō* was echoed by their interior decor, and when Father Gregorio visited Sō Yoshitomo, 'I was astonished to see the beautiful things he has; they surely did not seem to be of temporary use but looked as if they were intended to stay there all one's life.' This would have been at Jama, Ungcheon's support castle. The Korean winter was, however, an enormous trial to him:

> The cold in Korea is very severe and without comparison with that of Japan. All day long my limbs are half benumbed, and in the morning I can hardly move my hands to say mass, but I keep myself in good health; thanks to God and the fruit that our Lord is giving.

At Gijang he visited Kuroda Nagamasa, whose Christian piety comes in for special praise. His men listened to two sermons a day, and in the case of Nagamasa himself:

Left: The sloping stone wall of the keep of Gijang, typical of the native Japanese design imported into Korea as the *wajō*.

Right: A redrawing of a remarkable contemporary document showing the firing angles and ranges available in the defence of the *wajō* of Ulsan.

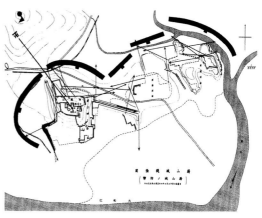

In order to meditate on them at his leisure, he withdrew each day at certain hours, which were set aside for this purpose, to read his books of devotion. … Being such a great lord and such a leading soldier and commander, and busy in affairs of war, never did he abstain from fasting all the days ordered by the Church, without counting others which he added on account of his devoutness, all of which he accompanied with the secret disciplines which he practised.

Father Gregorio concludes his brief correspondence with some perceptive observations of life in the *wajō*:

All these Christians are very poor, and suffer from hunger, cold, illness and other inconveniences very different from conditions in other places. Although Hideyoshi sends food, so little reaches here that it is impossible to sustain all with them, and moreover the help that comes from Japan is insufficient and comes late. It is now two months since ships have come, and many craft were lost.

Illness took its toll of high and low alike, and one of Yi Sunsin's reports notes, 'The Japanese in Ungcheon took new positions, stationing 1,000 men or 800–900 men in each place. Many of them have died of illness or fled home while undergoing hardships in building houses and city walls.' In another report on the Ungcheon actions, he noted that 'the enemy's fighting strength has recently been greatly weakened with many war dead and wounded'. Infectious diseases were rife in the Japanese army and had already claimed many lives. A letter sent home by Date Masamune reports an outbreak of beriberi, which killed eight out of ten sufferers, and in another letter three days later he refers to deaths occurring 'because the water in this country is different', which may imply an outbreak of cholera.

Ill-treated inhabitants of the *wajō* sometimes made their grievances felt, and on 16 February 1596 Yi reports hearing of a 'conspiracy to mutiny in the Japanese camp'. Some actually deserted and went over to the Korean side. Admiral Yi notes in his diary on 14 November 1595 that a group of renegade Japanese were employed to plaster the ceiling of his headquarters! Three months later we read:

Early in the morning five surrendered Japanese entered camp. On being questioned about the reasons for their escape, they explained that their commanding officer was a cruel fellow, driving them hard, so they ran away and surrendered. The large and small swords in their possession were collected and put away in the attic of the pavilion. They further confessed that they were not Japanese from Busan but Japanese under the command of Shimazu on Gadeok Island.

There is an extraordinary entry in Yi's diary, which reads:

> After dark the surrendered Japanese played a drama with the make-up of
> actors and actresses. As Commanding Admiral, I could not attend, but since
> the submissive captives wished to entertain themselves with their native
> farce for enjoyment of the day, I did not forbid it.

Yet life in a *wajō* was not all misery. Some samurai performed the tea
ceremony, played *go* (a board game), and generally tried to behave as if they
were back in Japan. As the *Wakizaka ki* (the chronicle of the Wakizaka family)
notes, 'It was very peaceful inside our camps, so on occasions some people
amused themselves by putting on *sarugaku* [comical theatrical] performances.
Others danced, or passed the time with tea ceremonies and the pleasures of
drinking bouts.' Of all the activities in which the occupying forces indulged
themselves, none was more dramatic than tiger hunting, but aside from these
diversions there were numerous raids on Korean settlements, and one of Yi's
reports from 1594 reads, 'They kill, rape and steal in a more cruel manner
than before.'

But not all these incidents were everything that they seemed to be. Yi's
diary entry concerning one such raid in 1593 says that 'the supposed Japanese
were found to be a large group of Korean refugees fleeing from Gyeongsang
province, who, having disguised themselves like the Japanese war dogs,
plundered private homes as they ran amok in all parts of the town'. In
October 1597 Yi's diary noted:

> During breakfast some Dangpo abalone divers stole the cattle in the field
> with the false alarm, 'The Japanese thieves have come! The Japanese thieves
> have come!' Since I knew it was a ruse I had two fellows among the
> shouting false alarmists arrested and ordered their heads to be cut off and
> hung up high for a public warning. The sailors and people calmed down.

Most incidents, however, were unquestionably Japanese raids. In March 1594
we read of 'torch-bearing robbers' haunting Haeundae, the beach area near
Busan, and five enemy sailors being apprehended and one killed at Nokdo.

WATCHING THE *WAJŌ*

During the occupation Japan and China were theoretically at peace, and talks
were continuing, a situation that was particularly frustrating to the Koreans.
Admiral Yi Sunsin longed for the opportunity to attack the *wajō*, but knew
he could not do it without Chinese support:

> Though I swore with other captains of war to avenge our slaughtered
> countrymen upon the enemy by risking our own lives, and we pass many

days on land and at sea in this resolution, the enemy has taken his positions in deep trenches and high fortresses on steep hills inaccessible to us.

A month later, however, Yi disregarded any possible Chinese qualms and made a demonstration outside Jangmunpo, but there was no reaction from on land so the Koreans simply burned two Japanese ships. A few days later he attacked Jangmunpo again, having made a useful alliance with some very effective Korean ground troops:

> I ordered out several hundred sharpshooters to land at Jangmunpo to challenge the enemy. Late in the day I led our central force to the scene of battle for a joint action on sea and land. Much frightened, the disheartened enemy hordes scattered and ran.

Yi continued to monitor troop movements and analyse intelligence reports. In April 1595 he notes receiving information that 'Hideyoshi has resolved to send more reinforcements across the sea in order to build permanent forts and barracks at Busan', but this is followed by reports concerning the evacuation of the three forts on Geoje Island in August. This indicated to Yi that the occupation forces were being concentrated into fewer areas, but there were still occasional armed clashes, and during the first month of 1596 a Japanese ship trying to land was driven away by Yi's blockading force.

THE *WAJŌ* AS ECONOMIC CENTRES

Throughout the time of occupation the Korean navy, assisted by guerrilla bands, largely succeeded in achieving the Korean government's overall aim of keeping the Japanese confined to barracks. It would appear that Hideyoshi was quite content to accept the status quo, with no advance being made by Japanese troops while peace negotiations continued. As a result, the areas immediately adjacent to the *wajō* remained the only pieces of Korean territory that could be regarded as 'occupied'. It would, however, be a mistake to regard the *wajō* as isolated fortresses hemmed in by hostile troops. In some cases Korean people who had initially fled before the Japanese advance returned to the *wajō* and settled nearby to work the land. They accepted Japanese rule and paid taxes to Japanese tax collectors. At its height Gimhae Jukdo was surrounded by over 600 houses, and trade flourished at Ungcheon. Ungcheon had a market and was extremely prosperous, giving the area directly adjacent to the *wajō* the appearance of a castle town.

OPERATIONAL HISTORY

THE REVELATION OF STRENGTH: BUSAN 1592

In September 1592 Admiral Yi Sunsin carried out a brave attempt to destroy the Japanese fleet lying at anchor in Busan. Before this time Yi had not dared venture to the east of Gadeok Island, and the scale of the challenge facing the Korean fleet at Busan is quite amazing. In none of his previous victories had Yi had to contend with more than 100 enemy ships at any one time, but his arrival off Busan revealed an enemy armada of over 400 vessels. 'Yi Okki and I roared, "Do or die!" and waved our war flags,' writes Yi in his report to the Korean court. Four Japanese ships lying outside the main anchorage became easy targets, but when the Korean fleet sailed in closer they came under heavy fire both from the ships themselves and from shore batteries, and Yi realized to his dismay that the *wajō* in Busan had been equipped with cannon seized from captured Korean castles, because 'cannon balls the size of Chinese quinces, or large stones as big as rice bowls' came flying over. Yi returned fire, and managed to silence the shore positions.

Yi also lamented the death of Cheong Un, a captain from Nokdo who was killed by being hit by 'a large fire ball of the enemy', which implies that among the artillery pieces acquired by the Japanese were some specimens of the mortars with delayed-action fuses. Alternatively the expression could mean the simple fire bombs used in Japanese naval warfare that were flung by hand or with the help of a net on a pole to give greater range. Five captured Korean cannon are mentioned in Yi's list of weapons taken from captured Japanese ships. Two were 'earth mark' cannon, and two of the others were of the 'black' variety. In the end Yi's concern for the local inhabitants, together with the size of the Japanese fleet, prevented Busan from being a more complete victory than it actually was. Yi was wise enough to realize that an operation like Busan could only be really effective if he was acting with the support of ground troops, and as of September 1592 such an action was not yet possible. But to the Japanese the repulse of the attack was a revelation. It proved that the *wajō* were effective in the role they had been given: that of defending a harbour against attack.

図ぅ馋遅をを戦の蔚軍ぁ大ぁの明
山

THE VINDICATION: UNGCHEON 1593

Early in 1593, while Seoul was being reclaimed by the Ming army, Admiral Yi Sunsin had been patrolling the sea around Gadeok and Geoje islands and observed large Japanese troops concentrations around Ungcheon, where ships were gathering and fortifications were being built. No Japanese warship was tempted to come out and engage the Korean fleet, so Yi went on to the offensive and launched his first assault on Ungcheon on 12 March.

> Our warships darted forward with one accord from right and left while shooting cannon balls and arrows like thunder and lightning. This was done twice a day, killing the enemy robbers in countless numbers.

Over four successive raids on Ungcheon, Yi inflicted much damage from a distance, but his reports also record his frustration at being unable to do more. For example, during his third raid he notes with satisfaction the performance of a turtle ship, whose crew killed 100 Japanese. The casualties included the commander, who was pierced through by one of the large wooden arrows fired from a cannon. Set against this is his clear exasperation at the absence of Korean or Chinese ground troops with whom he could have carried out a

The Ming army lays siege to the *wajō* of Ulsan. Good detail of fortifications is included in this section from the *Ehon Taikōki*. We see the typical stone bases, the long white walls, and the crude timber gateway towers with brushwood fencing for an outer defence.

combined operation. In spite of several requests the only response was the arrival of Gwak Jaeu's guerrillas, whose small force Yi regarded as insufficient. Yi therefore mounted a limited amphibious operation of his own. 'I ordered out a dozen warships manned by monk captains and sharpshooters to make landings at strategic points,' he writes. 'Our valiant monk soldiers jumped up brandishing swords and thrusting spears and charged into the enemy positions, shooting guns and arrows from morning to night.'

The most exasperating aspect of the situation was the evidence before his own eyes that the Japanese army was in a very sorry state and could have been easily swept into the sea, but once again the strong defensive qualities of the *wajō* had been demonstrated.

THE ULTIMATE TEST: ULSAN 1598

The siege of Ulsan was the largest operation ever conducted against a *wajō*, and its defence is more remarkable when one considers that at the time of the Chinese attack it was still unfinished. The *wajō* of Ulsan lay on a broad river estuary, which gave easy access to the sea. Katō Kiyomasa delegated its defence to a garrison of about 7,000 men and returned to Seosaengpo. Work began at a furious pace in late November 1597 to make a strong castle out of the prominent hill about 50m in height that overlooked the river, so squads of Japanese began raising earthworks and ditches, cladding the sides of the hill in stone, and building fences and barracks from timber cleared from nearby forests. By early January 1598 the increasingly severe winter weather was beginning to hinder the construction work, and the arrival of the Ming just before dawn on 29 January 1598 found a large proportion of the Japanese army still encamped in the flimsy barracks outside Ulsan's enceinte. Having been advised by their scouts that the Japanese defences were still incomplete, a Chinese flying squad was sent on ahead of the main body to do as much damage as possible. Fire arrows hit the temporary barracks buildings, which soon caught fire. The monk Keinen was fortunate in being well inside Ulsan Castle when the dawn attack on the outside camp happened. 'At the Hour of the Dragon smoke was rising on the eastern side of the castle, and I could hear the sounds of gunfire. The Chinese had advanced and set fire to the huts of the troops from Chūgoku.'

The survivors of the night attack took refuge within Ulsan's incomplete walls while rearguard actions held off the attackers. The pursuit of the stragglers continued up to the unfinished gates. Foot soldiers fired arquebuses from the ramparts to cover the withdrawal, but the Chinese 'were not discouraged by this, and, trampling over the corpses, forced their way in', and the bar of the gate broke under the weight of the soldiers climbing over it. To divert the Chinese attack another gate of the castle was opened and a sally was made on to the Ming flank. As the two armies separated firing began again, which finally drove back the Chinese. They made no further advance against Ulsan that day, but contented themselves with burning down the temporary barracks and then withdrew. The success was reported back to the Korean government, whose ministers were pleased at the news, although it was stressed that Seosaengpo was a more important target than temporary Ulsan.

The situation inside Ulsan was not encouraging. The garrison had no more than three days' supply of food, and another major attack was expected. A messenger had been sent to Seosaengpo to inform Katō Kiyomasa of the situation, and his response was swift. After despatching a request to Busan for reinforcements, Katō Kiyomasa sailed to Ulsan. During the assault that followed, Keinen found himself in the thick of the fighting for the first time, and gives us a vivid eyewitness description of how 'the castle was surrounded by countless numbers of troops, who were deployed in a number of rings that encircled us. There were so many of them covering the ground that one could no longer distinguish between the plain and the hills.' Because some of the gates were still missing the Chinese were able to swarm inside the outer baileys, and began loosing fire arrows from outside the walls. The result was that the bedding, storage boxes and many other 'treasured possessions' went up in flames. The smoke was so dense that the defenders could not keep their eyes or mouths open, and thousands of labourers who were late returning to the castle were caught in the conflagration and died. By now thousands of Chinese soldiers were climbing up the walls. They were eventually driven back, but at the cost of 660 Japanese casualties.

The defenders then shut the gates of the inner fortress, a small area now marked by the hill on which the ruins of Ulsan *wajō* sit. Katō Kiyomasa could only wait for reinforcements, hoping that the awful weather might also help in persuading the Chinese to withdraw. The Ming set up siege lines to starve out the defenders, and watched all the approaches by land and sea in case of a relief attempt. Cannon were used, and might have proved decisive had the defenders' fire not prevented the gunners from transporting their heavy pieces even closer to the walls. One cannonball hit Katō Kiyomasa's bodyguard, cutting him so quickly in half at the waist that the part of his body below the waist was left standing.

Being unable to batter down the gates or to make a breach in the walls, the Chinese artillery tactics were replaced by human waves launched against the parapets. Terrifying assaults were delivered regularly over the next ten days. As one furious surge of men was driven back another wave swept up to replace it, the dead bodies of their predecessors taking the place of scaling ladders as they clambered up the huge mound of corpses. 'They would put a large hook up on the wall and 50 or even 100 men would take hold of the attached rope to pull the wall down,' wrote the author of *Matsui Monogatari* in some amazement. 'When this happened we fired on them from the side, but out of 50 men five or ten still hung on and pulled to the end. It has to be said that they are extremely brave warriors.' On one occasion a detachment of Koreans carrying shields and bundles of brushwood approached the outer

bailey to make an arson attack on the palisade, but they were spotted and received volleys of arquebus balls for their pains. Concern was also expressed that the Japanese arquebus fire was being stopped by the solid Chinese shields, so to test them arquebuses were trained on the middle of the shields and it was noted at which range they could be pierced, as shown 'by the blood flowing'.

The siege was witnessed by Yu Seongnyong, who writes in *Chingbirok*, 'Every day this kind of battle was repeated, and the bodies of Chinese soldiers and our own began to pile up under the walls of the fortress.'

As Ulsan had no well within the inner castle the torments of thirst were soon added to the intense discomfort of the fierce Chinese attacks. Water-gathering parties slipped out of the castle by night and brought back supplies from ponds choked with corpses. 'But just when we were really craving for water,' writes Keinen, 'it began raining heavily and everyone in the castle could wet their mouths. The water fell like shed tears on to their helmets, and we washed our hands in the water that cascaded over us.'

Flocks of scavenging birds descend on the abandoned Chinese camp, a sign that the siege of Ulsan was finally over. (From the *Ehon Taikōki*)

When the temperature dropped below freezing that night a strong wind arose that brought about a wind-chill factor so severe that it affected the fighting spirit on both sides. The pause in the attack, and the intense cold, made the defenders realize how tired they were. By now all food was practically exhausted except for roasted strips of meat cut from dead horses cooked over fires made from broken arrows, piles of which lay several feet deep. Foraging parties had been reduced to searching the bodies of dead Chinese for grains of rice. The following morning, fooled by the deceptive warmth of a brief spell of winter sunshine, the exhausted soldiers huddled in the sunny places on the ramparts and fell asleep. The *Chosen ki* tells us:

> Both friend and foe are silent. Nevertheless inside the castle we have
> maintained our defences by day and night without any sleep. Here and there

inside the castle, at the sunny places on the walkways and at the foot of towers, with no distinction between samurai, *ashigaru* or labourers, 50 men at a time may be found crumpled under the unbearable hunger, thirst and cold. In addition there are a number of men who have let their heads drop and lie down to sleep. Other soldiers go on tours of inspection with their spears, and when they try to rouse men who have not moved all day by using the butt end of a spear, the ones who stay completely bent over have been frozen to death.

The conditions made both sides ready to parley, and the resulting offer by the Ming of a ceasefire was accepted by Katō Kiyomasa as a way of buying time, because the plight of Ulsan was now known to the rest of the Japanese army. Mōri Yoshinari, accompanied by ten samurai, sailed round from Seosaengpo and rowed up the river as far as was possible, where they waved their banners towards the ramparts, hoping that they had been seen. Two days later a large scouting force arrived in the estuary to identify a suitable landing place for a relieving army. They disembarked briefly on some high ground and again waved flags towards the castle. This time they were definitely noticed, and the garrison waved back to them. 'I was resigned to my fate,' writes Keinen, 'when at early dawn we saw the tips of the banners, and there was much rejoicing.' Greatly relieved at the sight, Katō Kiyomasa broke off his negotiations with the Ming, who resolved to make one final attempt to take Ulsan before the new army advanced upon them. Keinen watched in some excitement as the night attack unfolded:

> From early dawn they attacked anew, loosing fire arrows and firing arquebuses and cannon, and set up scaling ladders at places where they could climb the stone walls. We threw down pine torches, cut down their climbing implements and fired at them.

Soon intelligence reached the Chinese command of the huge relieving army that was approaching from behind them. The newcomers fell on their rear, and the result was a considerable Japanese victory. As dawn broke the following morning the defenders of Ulsan were heartened by the welcome sight of flocks of scavenging birds descending upon the now abandoned Chinese camp. The siege of Ulsan was over.

THE FINISHED PRODUCT: SACHEON 1598

The siege of Ulsan convinced many within the Japanese High Command that a withdrawal from Korea was the only course of action. Yet troops were to stay in their *wajo* throughout 1598, even though many were withdrawn, and only ten generals out of the 30 who had been involved in the second invasion remained in Korea by the time of Hideyoshi's death in September.

The allies realized that a major push against the *wajō* would dislodge the Japanese permanently, and Sacheon provided the penultimate battle. The *wajō* of Sacheon was built on a promontory where it overlooked the harbour and provided a safe anchorage. The approach to it was a narrow path, just as the Japanese preferred. Sacheon was defended by the Shimazu of Satsuma Province in southern Kyūshū under Shimazu Yoshihiro and his son Tadatsune (later to be known as Iehisa). Other Satsuma retainers held four small outposts to the north, including the old castle of Sacheon. There is an amusing anecdote concerning the building of Sacheon in *Jozan Kidan*, which tells of an argument between the veteran Chosokabe Motochika and a younger samurai about where to place the gun ports in the *wajō*'s gatehouse. Chosokabe maintained that gun ports should be inserted 'at a level between a man's chest and hips'. His colleague disagreed, saying that the gun ports should be placed high up on the walls, because low gun ports would allow enemy scouts to peer into the *wajō*. 'Let them!' was Chosokabe's reaction. 'Then they can see how strong it is!'

When the Chinese approached the lines Shimazu Yoshihiro evacuated all three forward positions for the new *wajō*. Young Shimazu Tadatsune was for making an immediate attack, but his father forbade it. He reasoned that the Chinese army would wish to waste no time in attacking anyway, and the men of Satsuma were ready for them. This assumption proved to be correct, and the

The Chinese attack on the main gate of Sacheon, showing the moment when there was an explosion that destroyed, among other things, the combination cannon and battering ram that was being used to breach the entrance. (From the *Ehon Taikōki*)

Ming army, in three units of right, left and centre, moved in for an attack at about 6 o'clock in the morning on 30 October 1598 with a total of 36,700 troops. The Shimazu father and son monitored their movements from the two towers flanking eastern gate. Under strict orders from Yoshihiro, the Japanese held their fire, and as one or two men fell dead from Chinese arrows Tadatsune was again for launching an attack, but once more his father urged caution.

By now the Chinese were approaching the walls, and were also attacking the main gate with a curious siege engine. *Seikan roku* calls it a 'wooden lever', while the chronicler of Kawakami's Korean campaign talks of 'gunpowder jars'. It was probably a combination of an iron-tipped battering ram mounted on a carriage with a cannon. The joint effects of cannon ball and ram smashed the gate, and soon thousands of Chinese soldiers were milling round the entrance and climbing up the castle walls. 'Lord Yoshihiro, who saw this, gave the order to attack without delay,' writes a commentator on behalf of the Shimazu, 'and all the soldiers as one body fired their arquebuses and mowed down the enemy soldiers who were clinging on to the walls.'

At that precise moment there was an enormous explosion in the allied ranks. Japanese accounts claim that they had managed to destroy the combined ram and cannon, causing its stock of gunpowder to explode with great fury right in the middle of the Ming host. A separate Shimazu chronicle implies that the engine was destroyed by a firebomb thrown from a mortar or a catapult, because:

> We flung fire against the gunpowder jars, many of which had been placed within the enemy ranks. It flew from one jar to another, and the tremendous noise was carried to our ears. Consequently the alarming sound terrified all of the enemy who were in the vicinity.

Chinese accounts state that the explosion was caused by the accidental ignition of the Japanese gunpowder store as a certain Peng Xingu forced his way in through the smashed gate. Whatever the reason, the explosion proved to be the turning point of the battle. Seeing the confusion in the Chinese ranks, Shimazu Yoshihiro led out his men in a tremendous charge. Many Chinese were cut down, but with admirable organization and discipline the army regrouped on a nearby hill and took the fight back to the Japanese. Some Japanese units had now become detached from the main body, and although at risk from a Chinese attack they quickly realized their opportunity and attacked the rear ranks of the Chinese where the poorest-quality troops were stationed. Soon the Ming baggage carriers had broken and were causing unintentional havoc in their own ranks. Yet still the fight continued, and the Shimazu remained outnumbered by three to one until the approach of a relieving army from Tachibana's *wajō* at Goseong tipped the balance in Japan's favour. Thousands of Chinese were killed or pursued back as far as the Nam River, where very few stragglers managed to cross and reach the safety of Jinju.

Once again a battle had been lost. Sacheon has usually been trumpeted as Japan's greatest victory over Ming China, but the real victory came shortly afterwards and was a Chinese one. In spite of the enormous Chinese losses, remembered today by the huge burial mound at Sacheon, the siege continued, and it was not long before the isolated garrison decided to withdraw as part of the overall evacuation from Korea that was now inevitable. The Shimazu slipped out of the *wajō's* harbour, leaving an empty castle for the Chinese. The sacrifice had been terrible, but Korea was almost free.

COMBINED OPERATIONS: SUNCHEON 1598

Suncheon had long been the finest remaining *wajō* in Korea. It held 13,700 men, and was well supplied with food and ammunition. Almost 500 ships lay at anchor in the harbour, waiting for the moment when they could safely evacuate the Japanese army. The operation against Suncheon was designed to be a combined land and sea operation between the Chinese Western Army and the naval commands of Admiral Yi and his Ming ally Chen Lin. Relations between the two admirals had not always been cordial, but there was sufficient co-operation for the joint fleet to secure Jang Island, which lay within sight of Suncheon Castle and on which the Japanese had stored some equipment and provisions. The fleet then proceeded to surround the *wajō* and sat there as a floating siege line while the Ming army made similar preparations on land.

The other arm of the attack on Suncheon was to see the employment by General Liu Ting of a weird and wonderful collection of Chinese siege engines, including movable shields, siege towers and the so-called 'cloud ladders': wheeled vehicles from which a hinged ladder could be folded out to hook on to a wall. The assembly and installation of these heavy contraptions took several days before the combined operation was ready to be set in motion. Supremely confident, Liu Ting offered 60 gold pieces to any Chinese soldier who brought him a Japanese head.

On the same day as the battle of Sacheon, the two forces made their final preparations for an attack at dawn the next day. 'At 6.00 am we opened an all-out attack,' wrote Yi. 'Our naval craft advanced to the very front and fought the enemy until noon, inflicting countless casualties upon him. In this battle we also suffered some losses.' While the two navies bombarded Suncheon from the sea, the Chinese soldiers slowly heaved the cloud ladders and siege towers towards the land walls. Fierce and accurate arquebus fire meant that few of these lumbering monsters got through to clamp their hooks against Suncheon's parapets, and those that did were met by desperate resistance. Realizing how much faith the Chinese were placing in their siege machines, Konishi Yukinaga's men dared to sally out of the gates and take on the operatives in hand-to-hand fighting. The lack of an alternative plan of assault was soon made plain. With their siege engines stranded and useless the Chinese pulled back to their lines, while on the sea the turn of the tide provided its own contribution to a temporary allied withdrawal, and the bombardment ceased.

Frustrated by this reversal on land, Liu Ting sent a message to Admiral Chen Lin suggesting a night attack on Suncheon from the sea. Admiral Yi had grave misgivings about the proposal, but Chen Lin was determined, so Yi was forced to provide support for the Chinese advance. Timing the assault to coincide with the incoming tide just after midnight, Chen Lin rowed in and opened up a close-range bombardment with heavy cannon, which knocked out a considerable section from the Japanese palisades. But within an hour the tide turned, and 30 Chinese ships ran aground. Not realizing that the beaching of the Chinese ships was a mistake, the Japanese troops interpreted the accident as a dramatic attempt at an amphibious landing that had no doubt been timed to coincide with a night attack from the land. The Chinese soldiers on board, however, had no such intentions, and sat there in great fear while they waited for the tide to rise and free them.

The Japanese succeeded in capturing five Chinese ships, and when the tide rose the garrison of Suncheon launched raids against other vessels as they pulled back. The samurai were only driven off when Yi's ships went to Chen Lin's rescue. The following morning Yi prepared for an attack of his own, but a strong westerly wind blew up and prevented any approach being made for the next two days. Yi was then told that General Liu Ting, who had no doubt been informed of the simultaneous disaster at Sacheon, had abandoned the last ever siege of a *wajō* and retreated north. Yet within days Suncheon was evacuated anyway as the curtain came down on the Korean invasion.

Although all three of the great sieges of 1598 against the *wajō* were individual failures in that they involved military defeats for the Chinese and Korean armies, they played their part in securing the overall objective of forcing a Japanese withdrawal from Korea. By confining the Japanese to the security of the *wajō* the allies had prevented them from launching attacks and gradually wore them down by a process of attrition. Had Busan not been secured so well the Japanese might have been expelled earlier. What the *wajō* had given the Japanese was time, and it had been clearly demonstrated that their design was so strong that none could be overcome by force of arms. Throughout the whole of the Korean operation no *wajō* was ever captured, yet in spite of this it was also appreciated that the only parts of Korean territory that Japan would ever own would be the *wajō* themselves. This finally swayed the commanders who were forced to defend them and did their duty so well. In time this fact was appreciated by Hideyoshi himself, although because of his deteriorating mental condition the command to withdraw had to wait for his death.

AFTERMATH

It might be thought that the bitter experience of the defeat of the Korean castles in 1592, and the repulse of three massive attacks against the *wajō* in 1598, would have led to a revolution in Korean castle design. But this did not happen, even though far-sighted statesmen such as Yu Seongnyong applied their minds to the vexed question of wall construction and maintenance. Musing on the subject by the banks of the river near Anju while the Japanese were ravaging his country, Yu came up with a proposal for walls that contained gun portals and towers separated by 600 or 700 paces, with a pile of cannon balls stacked ready beside the big guns 'like chicken's eggs':

> Then when the enemy approaches the walls, he will be hit by a cross fire from the guns. Not to speak of men and horses, even metal and stone could not escape being pulverized by this. ... All you would have to do is to have several dozen men man the gun turrets, and the enemy would not dare draw near.

Had his ideas been adopted, and both time and the devastated Korean economy were clearly against him, then the returning Japanese in 1597 might have had to face strongly fortified towns. Namweon certainly had towers that allowed some flanking fire when the Japanese attacked it in 1597, but this was probably due to the rapid rebuilding carried out by the Chinese army rather than as a result of Yu's recommendations. Instead a lack of will, and an even more acute lack of resources, meant that Korea faced the second invasion under the traditional policy of 'strengthen the walls and clear the countryside'.

In Japan, however, the experience of three massive sieges had vindicated the faith the Japanese had put in their own style of castle, so we look in vain for any change of direction in Japanese castle design arising out of the Korean experience. Castles certainly grew in size, but this was a trend that was well under way even before the Korean campaign began. In essence the Korean War confirmed the suitability for Japanese purposes of Japanese castles, a situation that was only to be shaken by the siege of Osaka, when

Hirosaki is the most northerly of the original castles on the main Japanese island of Honshū, and its isolation went some way towards saving it from demolition during the Meiji Period. Hirosaki's most important feature is the large keep that is built at one corner of the inner bailey.

European cannon were brought to bear upon a Japanese castle for the first time and played a decisive role. But this was over a decade in the future, and of far greater consequence for the appearance of Japanese castles was the effect of the new requirement enforced by the Tokugawa subsequent to 1603 that a castle should serve a political purpose in addition to its military functions.

CONCLUSION

The bombardment of Osaka Castle during the winter of 1614–15 marked the emergence of a new and successful way of attacking Japanese castles. Yet decisive political changes were to ensure that the experience was never to be repeated. Apart from the siege of Hara Castle during the Shimabara Rebellion of 1638, when a Dutch ship reluctantly fired cannon at its walls, the control exerted by the Tokugawa family ensured that no other castle was to come under attack by any means for over two centuries. In place of conflict, the triumph of the Tokugawa meant that the castles of Japan became the focus of the castle towns that had grown up beside them, and these in turn were to become the Japanese cities of today. Commerce and culture flourished, particularly in Edo and Osaka, yet even in the smallest castle towns the old fortress with its proud *daimyō* was to serve as the nucleus of civic life.

This state of affairs lasted until the early 19th century. The increased appearance of the ships of Western nations in Japanese waters posed a threat to the *shōgun* and to Japan's self-imposed isolation. One response to the challenge was to strengthen the defences of certain strategic fortresses. Between 1849 and 1854 Matsumae on Hokkaidō was completely rebuilt with reinforced walls to withstand a possible bombardment from Russian ships. Matsumae's overall design, however, remained that of the traditional Japanese castle with keep and towers, but not far away in Hakodate something very different took shape between 1857 and 1864. This was the Goryōkaku, Japan's first and only star-shaped fortress.

Yet the fighting that attended the birth of modern Japan in 1868 did not come about as a result of foreign aggression but took the shape of the Boshin War: a fierce civil war between the *daimyō* who favoured the abolition of the shogunate and the restoration of imperial rule, and those who stubbornly fought on in the name of the Tokugawa even when the last *shōgun* had abdicated. Castles played a major role in this conflict, which was both the last flourish of samurai warfare and Japan's first modern war. As both sides had tried to modernize their armies by acquiring European and American artillery, it is not surprising to read that the damage to the ancient fortresses was considerable. Most of the fighting took place in northern Japan, where

Aizu–Wakamatsu, Shinjō and Yokote were among several castles destroyed in the fighting or burned to the ground by the victorious army. The final battle of the Boshin War took the form of a siege of Hakodate's Goryōkaku in 1869, while the Satsuma Rebellion of 1877 included a siege of Kumamoto.

These wars showed the government of the new Meiji emperor that during modern times castles could act as a focus for rebellion just as they had done in the past. In order to demonstrate their loyalty many municipalities demolished their castles, which were officially regarded as the symbols of an old-fashioned and discredited system that modern Japan had left behind. The ones we see today that escaped this voluntary and patriotic destruction owed their survival to one or more of several possible factors: local sentiment, the absence of any possible military threat or even a simple lack of funds for demolition.

The final phase of destruction happened during the bombing raids of the final year of World War II, when many castles along the Pacific coastal area were lost forever. Castles in more remote areas such as Matsue and Matsumoto were untouched, but the overall destruction was considerable. Japan's economic revival led to the rebuilding of several castles during the 1960s. Ferro-concrete

The 'snout' of the corner of the stone base-cum-wall of Hirado Castle is shown here. Note the massive stones, the *ne ishi* or root stones, at the foot. The harbour of Hirado may be seen in the distance, and there are the traditional pine trees planted behind the line of the wall.

Matsumae Castle was the last of the old-style Japanese fortresses. It received strengthened walls in case of a Russian attack, but the design remained that of the traditional castle. It is shown here in the commanding position it enjoys overlooking the sea.

was then the preferred medium of reconstruction, often with scant regard for the original design or even its location. The past 20 years, however, have seen a welcome trend whereby castles, or at least parts of them, have been meticulously recreated using wood to authentic designs obtained from original drawings and plans. Kakegawa and Shirakawa are superb examples of this welcome development. Fine restoration work has also been done on such wonderful original specimens as Himeji and Hikone, so that the graceful developed style of Japanese castle may be enjoyed today as never before.

Another positive development has been the excavation and partial reconstruction of several Sengoku *yamashiro*. No attempt has been made in these cases to create a keep that never existed. Instead the visitor can study reconstructed ditches, bridges and simple gateways. The former castles of the Hōjō family around modern Tokyo such as Hachiōji, Hachigata and Sakasai provide some of the best examples. Such excavations have finally revealed the enormous size of some *yamashiro*, and the impressive way whereby a *daimyō* could utilize existing topography for military purposes. Similar excavations have also taken place at the sites of most of the *wajō* in Korea, although political sensitivities have ensured that none has been rebuilt. They nevertheless provide a unique insight into the overall plan of the stone walls of Japanese castles as they evolved from the elaborate *yamashiro* of Hachijō and Yamanaka. Himeji and Hikone then show us what could happen when these massive stone bases had superstructures raised above them to provide the final appearance of the fine and formidable strongholds of the samurai.

VISITING THE FORTIFICATIONS TODAY

THE EARLY CASTLES

The sites of the early fortified places described in this book are by no means as well known nor as accessible as the famous later Japanese castles such as Himeji and Hikone. Nevertheless, a combination of preservation and restoration, which in nearly all cases is done sensitively and well, makes a visit to the early sites a very rewarding experience.

The Jōmon site of Sannai-Maruyama, which may have been fortified, may be visited in Aomori, where an openwork tower has been reconstructed. For the fortified sites of the Yayoi Period the visitor has several options such as Otsuka, now in the city of Yokohama, which shares its site with an excellent museum, and the amazing Yoshinogari at the other end of Japan. The Jizoden site in Akita, rebuilt by local volunteers, is much smaller than Yoshinogari but very well done.

The Yayoi settlement of Yoshinogari in northern Kyūshū is one of the world's most spectacular restored archaeological sites. No expense has been spared in recreating the appearance of its fortifications, storehouses and dwellings. It first attracted national attention following an extensive archaeological dig in the late 1980s, and once the public were allowed access tens of thousands of people began to visit the site. Visitor numbers have prompted the installation of car parks and other facilities round the edge of the site, none of which have detracted from the settlement itself, preserved within its fences at a considerable walking distance away.

A visit to Dazaifu in northern Kyūshū provides the visitor with a rich mixture of preserved sites and excellent museums that together tell the story of Japan's response to the threat of invasion during the 7th century AD. Mizuki, although pierced by a motorway and a railway line, is very impressive, and has more for the visitor to see than is provided by a long walk up the mountainsides to find the remains of Ono and Kii castles.

A comparatively simple gatehouse is shown here in autumn colours at Kubota Castle in Akita in northern Japan.

Not far from Mizuki is a bare field that is the site of what Mizuki was built to protect, the regional government headquarters of Dazaifu. There is a small museum next to the site with helpful displays in Japanese and English. A few miles away is the moderately interesting Dazaifu Historical Museum, which is now eclipsed by the airport-like building with which it shares its car park. This is the magnificent Kyūshū National Museum, opened in 2005 and designed to rival the other national museums in Nara, Kyoto and Tokyo. The emphasis is very much on Japan's relations with its continental neighbours, which were conducted by and large through Kyūshū. The permanent gallery includes a model of the building of Mizuki.

The sites of the northern fortresses built against the *emishi* are also worth visiting. Tagajō, near modern Sendai, has little in the way of reconstruction, but a short walk away is the Tōhoku Historical Museum, with very good exhibits relating to the castle. In the city of Akita one may visit the site of Fort Akita. Part of the wall has been reconstructed, and there is a small museum where visitors are made very welcome. Hotta lies a short journey to the south near the city of Omagari. Here is a well-maintained site and a small museum, and there is an excellent spa complex (the Saku no Yu) next door to rest the weary traveller. In Morioka City is the finest Nara Period reconstruction of all: the castle of Shiwa. Here there is a wall, a gateway, several fighting towers and a full-sized reproduction of the shuttering that was used to ram the earth walls.

If one takes the train south from Omagari one arrives at Gosannen, which is the modern name given to the pleasant rural area that once saw the violence of the Gosannen (Later Three Years') War. The hill on which Kanezawa fortress was built may be climbed, and a short distance away is the site of Yoshiie's siege headquarters, which is now a pleasant park.

North of Sendai lies the town of Hiraizumi. There is almost nothing left of Yanagi no Gosho, the Oshu Fujiwara's palace, but the temple of Mōtsuji, with its beautiful lake, brings back echoes of the glory of these northern lords. Yet even Mōtsuji is surpassed by the Konjikidō, the exquisite Buddha-hall that is the centrepiece of the Chūsonji temple. This building, one of the few survivors from Heian Japan and the finest of them all, is so precious that it has been encased within a protective outer building for centuries. It is now housed within a reinforced concrete bunker and is viewed through plate glass, but is still one of the most marvellous sights in Japan.

To gain a very good impression of the fortifications of the northern Fujiwara it is necessary to take the train north from Hiraisumi to Esashi, where a shuttle bus will convey you to the Fujiwara Heritage Park. This former film set reproduces the castles and palaces of the Heian Period better than anywhere else in Japan. Some of the detail is so good you will think you are in a perfectly preserved Kyoto temple.

Of the 14th-century fortresses, Kasagiyama is well worth a visit. There is a temple on the mountain called Kasagidera, where the buildings are integrated into the dramatic rock formations into which images of Buddha have been carved. The defences of Kamakura, which make such good use of the natural geography, are easily explored on foot through the gullies carved out of the soft rock, and it is possible to walk or cycle the whole circuit of the former walls that were breached in 1333. Akasaka has little to see but a few lengths of ruined wall. Chihaya has little more, but its spectacular mountain setting gives a very good impression of Kusunoki's strategic layout.

Ichijōdani is near the modern city of Fukui, from where the peaceful and attractive valley is reached easily by train. It is possible to begin at one end of the valley at the small but interesting museum, and then walk on a footpath that follows the road through rice fields, examining the excavated remains along the way until the site of the Asakura mansion and the reconstructed street is reached. The *yamashiro* is gained after a long climb.

For an interesting display about a settlement contemporary with Ichijōdani I recommend a visit to the reconstruction of Kusado Sengen, a medieval village reminiscent of the UK's Jorvik, inside the Hiroshima Prefectural Museum in Fukuyama.

The excavated castle sites of the Sengoku Period described above are nearly all well off the beaten track. The Takeda fortress of Takane involves a

A wide-angle view of Shirakawa Castle, destroyed during one of the first battles of the Boshin War in 1868.

long train journey on the tiny but beautiful Iida line from Toyokawa, which passes through the battlefield of Nagashino. Takane Castle is within walking distance of Misakubo station. Of the Hōjō fortresses, Yamanaka is best approached by bus from Mishima station, a marvellous journey that provides increasingly better views of Mount Fuji the higher the bus climbs. Hachigata has a museum and some reconstruction, but for a stunning reconstruction Sakasai is without parallel. It is, however, very remote and a hire car is recommended. Hachiōji is easily reached by the Chuo Line from Tokyo station. It lies within an attractive wooded valley with a waterfall. Some walls, a bridge and a gateway have been reconstructed.

The site of Tsutsujigasaki, the fortified mansion of the great *daimyō* Takeda Shingen, now houses the Takeda shrine.

FORTIFIED TEMPLES AND MONASTERIES

All the fortified temple sites are accessible. They are described as follows, along with other important foundations that shed light on their design and development.

The great monasteries of Nara and Mount Hiei have been rebuilt over the centuries. Kōfukuji, Tōdaiji and the Kasuga shrine lie next to each other in Nara park. All are very much worth visiting, the Nandaimon (Great Southern Gate) of Tōdaiji and its Daibutsuden (Great Buddha Hall) being the highlights. The Kōfukuji contains two fine old pagodas. Next to Kōfukuji is the pond of Sarusawa that acted in its defence.

The temples of Enryakuji and Miidera are easily visited from Kyoto. A cable-car operates from the Kyoto side and a funicular railway from Sakamoto. A visit to Enryakuji involves a lot of walking as the temples are spread out between three main areas. The Konponchūdō is the central focus, while the Rurido (Lapis Lazuli Hall) in the Saito area is the only original building to have survived Nobunaga's attack in 1571. The Shakado in Saito was formerly at Miidera. The Shintō shrine of Sanno, the mountain king, lies on the Sakamoto side. Miidera temple may be found down towards Lake Biwa.

As noted earlier, one has to visit two places to see the surviving buildings of the important Negorodera. The pagoda is still on its original site. The *kondō* is at Daigoji temple to the south-west of Kyoto, easily accessible nowadays since the extension of the underground line out to Daigoji.

One Jōdo Shinshū temple contemporary with Ishiyama Honganji, the small Shorenji in Takayama, has survived in its entirety. Located just below the castle hill, the Shorenji was moved to its present position in 1961 to save it from the floodwaters of the Miboro dam. The *hondō* is a very delicate building constructed in 1504. There is also a bell tower, a drum tower and a gate together with a perimeter wall.

The site of Yoshizaki Gobō is very well preserved, and is one of the most rewarding places to visit, particularly for anyone interested in the life of Rennyō. It is difficult to get to by public transport, but easy to access from the motorway. The town also has two museums. The first, the Rennyō Kinenkan, occupies an attractive position on the lakeside and has a garden and tea house. The second is located on the ground floor of Yoshizakiji, a modern temple of quite appalling ugliness. Inside are the originals of some of the most important scroll paintings and documents about Rennyō that exist anywhere in Japan.

The Nagashima delta has changed greatly over the centuries from typhoons and the shifting of rivers, but the windswept reed beds that fringe the area are very evocative of the times of the *monto*. The island of Nagashima lies on the railway line between Nagoya and Ise. One gate of the later Nagashima Castle may be seen, and the rebuilt Ganshōji, which is the perfect image of the fortified temple, contains a memorial to the Ikkō-ikki. Even better is the Honshōji near Anjo, which has a fine corner tower.

Torigoe is the most interesting place to visit in connection with Ikkō-ikki fortified temples. The site is well preserved and restored, and at the foot of the hill is the Ikkō-ikki Museum. An Ikkō-ikki Festival takes place every August when the villagers dress up in period costume. The castle site is reached after a long steep walk. Parts of the fortress have been restored, and there is a moving memorial to the Ikkō-ikki.

The site of Osaka Castle contains the site of Ishiyama Honganji. There is a memorial to the Ikkō-ikki in the grounds and items relating to Ishiyama Honganji in the museum in the keep. The Osaka Museum of History is situated across the road. From the keep of Osaka a good impression may be gained of ho160w Ishiyama Honganji stood within a network of defensible waterways.

Tondabayashi has preserved within its historic centre a glimpse of old Japan in the shape of its former *jinaimachi*. The Koshoji temple has its main gate opening on the east side of the precincts and includes a bell tower and a drum tower on the south and north parts of the precincts respectively. Entering from the main gate, the *hondō* is in front with the reception hall and the priestly living quarters (including a study) on the right-hand side of the main temple. The existing temple was rebuilt in 1638. A walk round the outside of

Tondabayashi shows how the slope down to the river and bamboo groves could have been utilized in the town's defence.

The two Jōdo Shinshū temples of Higashi Honganji and Nishi Honganji in Kyoto are the nearest one can get nowadays to experiencing what Ishiyama Honganji must have been like. Each has a pair of main halls, but Nishi Honganji's *goeidō* was built in 1636. Higashi Honganji is quite near to Kyoto station and ideal for a quick visit, even though its buildings only date from 1864. The *goeidō*, one of the largest wooden structures in the world, measures 76 by 58m and covers an area of 927 *tatami* mats. There is a model of the Ishiyama Honganji in the Namba Betsuin in Osaka, and a cut-away model of its main hall in the National Musuem of Japanese History in Sakura near Narita Airport.

The site of the battle of Ueno is present-day Ueno Park in Tokyo. The Kan'eiji temple that was the focus of the attack was rebuilt but relocated to a nearby site to the north-west. The Kuromon gate may be seen at the Entsuji temple in Minowa, which is on the Hibiya subway line from Ueno.

The rebuilt keep of Kaminoyama Castle with Mount Zaokai in the background. Kaminoyama lies to the south of Yamagata, and saw action during the Tōhoku Sekigahara campaign of 1600 and the Boshin War of 1868.

THE DEVELOPED JAPANESE CASTLES

All the castles of the 'developed form' discussed in this volume are open to the public and accessible. The following list sketches in a few more extra details about the best sites. For precise locations, opening times, etc., the reader is referred to the internet or a reliable guidebook. As the sites are so numerous I list them below in alphabetical order. This is not a definitive list of all the castles in Japan.

AIZU-WAKAMATSU
Aizu-Wakamatsu has been rebuilt in concrete and is best viewed from afar. There are several museums and memorials in the city concerned with the siege of 1868 and the heroism of the White Tigers.

AKITA
Kubota Castle, the correct name for Akita Castle, has a rebuilt tower and gateway and a very good museum devoted to the Satake family.

AZUCHI
Only a stone base remains of the great Azuchi Castle, raised by Oda Nobunaga as one of the wonders of Japan, and burned to the ground when he was assassinated only six years later. For this reason no one can be certain what Azuchi actually looked like, but the consensus of opinion is that this revolutionary building had seven storeys, of which the uppermost one was octagonal and richly decorated. There is a museum at the site, where the upper storeys of the castle have been beautifully recreated.

BITCHŪ-MATSUYAMA
Bitchū-Matsuyama is the highest *yamashiro* in Japan, being located on top of Mount Gagyu at 425 metres above sea level. There was a simple fort on its summit as early as 1240, but the evolution of the present castle really dates to the Sengoku Period, when Mimura Motochika covered the top of the mountain in a Sengoku *yamashiro* complex. In 1600 the Tokugawa shogunate rebuilt it, and further work was done under its new lord, Mizunoya Katsutaka. Ruined during the Meiji Restoration, it has been superbly restored since 1929, and provides one of Japan's most spectacular castle sites. It is particularly beautiful under snow.

EDO
As the seat of the Tokugawa *shōgun*, Edo was the most important castle in Japan at the time. It is now the imperial palace in Tokyo. Not much of it can be seen by the public except for the outer walls and gates, which are enormously impressive on account of the vast areas of space enclosed within

them. Its keep burned down during the great fire of 1657. Several gardens and public buildings are located in the outer works, allowing the visitor an opportunity to appreciate its original size.

FUKUYAMA

Located right next to Fukuyama station, Fukuyama Castle is a concrete reproduction with a good museum. The excellent Hiroshima Prefectural Musuem of History is nearby.

FUSHIMI

Fushimi Castle has had a chequered history. It was first built in 1594 by Toyotomi Hideyoshi to allow him to dominate Kyoto, and was among his favourite residences. It was to be the meeting place with the Chinese ambassadors who were coming to negotiate an end to the Korean War, but an earthquake flattened most of the buildings in 1596. They were hastily rebuilt, and in 1600 Fushimi suffered one of the most celebrated sieges in Japanese history when Torii Mototada held it for the Tokugawa. In 1623 Fushimi was dismantled, and many of its finest buildings and interiors now form part of other castles and temples. In 1964 it was 'rebuilt' in concrete as Fushimi Momoyama Castle in a less than satisfying way, and has now been demolished.

GIFU

Gifu, formerly Inabayama, was Oda Nobunaga's headquarters, and is located on top of a mountain. The keep is a modern reconstruction, but as the town is at the foot of the mountain it gives a good impression of the relationship between castle town and fortress.

HACHINOHE

In Hachinohe city, Nejo castle has been excavated and partly restored as it would have appeared in the 14th century.

HAGI

Once the centre of the Restoration movement in the 19th century, only the stone base of Hagi Castle remains.

HAKODATE

The Goryōkaku provides a unique castle experience in Japan and amply rewards the effort taken to reach Hokkaidō. There is an excellent museum, and an 'aerial view' of the castle may be obtained from the nearby observation tower.

HAMAMATSU

Tokugawa Ieyasu's Hamamatsu Castle has a reconstructed keep.

Detail of the windows of the gatehouse of Yamato-Koriyama Castle.

HIKONE

Hikone, near the shores of Lake Biwa, is one of Japan's best preserved and most interesting castles, and rivals Himeji in everything but size. The keep, built by the Ii family, is original, and is believed to have been moved to Hikone from Otsu, where it was erected in 1575. There are several other towers and gates in excellent repair. The castle museum houses the famous red-lacquered armour and other items belonging to the Ii *daimyō*.

HIMEJI

Himeji is one of the finest castles in existence, and provides an excellent 'castle experience'. The keep that we see today dates from Himeji's rebuilding in 1601 by Ikeda Terumasa, Ieyasu's son-in-law. The work took nine years, and somehow it has miraculously survived. All the features of a Japanese castle discussed in this book may be found in Himeji, from stone-dropping holes to weapon racks, making it deservedly the tourist attraction that it has become. The walk up to the keep via the tortuous succession of gates and walls is an education in itself.

HIRADO

Hirado Castle, on the island of the same name, holds an attractive position looking down on the harbour. The keep has been restored, but all the stone walls are original. Nearby is the superb Matsuura Historical Museum, housed in the *daimyō*'s former *yashiki*.

HIROSAKI

Hirosaki lies in the far north of Japan and has a very picturesque keep, well known for its views among cherry blossom. It was originally built in 1611, but was struck by lightning and left in ruins until being rebuilt in 1810.

HIROSHIMA

Hiroshima Castle's keep was rebuilt in concrete after the atomic bomb removed everything except its stone bases. A few years ago one section of the outer defence wall was rebuilt in wood.

IGA UENO

Although its stone bases are impressive, Iga Ueno Castle is less interesting than the wealth of 'ninja culture' round about.

IMABARI

Although its keep is modern, the wide moats round the walls of Imabari's rectangular walls make it very attractive.

INUYAMA

Inuyama, which dominates a wooded outcrop over the Kiso River (the 'Japan Rhine' to the tourist guides) north of Nagoya has one of the most romantic settings of any Japanese castles, although the immediate riverside view is now almost spoiled by modern accretions. It was originally established in 1537, and the present keep, which is one of the best surviving wooden originals left in Japan, was built by the Naruse *daimyō*. The Naruse family still own Inuyama Castle, making it the only Japanese castle still in private hands. Its interior is

This is the perfectly preserved interior of Inuyama Castle. Here we see the *daimyō*'s chamber, situated within a wooden walkway that extends right round the keep. Concealed guards would be stationed behind the wooden screens.

most interesting as it accurately reflects life in a keep during the early 17th century. The *daimyō*'s residential quarters are on the first floor. They are divided into four rooms in classic Japanese style, while round the outside of them is a polished wooden corridor called the *musha bashiri* or 'warrior's run', where guards could maintain a constant watch. The second floor was used for storing armour and weapons, while the third floor houses more private rooms. The fourth storey, which has an external balcony, offers clear views in all directions for many miles around.

IWAKUNI

High on a mountain, Iwakuni's concrete keep is less interesting than the famous bridge at the foot of the mountain and a very good museum also at ground level.

KAGOSHIMA

An outer wall with bullet holes is all that survives of Kagoshima, but the museums round about are very good. The Reimeikan contains a model of the original castle.

KAKEGAWA

A welcome trend has in recent years been the rebuilding of Japanese castle keeps using the correct materials and based on the plans which the *daimyō* was required by law to keep. I shall never forget my surprise on turning up at Kakegawa Castle in 1997 with an out-of-date guidebook expecting to find a stone mound, only to see the complete keep appear before my eyes! For this reason Kakegawa is well worth a visit.

KARATSU

Although the keep is a modern reconstruction Karatsu is very interesting from its location beside a harbour.

KIYOSU

Since the author's first visit to the site of Kiyosu Castle in 1986, which is bisected by Japan's famous Bullet Train, the keep has been rebuilt a quarter of a mile away and houses a museum about Oda Nobunaga. On the original site there is a fine statue of Nobunaga.

KOCHI

Lying on the southern coast of Shikoku, Kochi does not receive as many visitors as it deserves. The keep was built in 1747 in exact imitation of the original that was destroyed by fire, and contains fascinating domestic apartments. From the outside it looks like a three-storey structure but it actually has six floors inside.

KOFU

As well as the site of Tsutsujigasaki, Kofu has a castle that has been rebuilt in recent years.

KOKURA

Kokura burned down during a fire in 1837. Parts of it were rebuilt in 1839, but it again suffered destruction in the turbulent times leading up to the Meiji Restoration. It has been rebuilt in modern times. Kokura was first created in 1602 by Hosokawa Tadaoki, and has a keep with the unusual feature of a fifth storey that is larger than the fourth.

KOMAKI

A concrete keep, modestly describing itself as a museum and not even a castle, lies on top of Komakiyama, from where there is a great view as far as Inuyama Castle.

KUMAMOTO

Kumamoto is one of Japan's largest and finest castles, and its combination of dark wood and white plaster make it look most attractive as a 'black and white' castle. It was built by Katō Kiyomasa, whose experience in the Korean War led him to incorporate into Kumamoto many of the lessons of siege craft that he learned the hard way at the hands of the Chinese army. Little details of food supply, such as 120 wells, nut trees in the courtyards and edible floor-matting, are not as apparent to the visitor as the stone-dropping holes and spikes on the keep, and above all the tremendous succession of massive stone bases built with pronounced curves. The present keep is a modern reconstruction, but the Uto tower in the northwest corner is an original. It was moved to Kumamoto from Uto Castle, where it formed the keep. The Uto tower lies on top of what is probably the most impressive stone base in Japan, which soars up from the moat. Also at Kumamoto is the superb 'long wall', which is made of wood and plaster and stretches for over half a mile in front of the Tsuboi River.

KUNOHE

The ditches and some sections of wall are all that remain of the castle that was the site of the last resistance to Hideyoshi in 1591.

MARUGAME

Marugame lies within an extensive complex of fine stone walls. There is a small museum in the keep.

MARUOKA

Maruoka has what is claimed to be Japan's oldest surviving keep, built in 1576. It was damaged during an earthquake in 1948 but repaired and re-assembled.

The roof tiles are of stone. Unfortunately the keep is all that survives of Maruoka, and unlike many other castle sites there are modern buildings quite close to it, making photography very difficult.

MATSUE

Matsue Castle was introduced to the outside world by the writer Lafcadio Hearn (1850–1904), who described it in his *Glimpses of Unfamiliar Japan* as 'a vast and sinister shape, all iron-grey, rising against the sky from a cyclopean foundation of stone. Fantastically grim the thing is, and grotesquely complex in detail.' Visitors today regard the charming Matsue as grim only in its existence as a 'black castle', with its walls covered in black-painted planks. It is one of Japan's best-preserved sites with an original keep, and was completed after five years' work by the *daimyō* Horio Yasuharu.

MATSUMAE

Matsumae is very remote, but if you are in Hakodate to see the Goryōkaku it is worth considering as a day trip. One tower has been rebuilt, but the site overlooking the sea is very pleasant.

MATSUMOTO

Matsumoto Castle boasts Japan's oldest surviving tower keep, which is one of the most beautiful buildings in Japan if not in the world. Its location in the heart of the 'Japanese Alps' spared it from bombing during World War II, and its setting is near perfect. Unlike most castles built on a hill, Matsumoto is a *hirajiro* – a castle on the plain, except that the immediate plain is beside the wide river that forms its moat. The moat is crossed by an exquisite bridge in Japanese style, which complements the graceful design of the keep. The hipped roofs are so designed to ease the burden of winter snow. With no subsidiary towers, walls and trees to detract from its impact, Matsumoto is visually stunning.

A fortress was first constructed on the site in 1504, and played its part in the expansion of the Takeda clan. It is to Ishikawa Kazumasa, however, that we owe the present magnificent castle. The complex we see today consists of the keep, an attached northern tower which balances it perfectly, and a small moon-viewing tower, and dates from 1593, with the present keep being finished in 1597.

MATSUYAMA

Matsuyama (otherwise Iyo-Matsuyama to distinguish it from the one in old Bitchu Province) was built by Kato Yoshiaki in 1601. The black walls and almost straight gables and roofs are quite striking. It has been very well restored, and its position on a long ridge provides a contrast with nearby Yuzuki. Yuzuki contains several reconstructions from an early period of castle design.

MORIOKA
Only the stone bases remain of this once formidable northern castle.

NAGAHAMA
Nagahama is a modern reconstruction but has much information about Toyotomi Hideyoshi.

NAGOYA
Nagoya Castle, located in the heart of one of Japan's largest cities, was something of a latecomer onto the castle scene, being built in 1612 for Tokugawa Ieyasu's ninth son, Tokugawa Yoshinao, who was appointed lord of Owari Province. The successive *daimyō* of Owari were the heads of one of the three most important branches of the Tokugawa family. Nagoya Castle reflected this importance, and rivalled Osaka in its appearance. Unfortunately it was almost totally destroyed in World War II, and the existing keep is a concrete reproduction.

NIHONMATSU
The main gate of Nihonmatsu has been rebuilt. There is little else to see except for the bronze memorial to the gallant youths who defended it in 1868.

The fortified gatehouse of Shiroishi Castle.

NIJO

Nijo Castle, which lies within the city of Kyoto, is unique among Japanese castles in that the keep has disappeared while the ornate palace has survived. It was originally built in 1603 to be the official Kyoto residence of the first Tokugawa shōgun Ieyasu, whose capital was Edo (now Tokyo). Nijo was completed by the third *shōgun* of the line, Tokugawa Iemitsu, who transferred some structures from Fushimi Castle. As a result, Nijo is representative of some of the best architecture and interior decoration of the Momoyama Period. Only the base of the keep (burned after being struck by lightning in 1750) survives in the *hon maru*, but there is also a small palace that dates from 1847. The focus of attention at Nijo, however, is found in the *ni no maru*, where the palace of the same name covers an area of 800 *tatami* (straw mats) and has 33 rooms. It was completed in 1626 and is almost entirely constructed from *hinoki* cypress, with wall and screen paintings by artists of the Kano school. The palace consists of five inter-locked complexes. On passing through (or beside) the Willow room, Retainers' room, Reception room and Third Grand Chamber the visitor arrives at the First and Second Grand Chambers, which are of important historical significance, because it was here that the 15th and last Tokugawa *shōgun* abdicated in 1867. Beyond this lies the Inner Audience Chamber, where the *fudai daimyō* were granted audience. These were the hereditary retainers who had supported the Tokugawa at the battle of Sekigahara in 1600. The *tozama daimyō*, who had opposed him, never got further than the Third Grand Chamber. The innermost rooms were the *shōgun's* living quarters, where he could sleep soundly in the knowledge that the slightest movement along the corridors by an assassin would be transmitted to the guards by the squeaking of the *uguisu bari*, the nightingale floor. The squeak was produced by metal clamps under the floorboards rubbing against the nails.

ODAWARA

Odawara was the great castle of the powerful Hōjō family, besieged in 1590 by Toyotomi Hideyoshi. The present castle keep is a rather disappointing modern concrete reproduction containing Odawara Zoo.

OGAKI

Ogaki Castle, easily combined with a visit to the battlefield of Sekigahara, has an uninteresting museum and a fine statue of its onetime owner.

OKAZAKI

Tokugawa Ieyasu's former headquarters castle has been rebuilt in concrete and houses a very good museum.

Okayama

Okayama lies on the banks of the Asahi River, and is one of Japan's best-known 'black castles', although the fine keep is in fact a concrete reconstruction after the original was destroyed in an air raid in 1945. Ukita Hideie, the *daimyō* who became commander-in-chief during the Korean campaign, first raised it in 1597. Its base is an irregular pentagon and the keep itself is six storeys high. The original castle complex had an additional 34 towers and 21 gates, which was a large number for the time. It is best viewed from across the river.

Omi-Hachiman

The network of canals that defended Omi-Hachiman is the best feature of the site. There is a shrine on top of the castle hill.

Osaka

Osaka Castle is one of the most important fortresses in Japanese history. Toyotomi Hideyoshi built it in 1586 on the site of Ishiyama Honganji, the formidable fortress cathedral of the Ikkō-ikki. In 1614–15 it suffered perhaps the greatest siege ever seen in Japan. Much of it was burned at this time, but Osaka was rebuilt shortly afterwards, only to suffer more destruction at the end of the 19th century. Today a rebuilt keep, housing a magnificent museum, is the centrepiece of a vast complex of interlocking stone walls and moats at the heart of the city of Osaka.

Saga

Part of the outer defence works has recently been beautifully rebuilt and houses an excellent museum.

Sannohe

Sannohe, a castle of the Nambu daimyo, has been partly rebuilt.

Sendai

Nothing remains of Sendai Castle, but the interesting museum on the site has an audio-visual presentation with a full reconstruction. Date Masamune's statue stands on one side of the castle hill.

Shinagawa

The sites of the third and sixth artillery fortresses in Tokyo Bay have been preserved. The third fortress is now a public park joined to the futuristic Odaiba complex in Tokyo Bay. A good view may be obtained from the Rainbow Bridge that links Odaiba with central Tokyo, from where the sixth fortress, an isolated pentagonal bastion, may also be seen.

SHIRAKAWA
Shirakawa, to the south of Koriyama, is one of the best examples of a castle rebuilt in wood. The original was destroyed during the Boshin War.

SHIROISHI
Shiroishi, to the south of Sendai, was the headquarters of the Northern Alliance in the Boshin War. The keep has been rebuilt.

TOYAMA
The keep of Toyama has been rebuilt as a local history museum.

UEDA
Ueda lies on the old Nakasendo road, and was the site of the celebrated delaying siege by Tokugawa Hidetada, which kept him away from Sekigahara in 1600. Two corner towers and the walls remain, which are enough to justify a visit, and there is a very good museum.

UTSUNOMIYA
Utsunomiya has Japan's strangest castle reconstruction, consisting of a section of mound with two wooden towers.

UWAJIMA
Uwajima on Shikoku Island has one of the best preserved wooden keeps in Japan.

WAKAYAMA
Wakayama Castle was built on the site of Ota Castle, captured by Toyotomi Hideyoshi in 1585 after a daring operation involving flooding. It lies at the mouth of the Kii River, and owes its present appearance to Tokugawa Yorinobu, the tenth son of the first Tokugawa *shōgun*. Unfortunately, the original keep was destroyed in 1945, but it has since been reconstructed very well.

YAMAGATA
A splendid equestrian statue of the *daimyō* Mogami Yoshiaki greets visitors to the modestly rebuilt sections of Yamagata Castle. The museum dedicated to Yoshiaki is very good.

YOKOTE
A very plain concrete keep was rebuilt at Yokote, which is most interesting for its position surrounded by a river with many pronounced bends.

JAPANESE CASTLES IN KOREA

All the *wajō* sites are open to the public, although there is very little to see at some of them. Most are concentrated around the Busan area, a fascinating place to visit in its own right with a new subway system that takes in nearly all the local *wajō* sites. Busan *wajō* and Jaseongdae are pleasant little parks in the middle of the city. Bakmungu and Dongsamdong have no remains, but their sites may be seen from the harbour. Dongnae offers the Chungyeolsa shrine and some very pleasant mountain walking along the ridge of the *wajō* hill with superb views. The dramatic Gupo is on the subway line, but a distant view of Gimhae Jukdo, Hopo and Yangsan will suffice.

Out on the east coast a car tour may be made through Gijang, with its exquisitely preserved harbour and 'mother' and 'child' castle sites. The remains of Imrangpo are only visible in winter, but further north is the magnificent Seosaengpo. The modern main road marks the location of the sea coast in 1592, from where a castle mound rises up beside the rocks that once were lapped with water. Behind this mound stretch long walls up to the summit with a fascinating combination of interlocked stone walls. Ulsan's small hill has little left to see, but is very evocative of the siege situation.

South Korea's hunger for land is having a very strange effect on the *wajō* of the Ungcheon area. Over a period of years Gadeok Island is being joined to the mainland by a massive civil engineering programme designed to create land for factories and an extension of Busan harbour. Much of the promontory on which Angolpo is built has already disappeared. Ungcheon's harbour is now enclosed by a new breakwater along which tipping lorries trundle, but the *wajō* site itself will be preserved, even if it will end at dry land on the outer side.

There is little to see at the *wajō* sites on Geoje Island, but a visit may be combined with trips to the battle sites and museums to Admiral Yi's victories at Okpo and Hansando. The sea voyage from Busan is very enjoyable. More memorials of Admiral Yi may be included in visits to the *wajō* that lie furthest to the west. Sacheon lies in an attractive position, approached past the huge Chinese burial mound. Not far away is the fine Korean fortress of Jinju. Namhae is reached across the suspension bridge that crosses the Noryang Straits, while Suncheon lies on the road towards Yeosu, where there is a full-scale replica of the turtle ship. Suncheon is one of the best *wajō* sites. A land creation project like the one at Ungcheon is now complete and has preserved the site completely. The ruins are well maintained, and a new road now passes it on the seaward side, allowing a visitor the opportunity to view the castle as it would have been seen by Chen Lin's fleet in 1598.

SOURCES AND FURTHER READING

There are many books about Japanese castles available in Japanese with excellent illustrations, but most of these suffer from a very narrow perspective on the topic. In many cases they deal exclusively with the later stone castles, which provide the most photogenic subjects. There is a handy little volume in the Hoikusha Color Book series entitled *Japanese Castles* by Michio Fujioka. It was first published in 1968, and replaces the earlier *Castles in Japan* by N. Orui (Tourist Library Volume 9, 1935). The best monograph of the subject is *Feudal Architecture of Japan* by Kiyoshi Hirai (Heibonsha Survey of Japanese Art, Vol. 13, 1973).

More recent publications have extensive reconstructions of Sengoku Period *yamashiro*, but very few are concerned with the earlier castles. A notable exception is *Nihon no shiro* (Tokyo, 1966), which has reconstructions of the earlier sites such as Tagajō. One complication in recommending other books is that nearly all of them bear the title '*Nihon no shiro*'!

A number of books and academic articles in English cover the Yayoi Period finds very well. For example see C. Melvin Aikens and Takayasu Higuchi, *Prehistory of Japan* (New York, 1982); Gina Barnes, 'Mimaki and the Matching Game', *Archaeology Review from Cambridge*, 3 (1984), pp. 37–47; Koji Mizoguchi, *An Archaeological History of Japan 30000 BC to AD 700* (Philadelphia, 2002); Mark Hudson and Gina Barnes, 'Yoshinogari: A Yayoi Settlement in Northern Kyūshū', *Monumenta Nipponica*, 46 (1991), pp. 211–235; Keiji Imamura, *Prehistoric Japan: New Perspectives on Insular East Asia* (London, 1996).

The rise of the samurai, along with their fortifications, is covered in Bruce L. Batten, 'Foreign Threat and Domestic Reform: The Emergence of the Ritsuryo State', *Monumenta Nipponica*, 41 (1986), pp. 199–219; and Wayne Farris, *Heavenly Warriors: The Evolution of Japan's Military 500–1300* (Harvard, 1992); Wayne Farris, *Sacred Texts and Buried Treasures* (Honolulu, 1998); Karl Friday, 'Pushing Beyond the Pale: The Yamato Conquest of the *Emishi* and Northern Japan', *Journal of Japanese Studies*, 23 (1997), pp. 1–24.

My information about hygiene in early castles comes from the museum in Akita, together with a fascinating article by Akira Matsui et al., 'Palaeoparasitology in Japan – Discovery of Toilet Features', *Mem Inst Oswaldo Cruz Rio de Janeiro*, 98 (2003), pp. 127–136.

The operational history of the early castles may be found in Helen Craig McCullough, 'A Tale of Mutsu', *Harvard Journal of Asiatic Studies*, 25 (1964–65), pp. 178–211. Kusunoki Masdashige's sieges are covered in Helen Craig McCullough, *The Taiheiki: A Chronicle of Medieval Japan* (New York, 1959).

Very little is available in English or Japanese on the fortified temples, so much of my research has depended upon fieldwork and site visits, with construction details and layouts being obtained from leaflets and pamphlets available at the sites themselves. For example, the Ikkō-ikki Museum next to the site of Torigoe supplies material including the scaled maps that I have used in designing the colour plates.

Works in English covering the *sōhei* and *monto* include: Mikael Adolphson, 'Enryakuji – An Old Power in a New Era' in J. P. Mass (ed.), *The Origins of Japan's Medieval World: Courtiers, Clerics, Warriors and Peasants in the Fourteenth Century* (Stanford, 1997), pp. 237–260; David L. Davis, 'Ikki in Late Medieval Japan', in J. W. Hall and J. P. Mass (eds.), *Medieval Japan: Studies in Institutional History* (New Haven, 1974); Michael Solomon, 'The Dilemma of Religious Power: Honganji and Hosokawa Masamoto', *Monumenta Nipponica*, 32, pp. 51–65; Michael Solomon, 'Rennyō and the Ikkō-ikki', *Transactions of the International Conference of Orientalists in Japan*, 21 (1976), pp. 150–155; Shigeki Sugiyama, 'Honganji in the Muromachi-Sengoku Period: Taking up the Sword and its Consequences', *Pacific World: Journal of the Institute of Buddhist Studies,* 10 (1994), pp. 56–74; Stanley Weinstein, 'Rennyō and the Shinshu Revival' in J. W. Hall and T. Toyoda (eds.), *Japan in the Muromachi Age* (Berkeley, 1977), pp. 331–358.

For Kyoto and its defences see Nicolas Fieve and Paul Waley, *Japanese Capitals in Historical Perspective: Place, Power and Memory in Kyoto, Edo and Tokyo* (London, 2003) and Tatsusaburo Hayashiya, 'Kyoto in the Muromachi Age', in J. W. Hall and T. Toyoda (eds.), *Japan in the Muromachi Age* (Berkeley, 1977), pp. 15–36.

The development of castle towns and *jinaimachi* appears in James L. McClain, *Kanazawa: A Seventeenth-Century Japanese Castle Town* (New Haven, 1982) and James L. McClain and Wakita Osamu (eds.), *Osaka: The Merchants' Capital of Early Modern Japan* (Cornell, 1999).

For the siege weapons used against Japanese castles, see my books New Vanguard 43: *Siege Weapons of the Far East (1)* AD 612–1300 (Osprey, Oxford, 2001) and New Vanguard 44: *Siege Weapons of the Far East (2)* AD 960–1644 (Osprey, Oxford, 2002).

For a spectacular scene involving the siege of a Japanese castle of the developed form, see the movie *Ran* (1985), directed by Akira Kurosawa. For a Sengoku *yamashiro*, see Kurosawa's older production *Throne of Blood* (1957).

My main sources for the structure, history and appearance of the individual *wajō* are all in Japanese. Most important is the journal *Wajō no Kenkyu*, published by the Wajō Kenkyu Kai. Five volumes have been published so far. Each contains numerous articles in Japanese and Korean on the *wajō* with extensive photographs, maps and diagrams, with special attention being given to particular sites as follows:

Volume 1:   Geoje Island (1997)

Volume 2:   Suncheon, Ulsan (1998)

Volume 3:   Busan, Gimhae Jukdo, Seosaengpo (1999)

Volume 4:   Namhae, Busan (2000)

Volume 5:   Seosaenpo, Ungcheon, Myeongdong (2002).

In 2005 the organization published the proceedings of a symposium that dealt with the relationship between the *wajō* and Osaka Castle. It is entitled *Chosen no wajō to Osaka jo*, and includes an excellent account of Gupo. Suncheon is covered in the volume in the Rekishi Gunzo series called *Sengoku no Kenjo* (2004).

Of the few sources in European languages, the Jesuit eyewitness accounts of the *wajō* appear in Ralph N. Cory, 'Some Notes on Father Gregorio de Cespedes: Korea's First European Visitor', *Transactions of the Korean Branch of the Royal Asiatic Society*, 27 (1937), pp.1-45. Yi Sunsin's reports and diary are translated in Tae-hung Ha, *Nanjung Ilgi* (*The War Diaries of Admiral Yi*) (Seoul, 1977) and Tae-hung Ha (trans.) and Chong-young Lee (ed.), *Imjin Changch'o* (*Admiral Yi's Memorials to Court*) (Seoul, 1981). Yu Seongnyong's *Chinbirok* is available in English translation as *The Book of Corrections: Reflections on the National Crisis during the Japanese Invasion of Korea 1592-1598*, translated by Choi Byonghyon (Institute of East Asian Studies, Berkeley, 2002).

A full account of the Korean invasions appears in my book *Samurai Invasion: Japan's Korean War 1592-1598* (Cassells, London, 2002), where there is an extensive bibliography for Japanese sources. Since that book was released, several important articles on the Korean campaign have been published. Kenneth Swope has been a particularly fine contributor because of his use of Chinese source material. See in particular 'Turning the Tide: The Strategic and Psychological Significance of the Liberation of Pyongyang in 1593', *War and Society*, 21 (2003), pp.1-22; and 'Crouching Tigers, Secret Weapons: Military Technology Employed during the Sino-Japanese-Korean War, 1592-1598', *The Journal of Military History*, 69 (2005), pp.11-41.

GLOSSARY

amidadō	temple hall dedicated to Amida Buddha
ashigaru	Japanese foot soldiers
bakufu	The shogunal government of Japan
bonji	Sanskrit pictographs
chidori hafu	triangular gables on a roof
daimyō	Japanese feudal lord
eupseong	enclosed area of Korean town
fujō	castle beside a lake
fusuma	paper walls
goeidō	founder's hall in Jōdo Shinshū temples
gohei	paper streamers used in the Shintō religion
goma	purification and prayer ritual
gomado	temple hall for the performance of *goma*
gundan	regiment
han	territory held by a *daimyō*
hara-kiri	ritual suicide by cutting the abdomen
hashigokaku	style of castle layout having the inner area as the apex
heishi	soldier
hirajiro	castle built on a plain
hirayamjiro	castle built on a mountain and a plain
hon maru	inner bailey of a castle
hondō	main hall of a temple
honjō	central castle in a *daimyō*'s terrritory
ikkeshū	ruling family council of the Honganji
ikki	(1) riot; (2) league or organization
ishi otoshi	stone-dropping holes, like machiolations
jinaimachi	temple town
jizamurai	low-ranking samurai who also farmed
jokamachi	castle town
kangō shūraku	settlements protected by ditches
kara hafu	curved gables on a roof
karamete mon	back gate of a castle
kato mado	style of curved window
ken	length of about six feet or two metres
ko	prayer communities or fraternities
kofun	keyhole-shaped burial mounds
kōchisei shūraku	highland settlements
koguchi	a barbican gate with a pronounced turn

komainu	mythological Chinese dog
kondō	alternative expression for a main hall of a temple
kuni	provinces
kuruwa	successive courtyards of a Japanese castle
maru	enclosed area within a castle
masugata	defensible area between two gates
mikkyō	esoteric Buddhist sects
mizuki	water fortress
mon	family badge or crest; gate
monto	adherent of Ikkō-ikki
nawabari	'marking with ropes' castle design
ne ishi	keystone
nembutsu	literally 'Buddha-calling'; a prayer sequence
ni no maru	second bailey of a castle
Nio	images of guardian gods
ōtemon	front gate of a castle
ōyumi	siege crossbows; called *ishiyumi* when used to throw stones
raido	public area of a *hondō*, also known as a *haiden*
renkaku	style of castle layout with subsidiary baileys on either side
rinkaku	style of castle layout using concentric circles
samurai	Japanese warrior, equivalent to a European knight
san no maru	third bailey of a castle
sanseong	Korean mountain fortress
seichō	government office
seiden	middle building of a *seichō*
Sengoku Jidai	the 'Warring States Period' 1467–1615
Sengoku yamashiro	pre-stone style of castles of the Sengoku Period
shachi	ornamental gold 'dolphins' on a castle roof
shijo	satellite castle in a *daimyō*'s territory
sho	liquid measure – about four pints
shōgun	military dictator of Japan
shoji	sliding screens of wood and paper
shoya	village headman
shu	sect of Japanese Buddhism
shugo	*shōgun*'s provincial governor
sōhei	warrior monk or priest soldier
sotoguruwa	outer courts of a castle
sumi yagura	corner towers
Sutra	the Buddhist scriptures
tamon yagura	a long tower
tatami	straw mats
tenshu kaku	castle keep
teramachi	temple town
tokonoma	alcove
wajō	the name for a Japanese castle in Korea
waju	dyked community to prevent flooding
watari yagura	gatehouse in the form of a tower
uzumi	secret gate
yagura	tower
yakata	samurai mansions
yamashiro	castle built on a mountain
yashiki	*daimyō*'s mansion
zasu	chief priest

INDEX